CIGAR BARONS

CIGAR BARONS

ISABELLA

SAPPHIRE BOOKS

SALINAS, CALIFORNIA

Editor - Heather Flournoy
Book Design - LJ Reynolds
Cover Design - Fineline Cover Design

Sapphire Books Publishing, LLC
P.O. Box 8142
Salinas, CA 93912
www.sapphirebooks.com

Printed in the United States of America
First Edition – November 2019

This and other Sapphire Books titles can be found at
www.sapphirebooks.com

Dedication

To my wife, Schileen.
She indulges my passions.

Acknowledgments

My sincere thanks to:

All of the cigar smokers out there. I've never met a stranger at a cigar lounge, no matter where I go. They are a welcoming and fun group.

My editor, Heather Flournoy. She works hard at making me look good.

Jennifer Fulton for her vision and advice.

Nicaragua for being a wonderful host country and the inspiration for this book.

Morgan Hill and Cigars LTD for a great place to smoke.

To my beta readers, Akemy and Terri. You rock!

May your ash be long and the smoke sweet!

Prologue

Vuelta Abajo, Cuba. July 1957

¡Revolución!

Alejandro Huerta wanted nothing to do with it. He stood between the tobacco plants trying to ignore the whispers of discontent that invaded the orderly rows as the early morning mist retreated. Rumors of imminent rebellion had gone on for a year now. Fidel Castro's guerillas made regular treks through the fields recruiting fighters for the struggle.

Their talk sounded good. The Cuban president, Fulgencio Batista, was a bastard—greedy, brutal, and corrupt. His regime killed anyone who stood in its way. His big money backers had plundered the country. Foreigners owned more land than Cubans, and the Americans were at the front of the line.

Castro would change everything for the common man. That was the promise.

Alejandro had overheard Don Miguel, the plantation owner, talking with other *jefes* about Castro's plans. The new revolutionary government would take over cigar production. Some of the big farms would be granted the honor of making Cuban cigars for the world. The smaller farms would be snatched up and merged into state-owned plantations.

Alejandro's father had long ago given up on his boyhood dream of buying more acres and turning the Huerta's miserable plot of land into a cigar plantation.

But Alejandro had thought about little else since he first encountered the sweet, earthy aroma of cigar smoke floating from the shiniest car he had ever seen. He was eleven years old. After months of pestering, his father finally agreed that he could attend the schoolhouse on the Ferro plantation. He had arrived not long after dawn the next morning and spent the next hour watching a procession of servants march up the narrow path, holding umbrellas over the *jefe*'s children. Just as the school bell rang, a long red car swished to a halt at the gate. Raindrops bounced from its gleaming hood, rivulets of water spun from its chrome wheels. Alejandro ran to the gate for a better look. When the back door opened, a puff of blue, fragrant smoke emerged, followed by a tall man in a pale suit and cravat—Don Ferro himself. He scooped the other occupant into his arms, a girl in a dress as green as tobacco leaves with the kind of sash Alejandro's older sister should have been buried in: white silk, huge bow, long ribbons floating behind.

She noticed Alejandro as the driver rushed to hold a big umbrella over her father, the most important man in the area. Peeking over Don Ferro's shoulder, she smiled, and Alejandro was instantly embarrassed by his baggy, threadbare white linen pants and shirt, hand-me-downs from his father, and his mud-caked toes perched like bird claws over the edge of leather sandals he had outgrown a year ago.

He felt out of place. He wanted to learn to read and write. He wanted to know about the world, and carry books home so that he could study at night. But in that moment he knew he would never fit in with the children of the plantation owners, in their fine clothes.

Even the field boss's children wore proper shoes and socks and smelled of soap.

At lunchtime, he sat alone, watching his classmates open up wooden boxes filled with food as he unwrapped the cloth that held a chunk of cheese and bread. He was startled when the girl in the green dress came up to him. She extended her hand, a plump orange balanced on her small palm.

"Would you like it?"

If he was lucky, his mother gave him a piece of fruit occasionally, but times were lean for the Huerta family and there were five children to feed, not including himself.

The girl must have read his nervous hesitation as good manners, assuring him, "I don't want it. The peel makes my fingers smelly. My name is María . What's yours?"

Before Alejandro could reply, an older boy came up, plucked the orange away, and snarled, "Go beg somewhere else." He shoved Alejandro off the bench so hard that a glob of half-chewed bread flew from his mouth as he landed on the wooden floorboards. Laughter erupted around him. He recognized a few of the mocking faces, boys from families almost as poor as his own.

Later, Alejandro learned the bully's name: Fernando Calderon.

He never got in any trouble. The Calderons were cigar barons.

A bead of sweat rolled down his cheek and Alejandro moved his thoughts back to the present. The anger never left him. It simmered beneath the calm face the world saw. It kept him up at night, making plans, and it kept him alert each day, waiting for his chance to pocket seeds from the plants he thought would produce the best cigars. One day he would plant them and watch the bright green leaves unfurl on land he owned.

He yanked off his weathered straw hat, pulled his bandana from around his neck, and wiped the sweat from his forehead. The Ferro plantation spanned two hundred acres of red soil in a valley that trapped the humidity. The soil was so deep and rich in minerals and sand that he'd heard Don Ferro proclaim that only he could produce the best Ligero tobacco. So dark, that when rolled the oils from the tobacco left the rollers' fingers coated in the black substance.

Alejandro's father said this was the best tobacco-growing land in the world. There was a time when the Huerta family owned a prosperous farm near San Juan y Martinez. Huerta ancestors had produced cigars for Spanish royalty. A hundred years ago, their farm was one of thousands supplying the cigar factories of Havana. Like most growers, they were forced off their land during the Ten Years' War and imprisoned in General Wyler's concentration camps. Alejandro's grandfather escaped and joined the *mambisis* to fight the Spanish occupation. The family had lost everything but their pride.

Now, according to Alejandro's father, Castro and his 26th of July Movement would finally take power from the hands of dictators and return it to the people. Alejandro did not share his optimism. The history books he'd borrowed from the schoolhouse filled him with misgivings. Castro's promises were nothing new. From Lenin and Stalin to Chairman Mao and Mussolini, revolutionaries always claimed to bring the government to the people. Yet as soon as they seized power, they became despots, as evil as the regimes they had replaced.

Why should Castro be any different? And whether he became a benevolent dictator or another tyrant, the Huertas would still lose their farm, for the greater good.

The sky, blue as the ocean just north of him, promised another sweltering day. He had started work at dawn, hoping to beat the heat of the day. While others took a siesta, he would be meeting María for another writing lesson. The plantation owner's daughter had taken pity on him when his father pulled him out of school to work in the fields.

Alejandro glanced up when he heard voices drawing closer, still talking of Castro and the changes he would make to Cuba.

"I hear he is going to recruit virgins to roll cigars on their thighs. Oh, what I wouldn't do to work in that factory," a man said.

"Perhaps María will roll one for you on her thigh?" another said. A slap on a back echoed in the wet air.

"Didn't you hear? She's going to marry Fernando from the Calderon plantation. Don Ferro thinks that it will keep both plantations in the family and Castro will allow them to be one of the chosen cigar manufactures in Cuba."

"You mean Señora Ferro wants María to marry Don Calderon's son. I heard her tell one of the maids that a match between the families would cement their position as the only Cuban cigar manufacturers privileged enough to make cigars for export." So close to Havana, Alejandro was sure Señora Ferro could almost hear the tinkling of champagne glasses as the upper crust toasted their good fortune.

Alejandro was aware of Señora Ferro's lofty goals for her daughter, but María had downplayed the talk when they'd spoken. He knew her distaste for Fernando went as far back as his brief stint at school, when he'd pushed Alejandro off the bench he and María had shared for lunch. His blood boiled as the memory flooded back. He wished he'd punched the bastard, but knew his father would pay the price for his anger, and he'd brought enough trouble to his family when he'd pleaded for an education.

Alejandro had overheard the *jefes* talking of the possibility of the Cubatabaco, an organization that would oversee cigar production once the tobacco was grown and passed on to the government for cigar production. Whatever happened, it wouldn't be good for his family or his dreams. An imaginary clock was ticking down in his head. He didn't have time to waste.

The thought of María marrying someone else wasn't something he had given much thought to. He'd had a few fleeting daydreams of the beautiful woman being the mother of his children, but marriage to someone else? Never. He had to come to terms with the fact that she had a firm grasp of his heart, and any ideas of her mother giving María to Fernando just to build a larger empire…Well, that had to be stopped. Now.

Besides, why hadn't she told him? What would he do now? His future had never looked more bleak.

"Hey, Alejandro. Daydreaming again?" Someone shook his shoulder.

"Oh, I think you crushed his dreams of marrying jefe's daughter," another said.

The group laughed until a voice boomed behind

them.

"Get to work, you lazy bastards. The day is getting away from us and we have this whole field to work. So, get your asses busy." The boss on horseback motioned his riding crop at the men. "Understand?'

"Sí, sí," they all mumbled, weaving away from the swish of the crop.

The boss backed his mount up. "Alejandro, the jefe wants to see you later."

"Me?"

"Are you deaf? After dinner, don't be late."

"Yes, jefe." Alejandro nervously wondered why he would be called to the big house. In the meantime, he crouched down and went back to pulling tobacco worms from the plants. Don Ferro didn't import the pesticides some cigar plantations did. He'd said the cost outweighed the benefits as far as he was concerned. Alejandro had heard workers from other farms had become sick from the petroleum-based bug killers, so he was happy to pull worms, squish them dead, and move on to the next plant. It signified where he was on the pecking order of work. Lowest of the low, but it paid something he could send back to his family.

≈ ≈ ≈ ≈

"If you drop that marble bust, I'll make sure you are cutting sugar cane." María could hear her father bellowing all the way up into her room. Moving to the edge of the stairs, she absently ran her fingers over the mirror finish of the mahogany rail of the balcony. Peering over the edge, she remembered a time when she'd press her face between the rungs of the stairs and wish she could go down to the massive parties her mother and father held—opulent, with music that played into the wee hours of the night as the liquor flowed and the laughing seemed never-ending. Tonight, though, she'd get her wish and join the festivities. Her leap into adulthood had come without any fanfare, without the customary elegance many of her girlfriends had when they turned seventeen. Her mother always seemed to be the center of attention and unfortunately, María was always shoved out of the way so her mother could bask in it.

"There is only one sun, *mija*. Your time will come," her mother said one evening when she locked María in her room. She couldn't fathom at her young age what her mother meant, but as she started to grow up, she slowly began to understand. While María always envisioned the world as her oyster after she finished school, including a trip to university, or a summer in Europe, she had a feeling something wasn't quite right for tonight's party. Her father was taking many of the lavish furniture pieces out of the main rooms and squirreling them away so they wouldn't be seen. Her mother would be furious when she found out.

She let her fingers trail down the handrail as she descended, imagining she was a princess, or perhaps a duchess in some far-off land, as she admired the grand entrance of the plantation that had been in her family for generations. Looming columns flanked the huge gothic staircase. Its deep, thick, burgundy carpet cushioned each step she took. The massive paintings her mother had agonized over for months littered every inch of wall. Each one had been replaced several times until just the right painting had been selected. Her mother's intent was to represent the wealth and status for an owner of an estate the size of theirs. The

marble floors were always polished to the point of
being dangerous, if one wasn't careful. Overhead, the
fan with blades the size of airplane propellers seemed
to swirl lazily, its giant palm fronds barely pushing air
around. Again, all for decoration. Whether it served a
functional purpose or not wasn't the question; it looked
beautiful. However, now it all seemed so…wasted.

She couldn't quite put her finger on it, but her
recent trip to Havana with her uncle Luis had opened
her eyes to a whole new world. It was alive and bustling
with fashion, art, music, flair, and fun. She smoothed
down the elegant black dress she wore, a gift from her
uncle with strict instructions to wear it, and wear it
often.

"Clothes should be fun. You should enjoy wearing
them, mija." He swished his hand around and pointed
to the women flitting through the fashion magazines
that littered the boutique, none paying any attention to
the gay man and his ingénue. "Do you think they care
what a dress costs?"

She shook her head.

"Of course they don't. Do you know why?"

"No."

"Because they have money and they spend it,
mija. They know that something is in the wind. I mean,
just look at this wretched place." He twirled a little,
his jacket flaring out. "We all know that change is
looming for Havana. So enjoy what you have, sweetie."
He pulled at one of the dresses the clerk was holding
up. "She'll try this one."

She was wearing that black silk dress now. The
tight lines caressed her figure and she liked the way
she felt in it. The hose and high heels were the addition
to the package she'd tried to reject, but her uncle had

insisted.

"Honey, you need to match, so you might as well get these now. Besides, when you mother was your age, she dressed like she was twenty. Don't let her tell you different."

Trying to stay out of the way of the servants, María sat up straight on the settee in the entryway as everyone bustled around her. Suddenly, she was the object of her mother's attention. "Sit up straight, mija. You need to present yourself as a lady. Remember, eyes will always be on you because of who your father is—a cigar baron." Her mother pushed on her lower back and pulled her shoulders back, forcing her chest out.

"Mother, please." She wiggled out of the pose.

"María." Her mother's eyes narrowed, boring right through María. "You are a Ferro. Act like one." She raised her hand as if to strike María, but María turned her cheek toward the hand, taunting her mother. "You've always been an insolent child." Her mother huffed and lowered her hand just as her father entered the room. They always seemed to be at odds lately, and she didn't know why.

María saw her father barking orders at the staff, his signature cigar wedged between clenched teeth.

"Where is Alejandro? I called for him to come and help with the preparations."

"He is on his way, jeffe."

María smiled at the mention of Alejandro's name. She hadn't seen him lately and they'd seemed to be at opposite ends of the plantation when it had come to their lessons. María was looking forward to today's lesson, but her mother had squashed it, announcing they were having an impromptu party.

María enjoyed their time together, as their

conversations were more than the usual superficial niceties she had with Fernando and the other kids from the neighboring plantations. Her conversations with her girlfriends as they sat together reading glamor magazines touting the latest fashion craze in Paris or some starlet or actor were fun, but Alejandro talked of the future, starting his own plantation and his own line of cigars that would carry the Huerta name. He had dreams, and she liked them. Fernando, on the other hand, only talked about his car, his inheritance, and himself.

Boring.

She'd walked out on him more than once, exasperated. Men were such phonies, she had realized quickly in school. Macho, arrogant, and self-absorbed. Women were arm candy, valued only to have their babies and put on parties like the one her mother planned for tonight. María wasn't going to be one of those wives. Havana held her interest with its university and nightlife. She wanted to live like her uncle. Endless festivities, friends, and travel.

"María, what are you doing here?" Her father bent down and kissed her forehead.

"Papa. What's going on?" She pointed to the furniture leaving the grand room.

"Ah, I just found out we have a special guest coming tonight. So, your mother decided we should entertain and make a big production out of his arrival."

"Who is it?"

His broad smile split around the cigar still wedged between his teeth. "I don't know, mija. I guess even I am to be surprised."

"Hmm, but why are you taking some of the furniture out of the rooms?"

"I've been told that we don't want to look like we are flaunting our wealth."

"But you've worked hard. Why should anyone care about our things?"

"Well it was your mother's idea, and you know how she feels about her 'stuff.' It's complicated, mija." He cast a sideways glance at her mother.

María suspected she wasn't the only one confused. The more her father tried to explain, the more she knew her mother was up to something. Before she could ask another question, Alejandro stood on the porch, his figure casting a long shadow on the floor of the entryway.

"Ah, Alejandro. Finally."

Alejandro pulled his worn straw hat from his head and worried it in a circle as he looked past her father and at María. Bowing his head, he said, "Sir, Señorita Ferro."

"Come, come." He grabbed Alejandro's shoulder and twisted him toward the kitchen. "I need you to help with the party tonight."

"Señor?"

"Am I speaking Greek? I want you to help with the party we are having tonight. Get cleaned up and change into the clothes on the back porch." He looked down at his watch. "We have about an hour before guests start to arrive. Hurry."

María smiled and waved at Alejandro, who shrugged his shoulders and cast her a dubious look. Her stomach suddenly filled with butterflies as he winked at her. They'd always had something special between them that made her think silly thoughts whenever they were together. Her father followed him as he went to get changed, barking orders as he left the room.

"María, what are you smiling about?" Her mother's voice sliced through her.

"Mother." She slid off the settee and smoothed her dress, then pushed back a few curls that fell into her face.

"Where did you get that dress?"

"Tío Luís."

"Go and take it off. It's too adult for you." Her mother grabbed her and tried to steer her toward the stairs.

Jerking herself away from her mother's grasp, she stiffened. "Papa's already seen it and said it's fine."

"Really. Huh, where is he? Miguel? Where are you?" her mother bellowed.

Miguel emerged from the dining room. "Que?"

"You said she could wear this?"

"She's not a child anymore."

Before her mother could utter another word, the roar of an engine pulled everyone's attention to the front porch. María followed her parents out into the setting-sun-drenched porch just as a sleek red sports car pulled in front of the plantation. The tobacco fields framed the elegant vehicle. Shielding her eyes from the sun, she could see a mustached man in a beret slide out from the driver's side, swagger and confidence oozing out of him like oil on a hot pan ready to sizzle. From the passenger side, Fernando was grinning from ear to ear as he jumped from his seat.

"Don Ferro," he yelled. He ran his hand down the fender and grinned. "What do you think? Ché…I mean General Guevara…" He turned to the general and bowed. "My apologies, General."

"Please, Ché is fine. I love the enthusiasm of the young, don't you?" He smiled a toothy grin, his moustache pulling at the corners. "Señora," He lifted María 's mother's hand and pressed his lips against it.

Fernando strutted over to Don Ferro and swept his hand wide. "What do you think? Quite a ride, no?"

María waited for her father to respond. She knew he wasn't much into cars, and the rolling tin can, as he often referred to them, wouldn't impress the Don. However, it was clear Fernando was smitten.

"María, come. Take a look."

"Aw, who do we have here?" Ché said, pulling at the hem of his military uniform and straightening out the creases from the contortionist position she was sure he'd been in for a while. There weren't any close towns as the plantation sat secluded from any bigger city, more due to its size than proximity.

Fernando tried to step forward, but María stuck her hand out and stopped him. She didn't need him speaking for her, and it irritated her that he would assume such a position.

"María Ferro. And you are?" She stuck her hand out and waited for the man to accept it.

He was slender and handsome in a rugged, machismo sort of way. His moustache quirked when he took her hand and looked into her eyes. She was sure women threw themselves at his feet with that gesture, not to mention the excitement surrounding the fact that he was currently one of the most wanted men in Cuba right now. The insurgency was going well—at least the bits and pieces she'd heard forecasted that it would be a matter of months before Fidel Castro and Ché Guevara would overthrow the government.

Was that why he was here, to recruit? Suddenly, her mind raced to Alejandro. They were looking for strong backs and weak minds. While he definitely didn't have a weak mind, he was young, determined, and could be vital to any attempted overthrow of the current regime. She needed to warn him. A wave of panic lanced through her. *Oh god.* This group wasn't against conscripting anyone they felt would help their cause.

"Señorita, it is a pleasure to meet you." He raised her hand to his lips and held it against her hand for far too long for her comfort, and clearly Fernando's as well, as he tried to move the general away.

"General?" Fernando wedged himself between María and Guevara. "Perhaps, I mean, you'd consider letting me take my fiancée for a ride in your car?"

There. He'd done it. He'd marked his territory, and she was furious.

A sideways glance caught her mother beaming at Fernando's declaration. There wasn't an engagement; they had barely seen each other at school. She'd be damned if she married someone she didn't care about, let alone someone who treated her like an object and not someone with a brain who could think for herself.

Bastard.

"I'm sorry, General, I need to help with the festivities. If you'll excuse me."

Turning on her heel, she didn't wait for a reply. Her mother guffawed behind her, struggling to say something, but with the general there, she'd mind her manners. Looking down at her hand, she wiped the back of it on her dress and writhed in disgust.

She needed to find Alejandro, and quick.

Chapter One

Present Day
Estelí, Nicaragua

Sofia ran her fingers over the huge lacquered humidor that sat on her father's desk. A simple brass name plate was etched with one word: HUERTA. It was the only adornment on the humidor. Its importance wasn't its size, but the wood that constructed the box. Sofia's great-grandfather had saved a few boards when he watched his small shanty be demolished. He'd built the rickety thing when he'd arrived in Nicaragua. All she knew was that her grandfather, Alejandro, hadn't intended to live in the wretched house as long as they had. According to the stories, her grandmother had conceived within days of their arrival, so the need for a roof over their growing family's head had been paramount. Lucky for him, the plot of land was cheap enough and that would be the start of the Huerta legend. Her father had built a small chapel on the site for his mother, the first extravagance in a life full of frugality. He'd been happy to witness the end of that part of his life and revel in the small success he was enjoying at that time. The humidor was the only reminder of his childhood he kept close.

Pushing the lid to the cedar-lined box up, scents of tobacco and cedar mixed, filling the air around her. Tears surfaced and quickly clouded Sofia's view of the contents. "Oh, Papa."

She caressed the toothy wrapper of a *Negrilla Diabla*, Bold She-Devil. The dark maduro wrapper earned the robusto cigar its name. The humidor was divided into thirds, with a third dedicated to his favorite Huerta cigar, The Reserve. Another third had her *Angel Blanca*, or White Angel, due to its Connecticut wrapper, and the last third held the Negrilla Diabla. The only cigar from her line missing from the humidor was her Conundrum, so named because it was such an enigma. Its traditional leather and creamy flavors at the start gave way to more chocolate and coffee undertones. She'd had a hard time branding it, so she went to the source to name it—her father. She'd shared a sample with him for his opinion. She'd never forget the look on his face as he smoked the first third. The creamy smoke eased out of his nose, and then he let the rest escape from his pursed lips.

"Well?"

Sofia held her breath as she watched him take another mouthful and hold it, his lips barely parting, letting the smoke escape, before he answered. "This is…"

She bit her lip and waited for the rest of his answer. He'd smoked thousands of cigars in his lifetime, so he was a consummate authority on all types.

"Got a delicate flavor that really…" He closed his mouth and pushed air through his nostrils. "It's very nice, mija."

"Nice?"

"It's…" He smiled. "It's very good."

Sofia controlled the urge to jump up and down at the compliment. Her father was known to be light on the praise, so a "very good" was great.

"It's really a conundrum, mija. It has such complex flavors that are really delicate, yet grow bolder toward the end. A conundrum."

"Then that's what I'll call it. Conundrum. Thank you, Papa."

They had sat in companionable silence smoking a few Conundrums.

"What are these, Sofia?" Manny asked, lifting one of the Negrilla Diablas to his nose and sniffing. "Are these yours?"

She nodded, wiping at the tears threatening to fall. "Yes, this is the Negrilla Diabla—"

"Ah, Bold She-Devil. Nice." Manny twisted the stick between his fingers, looking at the rounded triple cap, something that distinguished a Cuban cigar from others. "The size is perfect." It was a Robusto size, a ring gauge that was small enough so that women didn't think they were sticking a huge cigar in their mouths, but still big on flavors and guaranteed a good thirty minutes to smoke. She'd seen the oversexualized pictures in cigar magazines, models with big sticks in their mouths, or hands. Definitely a phallic symbol, she surmised, that appealed to the male gaze. She loved beautiful women, but had decided on more of a pinup-style label with a female devil and female angel on their respective cigars. Macho advertising wasn't an uncommon image, but it wasn't one she wanted to emulate in her own marketing campaign. Some of the new cigar companies were going with an urban, hip approach. She was leaning toward a sophisticated and polished package that promised being part of an exclusive community of like-minded individuals. She wanted to appeal to both men and women, their sense of style, and the cultural mystique surrounding the cigar industry. While she knew the romanticism of cigar history was important and robust, she also knew how cigar culture was evolving. Gone were the days of cigars being the sole property of wealthy men's clubs filled with smoke and crystal tumblers filled with high-end bourbon, where talk entailed stocks, bonds, mistresses, and backroom deals.

No, the industry was bigger than that, and she was breaking through beyond those smoke-filled lounges—or at least her cigars were.

Picking up the Blanca Angel, she ran it under her nose. The Connecticut wrapper would give it peppery notes. The thought made her laugh. It should have been the Negrilla Diabla, but they were named because of their wrappers and not the flavors when smoked.

"And this one?" He pointed to the one she held.

"Blanca Angel."

"White Angel. Fitting with the Connecticut wrapper. So, you have an Angel and a Devil. What are you saying, mija?" He gave off a belly laugh, picking up the Blanca Angel and sniffing it. "These are fantastic. Do you mind if I take one of each?"

"Not at all, Tío, please. I'd be honored to hear what you think about the line. I have one more, the Conundrum. I'll have it sent over to you."

"Conundrum. I like it." He ran his hand across her shoulders and pulled her in for a hug. "Your father would be so proud."

"Thank you." More tears fell.

"Oh, Sofia don't cry."

"I didn't know he had these in here," she said, wiping at the tears.

Manny wrapped his arms around her, pulling her close. He whispered in her ear, "He was so proud of you."

"Thanks." A few sobs let loose.

"Oh mija, don't cry. We are Huertas, and Huertas are proud Nicaraguans. We face the demon and fight it head-on. We do not surrender to our grief. We use it to build us up and propel us forward." Manny leaned back. "Conundrum, *por que*?"

Sofia smiled. "If you are fighting between the Devil…" She raised a Negrilla Diabla. "Or an Angel…" She held the other cigar in her right hand. "You have a conundrum. ¿Verdad?"

Manny gave off a raucous belly laugh so deep it shook his pony keg of a belly. "Si, Si. That's very clever, Sofia. RJ, isn't that clever?"

They both looked at RJ, who was pouring another liberal helping of rum. "Right, clever." He soured after tossing back another mouthful.

"Hey *compadre*. Slow down. You still have guests out there, and I'm sure Lina is tired of making small talk." Manny grabbed the bottle from the iron grasp RJ had on it. "Besides, we need to share some of Nicaragua's finest rum with our guest. *Sí*?"

Sofia wanted to shake some sense into her brother, but his actions right now were one of the reasons their father didn't trust RJ. Chances were he'd sell the business—or worse, lose it in a card game—putting all of them out on their asses. All of her father's sweat equity, time, and money gone just like that.

"I'll bring some Huerta cigars from our reserve collection. We should toast Father appropriately."

"Agreed," Manny said, spinning RJ in the direction of the door. "Come on, let's celebrate the life of Don Roberto, huh?"

As the door shut behind them, Sofia plopped

down into the huge leather chair reserved for the head of Huerta cigars. This was the view her father saw every day when he sat here, but now he would never see this again. Her heart seized at the thought and her mind flooded with all the good memories courtesy of her father. Now she was nearly an orphan, with only her grandmother left. It would be long before she took her place next to her parents in the family crypt. Sofia needed to steel herself when that time came. She buried her face in her hands, grief overtaking her. Just as she thought she'd controlled it, another wave washed over her. She stood, wishing she could give into it, but as Manny had said, Huertas pushed it down and used it to fight off the demons.

There was only one problem. Death was an evil mistress no one divorced.

❧ ❧ ❧ ❧

Her brother's message had been cryptic. "Sofia… uh…there's been an accident…uhm…Father's fallen off his horse and he's in hospital. I think you need to get home, now." When she called him back it had gone to voice mail and RJ hadn't returned her call. A call to the house and a quick discussion with her grandmother had confirmed her worst fears. Her father had been hurt in a horse-riding accident and wasn't expected to make it.

Her race home from Tampa had been quick. She'd had just enough time to get a rented corporate jet, toss her bags on it, and command the pilot to take her home the quickest way possible. Her father lay in a coma—the prognosis…she couldn't even go there. She prayed as she'd never prayed before. She begged, she bargained, she even promised to convert if that would save her father's life.

"We're on approach, Ms. Huerta." A flight attendant offered a sympathetic smile and patted Sofia on the shoulder. "Can I get you anything?"

"No, thank you." Sofia's mind was elsewhere. A hospital room. Her father on life support. She imagined standing next to him, his warm hand clasped firmly in hers. The beeping heart monitor. The squish, squish of the ventilator as it helped him breathe.

God, just get me there quick.

Don Roberto Huerta had been life-flighted to Managua, where he could get the best care money could buy. Looking down at the familiar landscape far below, Sofia calculated the time she had left to get to his bedside. Maybe twenty minutes. Forested land transitioned to tobacco fields and then to the cityscape of Managua. The plane skidded across the runway and taxied toward a waiting car. Julian, her pseudo-uncle, stood next to the company SUV. His stoic face gave nothing away.

Wordlessly, he opened the door to the backseat.

"How is he, Julian?"

He shook his head and looked away, obviously choked up. "Señorita Sofia..."

Fear crushed the air from Sofia's chest. She wondered if she was having a heart attack. "It's bad," she concluded flatly.

Julian lowered his gaze. His white knuckles confirmed the worst.

"I'm so sorry, Ms. Sofia."

Stunned, she sank into the back seat. Her father was dead. How was that possible?

Beyond the noisy thud of her pulse pounding in

her ears, she heard her bags being stowed, the driver's door closing, the tires gathering speed on the tarmac.

"What happened?" she asked numbly.

"They took your father off life support this morning. The doctor said he had no…" Julian tapped his head and mumbled something.

"No what?" When no answer came, she said, "Take me to my father, Julian. I want to see him."

☙ ☙ ☙ ☙

Sofia tucked a few errant strands of hair behind her ear. The warm, moist breeze had picked up and Sofia could smell rain. The small chapel suddenly seemed huge in front of her. The golden flicker of candlelight danced through the windows taunting her, beckoning her to enter. Sofia stood frozen in place and wondered if she could handle seeing her father, dead. A man so loving and full of life when she left for her trip to the United States, now lay beyond the simple wooden doors, never to take another breath. The priest had honored her request and promised to leave the church open so she could pay her respects in private. Now, her lips quivered, her feet refusing to move forward as her reserve started to crumble. While Sofia had a reputation for being made of ice when it came to business—a reputation she wanted to maintain—her inner composition was far from cold. This would be the only time she could grieve her father in the way she wanted.

Privately.

The small gravel crunched and popped under her high heels, each step louder than the last, until finally she reached the tile steps that led up to the church. She looked down at the red and blue serpentine pattern, boxed in by the cement grout, the pattern repeating until it finally met the wall of the church. She knew she was trying to distract herself as she admired the tile, but she knew what she had to do. She had to force herself to focus as she struggled to put one foot in front of the other until she stood before massive barriers between her and her father. Sofia jammed her purse under her arm, wiped her eyes, and stiffened her spine. She wrestled with the bulk of the door, heaving its weight against her shoulder. A sliver of light peeked out between the slabs of oak and leaked past the barrier, memories flooding past her with the smell of incense. She could see a younger version of herself in her youth kneeling on the prayer bench every Sunday morning. The door rested on her back, the weight of it pushing her farther into the church as if the hand of god was moving her toward her destiny. It closed with a thud behind her. The cool, cavernous interior was a sharp contrast to the warm, humid night that was being held at bay outside.

Eighteen pews lined the left and right sides, framing the large center aisle. She'd counted them repeatedly, squirming on those Sunday mornings. By twos, by threes, forward and backward, anything to keep her mind off the constant humming of prayers offered for the living, the dead, for good fortune, and penance that occurred the week before.

She recognized the large velvet clad confessional booth like a good friend, having spent a good many hours confessing her youthful indiscretions. The dark box with heavy curtains hid the occupant from the prying eyes of other church parishioners. Inside the dark room was a prayer bench and a pull screen opposite her face. When she knelt in front of it to confess her sins, she never saw the priest on the other side. Only hearing his voice was scary for a young child. All of this just so she could get a tiny wafer the next day. As she aged, so did her confessional sins. Hitting her brother, spitting in the fields, and when she had little to confess she started to make stuff up. Then she had something to confess the next time she sat in the confessional. The guilt had been too much, so she finally had to come clean. The priest admonished her for lying and gave her six Our Fathers and twelve Hail Marys, then asked her why she'd made up sins to confess. She sat in the confessional and shrugged her shoulders. The silence finally weighed on the priest and he dismissed her. The truth was something she wasn't ready to divulge—at least not to a priest—and she wouldn't for years.

Her gaze traveled to her left and to the simple casket directly in front of her, just in front of the altar. A small wooden prayer bench sat in front of the casket. She'd expected to pay her respects at home, but RJ had them move their father from the house to the church for the funeral tomorrow. His reason was bullshit: he didn't want his kids disturbing their father, or accidently knocking him over, or some other crap. If he acted like a parent, he wouldn't have to worry about accidents. RJ was an ass and his kids, well… She shook her head and pushed his family drama from her mind.

She was deliberately stalling.

A tight swallow, squeezing her lips together, she walked forward. The heady smell of incense burned her nostrils. A cold sweat swept over her body and the click of her heels on the polished tile cut through the silence of the church. The prayer candles were all lit, in memory of her father she was sure. Her chest heaved as she struggled to take a breath as each step moved her closer to her father. The lid had been left open and she could start to see his soft features. If she didn't know better, she would have just thought he was resting. She'd seen that face before. After a long afternoon in the factory, he'd catch a quick nap—resting his eyes, he often told her when she'd caught him in his office asleep.

Her hands rested on the end of the casket. At first, she could only stare at her father. She couldn't find anything wrong with him, and then she shifted her gaze and looked over his shoulder to the right side of his head. A dark bruise, trying to hide under a thin layer of makeup, had etched its way just behind his ear. Her stomach lurched and she fell to the prayer bench. She crossed herself and her head dipped, and her shoulder sagged under the weight of the final acknowledgement that her father was in fact, gone.

"Oh, Father," she whispered. Her plea, soft as it was, echoed around her. She rose on her knees and reached for her father's hand and clutched it tightly. "What am I going to do without you?"

She rested her head on her arm and sobbed as she still clutched his hand. He'd been the one to encourage her to start her own cigar line, to tell her that the only way she'd be taken seriously was to work her way from the bottom up. He'd shared stories of his father's life in Cuba as a young man, and his migration from the communist state to Nicaragua and the culmination of that journey. His greatest accomplishment, as he was always asked and answered, was finding someone, the love of his life, that would marry a poor upstart such as himself and the beautiful children she gifted him. Her father felt the same way about her mother, and

told Sofia many times she would feel the same way
when she finally found the love of her life. *Doubtful,*
Sofia thought, looking down at her father. He always
said the same thing whenever they talked about family:
every Huerta was born with cigars running through
their veins.

Thirty-five years wasn't enough. She felt cheated.

She stood and walked around the casket, then
leaned down, kissed his forehead, and stroked his thick,
graying hair. A tear fell on his face and then another,
and another. Her throat tightened, almost choking her.
Fear fingered its way into her thoughts. Whom would
she turn to for advice, for help, for the fatherly hug
he offered without judgment when she doubted her
decisions?

Her head tilted back, and before she could
stop herself she offered god a demented groan and
screamed, "Why? Why would you rip someone so
loved from their family?" A damnation was in order
but her father, a godly man, wouldn't allow it, even in
death.

"Why?" she said again as she threw herself over
the casket, sobs spilling out of her.

☙ ☙ ☙ ☙

RJ stood at the window of the church watching
his sister expel her grief. He wanted to feel bad, but
he just couldn't raise enough emotion. Besides, he was
the one who'd had to make the tough decisions when
the doctors broke the bad news about Don Roberto's
brain damage. His father could have been kept alive by
machines, but for what? He was not going to awaken
and greet his daughter, so RJ could not see the point

in delaying the inevitable. He looked down at his hand and let an evil grin cross his lips. He had held his father's life in his hands, and he took some satisfaction knowing it was a circumstance that the old man would never want to find himself in.

Sofia's hands, yes.

His, no.

A man's decision was left to the only man in the Huerta household and he had made it, whether Sofia liked it or not. She'd always been their father's favorite; now, she had no one. Through a cruel twist of fate, the playing field had been leveled and now they stood as equals. He would finally have an equal say in the business empire their family had built over two generations. Their holdings went beyond Huerta Cigars and the plantation established almost over three-quarters a century ago. There was a rum plant, and Crema, the ice cream company their father had started.

RJ had been a glorified errand boy for all of the companies at different times, but he'd shown his father he was leadership material. RJ had turned the rum plant around and made it into the profitable corporation it was today. Negotiating export deals with twenty different countries and a huge agreement with a big-box beverage company in the United States had seen it through the downturn in the world economy. Several other companies hadn't survived the crash, and RJ had seized on the opportunity to buy them for pennies on the dollar. Expanding Huerta's holdings and moving the needle on their influence in Nicaragua was all his doing, not Sofia's, and he had to remind his father often. RJ had finally twisted his father's arm into admitting he'd been right and could handle a Huerta business venture. He had pressed his father to let him run Huerta Cigars, but the old man wouldn't relent. Instead, he'd cut RJ off from the business, telling him to be happy with what he had because it could easily be taken away.

Bastard.

Now, one of them would have the opportunity to prove the old man wrong and he was certain once the will was read, he'd be victorious and Sofia would be out. She couldn't manipulate their father anymore. Those days were gone, and with them, her power. The business world was all about winners, and he would finally be able to prove to everyone he had what it took to lead Huerta to bigger things. RJ sat up straighter. He knew all eyes were on him. People would be coming to him for advice just as they had with his father. If they were lucky, he'd do business with them, but only if they paid him the respect he was due. The days of him being a doormat were over, and he was going to let the world know that fact once he assumed his rightful place on the Huerta throne. He wasn't above flaunting his newfound position under some people's noses. In fact, he would take great joy in watching them grovel, begging for his scraps.

As for Sofia, perhaps he would ship her off to the US to work on market expansion or send her on a publicity tour around the world—shit, he didn't want her acting like the company rock star. If she was lucky he'd let her keep her cigar brand, but only if she fell in line. Otherwise, he'd help her find a role she could live with. Perhaps he'd get her one of those little push carts for ice cream and she could hawk their product to tourists along the beach. Naw, that might be too good for her. He'd love to see her in an apron cleaning toilets at the factory. In fact, he'd pay to see her on her knees scrubbing the porcelain god.

RJ hesitated, tempted to stay in the church a little longer and revel in his sister's pain, but he had a speech to prepare for the funeral tomorrow. Once they'd dispensed with the will, he'd take his place as the rightful heir to the Huerta Company and then he'd dispense with his sister's nonsense.

Chapter Two

The combination of cold air and her sister-in-law's cloying perfume had Sofia's head swimming. Everything felt surreal as she glanced around the limo. Her younger brother Roberto II, or RJ as he liked to be called, was on his second drink. At eight in the morning. She wasn't surprised to see him slamming the alcohol. If she were married to the witch on his right, she would be in a constant state of inebriation as well. She let out a sigh. RJ's kids slapped each other and then wailed to their inattentive parents, who clearly didn't give a rat's ass about them. At four and five years old, they were at a stage where one minute they could be little angels, but then quickly flip that halo and sprout horns, which seemed to be permanently attached. Why Lina had bothered to have children was beyond her. It was clear she wasn't going to be winning any Mother of the Year awards anytime soon. The little rug rats had no manners. No surprise, as Lina could barely muster a "Thank you" or "Please" when she needed something. Every time Sofia saw the children at the family compound they were always screaming, hitting each other, or crying over some perceived slight. These kids were the poster children for contraception.

Sofia was about to say something to discipline the children when a fragile, weathered hand patted her arm, stopping her. As if she could read Sofia's mind, her *abuela* María offered a slight smile.

"They are young, mija."

"I know, *Abuelita*." Sofia raised the frail digits to her lips. "I know."

She had hoped that RJ would have reined in the little animals on a day such as today. but she wasn't surprised by his lack of involvement. In fact, she *was* surprised to see him at all. He usually rolled into the house about this time—the sneaky crawl past her father's office and into his bed usually happened around 8:30 a.m. Therefore, it was technically past RJ's bedtime.

The limo eased to a stop. The door swung open, showering the cool interior with warm, humid sunshine. Julian stood to the side of the door offering his hand to her. Sofia eased herself out of the vehicle, glad to be free of the makeshift romper room. The morning was already hot and her black dress was eating the sun that beat down on them. She bent down and gently helped her grandmother toward the door. She had to put her hand on her nephew to stop him from wedging himself past his grandmother and the door.

"Bobby, stop." She pressed her hand against the five-year-old's chest and forced him back into the car. "RJ, a little help here?"

She bit back what she really wanted to say to her brother, but her grandmother was waiting. Lucky for him. Otherwise, she'd tell him to get his offspring under control or she would teach them some manners.

"Abuelita." She helped her grandmother out of the car. The older woman's thin black veil promised to obscure any emotions that might surface on her face, but it was hardly needed. The mask that had taken decades to build was firmly in place. She admired her grandmother's ability to hide the pain.

Sofia pulled the sides of her dress down. A straitjacket would be more comfortable. It wasn't that she didn't like to dress up, but it was the occasion she was protesting. She couldn't hide her own anguish as the formality of what she was about to do finally hit her. Tears escaped and dripped off her cheek before her delicate handkerchief could catch the errant sorrow.

"*Señora, lo siento.*" Julian bowed toward her grandmother, the matriarch of the family, and helped steady her while Sofia collected herself. His own grief-stricken gaze split her heart wide open. He had been her father's right-hand man for decades, but now no one knew what the future held for the company, the workers, or her family.

"*Gracias*, Julian," was all her grandmother could say as she clutched Sofia's forearm, looking up at the small chapel. She had been here many times with her grandmother, sitting next to her as she knelt, praying. Rosary in hand, her abuela moved from bead to bead until she'd made the full circle and back again until she was sure God had heard her prayers. Peering down at the elderly woman who had lost her son, Sofia noted her grandmother clutched the same worn beads, a pewter crucifix dangling off the end.

"Thank you, Julian." Sofia squeezed his hand.

"Of course, I am at your disposal, *jefa.*"

Before she could correct him for calling her "boss," he hugged her and then walked to join the rest of the men who were milling about.

"What, no help here?" RJ yelled out, practically pouring himself out of the limo and onto the pebbled drive way.

Sofia bent down and jerked his arm. "Pull

yourself together, RJ. Everyone is watching."

"Fuck them, I don't care." RJ looked back into the limo and yelled, "God dammit, knock that shit off."

"¡Ay, dios mío!" Sofia heard her grandmother cough into her handkerchief.

"RJ," Sofia said through clenched teeth. "Everyone is looking and you're embarrassing our abuela."

She raked RJ with a terse glare, daring him to say just one word to her. She wasn't sure which limb of the Huerta tree he sprang from, but she often doubted their linked lineage. At least he had sense enough to look at their grandmother and offer a half-hearted apology, but afterward he went back into the limo, spewing a slew of curses.

Father José walked up just as she was ready to go back and straighten RJ out.

"Sofia."

"Father."

"Allow me to escort your grandmother inside."

"Of course." Sofia bowed her head slightly and then returned to the commotion in the limousine.

☙ ☙ ☙ ☙

The small chapel had been María's refuge where she spent her days praying for strength to continue a life without her Alejandro. She counted on her fingers the number of years her beloved had been gone, twice around and three more fingers for twenty-three years. His unexpected death at sixty-six almost wrecked her. If it wasn't for her two sons, Roberto and Manuel, she would have given up long before now. She had never wanted to live this long without him. They had been each other's everything after arriving in Nicaragua.

Alejandro had spent long days building his business, María close by his side at all times. She'd learned to plant the seeds, know when the leaves were just right for harvesting, and how to roll cigars during those lean years. They'd been the happiest of her life. She'd hoped that the grief would take her life when her husband died, but her sons, the factory, and grandchildren had all distracted her enough that she tolerated life.

However, the church now held the second misery of her life. The casket sat at the end of the aisle. María knew she'd be on her knees if she wasn't holding on to the priest's arm like a life preserver. She was drowning in her swirling emotions. Grabbing his arm tighter, she averted her gaze. The density of the incense, the sweaty bodies, and the heat of the day seemed to have a physical weight that lingered under her veil. If her fan worked any harder, the veil would be swept off her head. No parent should outlive their child. The grief was almost unbearable.

The news had swept her into the depths of despair, just as it had when news of her father's death had reached her from Cuba. They hadn't seen each other since she'd left. Her father had been given strict orders from her mother to never mention their daughter's name. María and her mother had shared coarse words on the one and only phone call she'd made to the plantation after she left Cuba with Alejandro. Word had traveled back to her through the cigar worker grapevine that after Castro's nationalization of the cigar industry, her father had been allowed to keep part of his plantation only after merging with the Calderons. While it wasn't the sprawling farm he once had, it was enough to keep them in the lifestyle her mother had enjoyed. Her mother had finally received what she deserved—a

merger with Fernando's family—and not one brought
by the forced marriage of her only daughter.
Alejandro booked a flight for them on the next
airplane to Cuba. It had been her first-ever flight,
and she couldn't tell if the butterflies flitting around
in her stomach were from her nerves or going home
and seeing her mother for the first time in a decade.
She had a death grip on Alejandro's hand from the
moment they'd taken off to the moment her feet hit the
ground. His patience had been extraordinary as they
circled Havana waiting to land. Her nose pressed to
the window gave her an exhilarating feeling of falling,
and she thought she could make out the cigar fields of
her father if the map in her purse was halfway right.
Crossing herself, she prayed that if they survived she'd
take a ship home and never fly again. The bumpy ride
was nothing compared to the jolt she received when
they finally landed. Besides, if God wanted them to
fly, he'd have given them wings and halos. Alejandro
pulled their bag and a small carry-on from the overhead
compartment, and reached down for her hand.

"Ready?" He offered a smile.

Her nerves weren't through with her stomach,
but she was successful in giving him a weak smile.

"I don't think so."

"It'll be okay. I'm here, and Fernando is
yesterday's news. Right?"

María pinched his cheek and kissed him. "He
will always be my mother's choice."

"I think I can live with that."

"Me, too." Pulling her wrap around her, she
shaded her eyes as she saw Havana from a whole new
perspective. Now she would just have to deal with her
mother and the Calderons.

A crowd of eager greeters stood around the airport entrance waiting for their loved ones to emerge from the terminal. Couples kissed, parents hugged their children, and people mingled, blocking the entrance. She was pulled along as Alejandro cut a path through the throng of people. A young man in work clothes stood at the airport door holding a sign with "Huerta" emblazed across it.

"Hola, we're the Huertas. Who are you?" Alejandro said, shouldering their luggage and shifting its bulk.

"Ah, Señor Huerta. I am here to take you to the rancho." The man grabbed the bag from Alejandro and then acknowledged María. "Señora Huerta. I am so sorry for your loss. Don Miguel was a wonderful man."

"Thank you. You are?"

"Oh, lo siento. My name is, Pablo. I work for your father." He dropped his eyes. "I mean, I worked for your father." He crossed himself before looking up. "This way please. We have a long drive to Vuelta Abajo and I'm sure your mother is anxious to see you."

"I doubt it," María said under her breath.

Alejandro pulled her under his arm and hugged her. "You aren't the same person you were when you lived here, sweetheart. *We* aren't the same people we were when we lived here. Cuba isn't the same place it used to be. So, let's remember that as we go home."

The air slapped her in the face as they exited the airport. It felt heavier, wetter than she remembered. The noxious smell of car exhaust was thick in the air and the traffic sped past them as if they were racing each other. A '55 Chevy sat waiting for them. It had seen better days. The blue paint had faded, and the multiple dents added character. She wondered where they acquired parts for the aging jalopies that zipped around the cracked streets. With Castro's embargo in effect, she was sure anything specialized was hard to get and car parts would be on that list of rare items to be found.

María shielded her eyes and looked around at the city. Havana was showing its age. The buildings were clearly lacking basic services and in serious need of repair, paint, and occupants, if the boarded-up windows were any indication. María noticed the large groups of men with vacant glances standing against the buildings lining the dirty streets, smoking and eyeing everyone who exited the airport. Some stood next to taxis waiting for a fare, and some hustled for customers leaving the airport. Havana was different. She could feel it. It lacked the energy and verve it had when she last visited. If this is what Havana looked like, she wondered what she'd find at the Ferro estate.

Family was everything to María. Her mother had made it a point to put it, along with money, power, and property, above all else in her small world. Surprising to María was that her mother never had another child. She had grown up close to her own grandparents, and aunts, uncles, and cousins were only a house or two away. Family gatherings were festive, even wonder-filled times in her life. However, as an only child, María often found herself alone with just her parents for company. According to her mother, family legacy was more important than friends, more important than almost life itself. Her father had built an empire to be proud of, and the revolution had cost him the one thing he valued almost as much as her: his cigar plantation. The land had a value that kept them grounded and prosperous, so losing that broke her father. He'd been allowed to stay and run the government-approved and sanctioned cigar business as a consolation prize for being a dedicated servant to Castro. Her mother pushed him to fight for their business, but the communist view of the world meant he would never "own" the plantation. The government was the benefactor of her family's hard work. His broken spirit was on display every night when he came home to his family. Her feet firmly grounded in family, it almost killed her to leave them and Cuba behind with Alejandro. She knew the future for her own family wouldn't be under a tin-despot dictator like Castro, but in the freedom that would allow her children to thrive and build their own opportunities. Alejandro had seen the future, and it wasn't in Cuba.

Seeing her Cuba in a state of poverty stabbed at her heart. Her memories of visiting Havana had been some of her most coveted. Time spent with her uncle and cousins in a vibrant, thriving city had been a wake-up call for María. Now looking at the streets and people, she was suddenly grateful for her husband's passion and vision. She hoped she could pass down the same values to her own children. A love for their country, for the business their father was building and the future, that was much brighter in Nicaragua.

A thought suddenly crossed her mind. What would she do if her mother asked her to stay in Cuba and help with the family farm? Would it be seen as her family obligation to stay? Her cousins had stepped up to help with the work that had become too much for her father, but what would happen to them now? She could only hope that her mother wouldn't ask and she wouldn't have to decline. She had her own family now, and there was no way she would come back, not even for her mother.

María shook her head to wipe away the memories of her father's ruined legacy. Those days had passed, and now she had to tune back in to the tragedy of her son's untimely death.

༄༅༅༅

The sweltering of the morning was choking RJ. He pulled at his black silk tie, trying to loosen it. It felt more like a noose around his neck. Perhaps his wife had planned for him to pass out and look the fool in front of everyone as he bit the floor.

The brats next to him fidgeted nonstop. He smacked the back of Roberto III's head, and it sounded more like thumping a melon at a roadside fruit stand. He often wondered if the kid had any brains at all, considering the stupid shit he'd been pulling lately. He'd caught the boy tying his shoes to the dog's feet, thinking it would be funny to shoot video as the poor mutt practically ran through a plate glass door trying to get the shoes off.

RJ shoved his family down the church aisle. Lina ushered the children into their reserved pew as he dropped to one knee, faced the altar and crossed himself, then slid in behind. He could feel hundreds of eyes on him as the mourners flowed in behind him and filled the rest of the quaint chapel. Across the aisle sat his sister and grandmother.

"Bitch."

"R.J..." Lina poked him in the ribs. "The children." RJ flashed her a dismissive look and clucked at the two brats still squabbling.

Everyone stood as the priest, in his robes and

vestments, and altar boys walked down the aisle swinging an incense bowl. RJ pinched the bridge of his nose. Incense and last night's rum weren't mixing well. Turning forward, he could see his father's face poking out of the casket.

"Did you have to bring her?"

"What?" RJ followed Lina's gaze across the church and spotted Estrella dabbing at her eyes.

"Christ, Lina. She was my father's secretary." *Really?* he thought. *I don't need this petty jealousy from a woman who has revolving sheets on her bed. Puta.*

"Yeah…but does she have to be here, now?"

RJ rolled his eyes. "She. Worked. For. My. Father, Lina… Fuck." The last word said loud enough that everyone in the church turned toward the arguing couple. He switched to a terse whisper. "Everyone from the company is here. Knock your shit off."

Lina tossed her hair and bent down to answer a question from her son. "No, honey. Dad's just sad that Papa's gone to live with your abuelita and the angels."

"Is that really Papa in the casket? I want to touch him," Roberto said.

RJ jerked his arm and pulled him down into the pew, then cuffed him on the back of the head. "You are not going to touch Papa, son. Now, sit down."

"Mama." He screamed so loud that RJ wanted to shove his fist down the little brat's throat to shut him up.

Christ, would this day never end? He ran his fingers through his dirty hair trying to avoid the stares of the crowd.

"Mommy, why doesn't Papa get up?" his daughter chimed in.

His temper finally got the best of him. Leaning

over, he grunted, "Shut them the fuck up or take them out of the building." He would gladly stomp out of the church and be done with the whole thing, however if he wanted to be seen as the new heir apparent of Huerta, he needed to stay and exude leadership and poise. His jaw bunched thinking about the job ahead. A sideways glance back toward his sister stiffened his resolve. *She'll be the first to go.* He didn't need any help when it came to running the Huerta holdings, or any advice, for that matter. If he was feeling generous, maybe he'd just buy her out of her half of Huerta assets and let her take her little cigar company and run. He'd make it clear if she didn't take the money he'd run her out of business. With his new connections with the other cigar families, he'd have enough clout to do it. He smiled at how ruthless he could be when he wanted something. Turning his attention to Estrella, his smiled broadened. He always got what he wanted...one way, or another.

"Sweetheart," Lina's voice jerked him back to his current-day reality. He watched her cup her daughter's chin and kiss her forehead. "Daddy will explain everything later. Right, Daddy?"

"Whatever," was all RJ could offer. No one, it seemed, wanted to be at this godforsaken service. Him most of all.

RJ thought about Estrella again as they exchanged glances. She offered him a brief smile before turning her attention back to the priest starting the funeral mass. He wished he were sitting there instead of next to the ball-and-chain he had around his neck.

RJ pulled at the noose again. *Fuck me*, he thought, looking at his father for the last time. He wished he could summon some tears for the bastard, but he just couldn't. He couldn't be further removed from the man he called Father than if he was lying next to him in his casket. They'd never had a true father/son relationship the whole time he was growing up. He blamed himself. His reckless teens had turned into his rebellious twenties, and he didn't even want to talk about his dirty thirties. He smiled at the memories. Well, maybe they weren't so bad, but they further ostracized him from the family. The icing on the frozen pond had been his marriage to Lina. Instead of the children bringing them closer, it had driven a wedge between him and his promiscuous wife. His father, though, was over the moon to have a third generation of Robertos in the family. His legacy—at least his name—would live on. His father put a high price on family and that had smoothed over the rift between them...for a time. It wasn't as if his sister, the *manflor*, was going to give him grandchildren.

Then suddenly one day, something changed. Each exchange with his father was strained, and suddenly a chasm so deep it couldn't be overcome developed between them. Everything RJ did to try to please his father was meet with scorn and revulsion. His comparison to his sister had become a daily occurrence. So, he avoided his father, slipping further into his cups. Rum, women and...well that's all he wanted lately, and the more of each the better. In fact, he couldn't wait for the funeral to be over so he could drink himself stupid and be rid of Lina and the kids.

A diversion. That's what he needed. The crowd around him stood for a prayer, startling RJ. He didn't recognize the foreigner in the casket and imagined his mother there instead. He often wondered what his mother was like, as he took these brief detours out of his screwed-up life. Was she kind and gentle, or cold and brisk like his father had been?

No, he imagined her to be loving and kind. He had her brown eyes and curly brown hair. He kept a picture of her on his desk and on his nightstand. He never wanted to be far away from her, even if it was only in spirit.

He wiped his mouth, craving a drink. Reminiscing did that to him. The memories were often too painful, so he dulled the hurt with alcohol. At least if he drank himself stupid he would be momentarily rid of the anchor around his neck drowning him.

Thoughts of his mother often haunted his dreams, urging him to be a better man. Now, he wondered if his father would be the nightmare he would never be rid of.

God, how could she have left him with these cold, heartless people? Didn't she love him? Unfortunately, he'd become one of them, the very thing he despised. His shoulders sagged in defeat.

They'd won, for now.

Chapter Three

W hat? That's got to be a mistake." RJ stood, knocking his chair backward.

"No, I assure you, sir, these were his exact wishes." The lawyer looked down his crooked nose and pointed to the line in the will. Moving his finger along with the text, he repeated, "See, two-thirds interest and the running of Huerta holdings is bequeathed to your sister."

"Why? Why would he do this to me?" RJ paced back and forth in his father's huge office. Sofía shook her head. Clearly, it seemed, he just now realized he would not be inhabiting their father's office anytime soon. "What about the rum production, or the ice cream company? Give those to Sofía and I get Huerta Cigars," he said, stomping his feet wanting his way like an impetuous child.

"Did you think Papa wouldn't find out about Lina?"

"What are you talking about?" RJ was clearly feigning shock at the question.

"Father was crushed when he found out the grandchildren, his only grandchildren, that you tried to pawn off as yours, were some other man's." Sofia swirled her tumbler and stared out the window.

People were still milling about, talking, drinking, and soon the music would begin. There was always a party—births, marriages, birthdays, deaths, any reason was a good enough reason to party. Her father would have wanted it that way, so she was happy to oblige the workers. Most of them had worked for her father for decades, and it was their way of showing respect to Don Roberto.

She looked back at her brother and wondered why she wasn't lucky enough to find out RJ had a different parent. If it wasn't for the fact that their mother had died shortly after having him, she would have sworn he was illegitimate. His womanizing, drinking, and the way he spent money clearly weren't the trademarks of a Huerta. At least not a Don Huerta.

Crossing the expanse of the office, Sofia plopped down in a leather chair in front of the desk, crossed her legs at the ankles, and pursed her lips. The glare she offered RJ only made him more defiant as he moved aggressively toward the desk.

Sofia put her foot on the edge of the desk, stopping him from getting any closer. The lawyer shuffled the stacks of papers and tried to be as inconspicuous as possible. He leafed through the bulk and pulled several pages that were tagged with sticky arrows. Laying them out in an orderly line, he looked at Sofia and started to say something as RJ interrupted.

"This is bullshit. I'm the man of the family now. All of this should come to me." RJ drunk-stumbled as he swung his arm wide, practically hitting Sofia.

"And you, you go into town whoring around. Picking up a little *señorita* or two. I'm surprised you don't have any more little bastards running around."

Sofia knew she was pushing his buttons, but she didn't have to pretend anymore. Out of respect for her father, she never mentioned her brother's indiscretions, or those of his wife.

"I can't have children," RJ finally admitted. Kneeing the chair next to Sofia, he sat down with a thud. "So, Father is going to leave my lesbian sister to run one of the biggest cigar manufacturers in Nicaragua?"

"Hold on. You thought you could pass your wife's children off as Huertas and no one would know?"

Sofia gripped the carved lion heads of the chair. She wanted to get up and punch him in the throat. Her father deserved more respect than RJ had shown him. He had been devastated when he found out, and he had sprung it on Sofia on one of their rides through the tobacco fields. Their weekly, almost daily rides had started when Sofia had purchased her own tobacco field in the US and then another small parcel next to the Huerta estate. Small, minute even compared to Huerta's grand estate, but she had his blessing when she announced she wanted to start her own boutique line of cigars.

"Sofia…" Don Roberto paused before the rest of the words had tumbled out. "Did you know Lina had affairs?"

"Knew, Papa?" Her heart seized as she registered what her father was saying. She thought *he* knew. It was just something Latino men were known for, at least that's what her abuelita had told her when she discussed Lina with her. "Yes, I'm sorry, I thought you knew."

Don Roberto reined his horse to a stop and searched her face. "No, I didn't know the grandchildren weren't RJ's."

"What?"

"So, you know about Lina, but did not tell me about the babies?"

"Papa, I had no idea. I'm sorry."

They sat facing each other, leg to leg. She wanted to reach out and touch the proud man who set rigid in his saddle. He had been so excited when RJ had announced that Lina was carrying an heir to the Huerta cigar dynasty. Adding the fact that it was a boy only made it more exciting for Don Roberto.

"Do you know how proud I am of your new line of cigars?" he said, changing the subject.

"I hope so, Papa." She smiled back at her father. He taught her everything she knew about the cigar industry and she couldn't be more thankful.

"You've worked this business from the dirt up. Getting out here and working beside the workers. And going into the drying rooms. Developing your own blends and learning to roll cigars. The workers look up to you."

She blushed at the compliment. She wanted to learn the business and did the only thing she knew how: work it. Coming home from college, she walked the fields with their foreman, Julian, asking questions, learning what made good tobacco; the difference between the leaves of maduro, ligero, and habano; how to judge the tobacco to get just the right Connecticut leaf outside the state. She rolled cigars with her own hands and knew the oily feel of a good habano versus a bad one.

While her blends were no competition against the Huerta line, she took pride in knowing she had a taste for the business, so to speak.

"I want you to take over Huerta when I'm gone," he said, matter-of-factly.

"Papa."

"Don't worry, I'm not going anywhere, Sofia." He smiled and reached over, patting her horse's neck.

"You've proven that you are the only Huerta ready to take over the business." He fingered the reins and then added, "The only one I can trust."

Sofia knew there would be implications from her father's decision. RJ wasn't one to sit down and take bad news lightly. RJ not only thought of himself as second-in-command, but he had always assumed and told everyone in the cigar industry that he would soon have control of Huerta Cigars. Perhaps RJ had a premonition, but more likely it was what he saw on the bottom of his bourbon tumbler at night.

"Have you talked to Abuelita about this?"

"You don't want the business?" he asked, a surprised look crossing his face before it was replaced with his typical stoic expression.

"Of course I do, but what about Tío Manny?"

"He agrees with me, and he'll have part ownership, too. But just for the first year." His toothy grin alleviated any reservations she might have had.

"Besides, sending you to business college means Huerta will move seamlessly into the twenty-first century where it belongs."

"Have you told RJ?" She worried how her brother would react.

"I will, in good time, mija."

"It's a man's world, Papa."

"You can handle it, Sofia. I've seen the way you've dealt with Vega."

Gerardo Vega made her skin crawl. He wasn't just one of the biggest cigar manufacturers in the Dominican Republic, he was one of the biggest lechers, too. He worked overtime any time he was around Sofia, trying to call her, ply her with alcohol, and do almost anything he could to get her into his bed. It was a behavior she was very familiar with. The cigar industry was a macho man's world, and their behavior was out for all to see at cigar conventions. While there were a few women who were starting to lead cigar companies or build their own smaller cigar boutiques, they only made up about eight percent of the industry. Women flocked to the men who owned cigar companies, thinking they epitomized Latino culture, virility, and machismo. Eye candy was not only ready and available, it was wanting.

She'd been working on a Huerta marketing campaign to get more women interested in cigars, and Vega had pushed her buttons at the last trade show in Las Vegas. The fact that he did it in front of her father made no difference to Vega—he was trying to make a point. The cigar business was an old boys' club and she didn't have the proper anatomy to join.

"I've heard talk that RJ's been meeting with some of the other families, trying to set up some kind of—"

"Cigar cartel?"

"Something like that," she said. Looking across the field she suddenly wondered if she could handle *all* of Huerta cigars. Don Roberto had started with only a few acres, and now he had a couple hundred of the best leaves in production. He didn't need to buy tobacco to produce his cigars. In fact, he could sell what he didn't need. Lucky for her, he was family oriented and she got first pick of the bales.

"He's already planning for when I die. Not smart on his part. Trust me, I know what he's doing."

"He thinks it's his by right of birth, Papa. He'll never agree to having me as the head of Huerta."

"He doesn't have a choice. It's done. All nice and legal, Daughter." He pulled his horse around and kicked the mare into a cantor.

While her father wasn't school educated, he was tobacco smart. He'd learned it from his Cuban roots that had emigrated to Nicaragua. By mid-winter he knew where he stood for production for the spring. He could pretty much tell exactly how many bales of tobacco they would produce that year based on records his father had kept and added to over the decades. He knew what to plant more of for his own production as well as everyone else's. What he couldn't use he sold to Americans wanting to start their own cigar lines with top-of-the-line tobacco.

Sofia spurred her horse to catch up with her father's.

"RJ spends money like he's earned it. His soft hands betray his shallow heart."

"What about the kids? They adore you."

"And I adore them. It isn't their fault their mother's a slut."

"RJ is no saint, Papa."

He took a deep breath and sighed. "I know. His mama's shame is palpable. She looks down on your brother and carries his shame even in heaven."

Her abuelita knew, too, yet clearly hadn't said anything to her son. RJ was like a frat boy everywhere he went traveling for Huerta business. Half a brain on cigar business, the other half on women.

"You know I can't give you grandbabies. Right, Papa?"

That had been the end of their conversation. Sofia didn't need to reiterate why, as he had given her his blessing long ago that it was okay for her not to provide grandchildren. Besides, he reminded her, that's why he had a son.

Sofia jerked back to the present when RJ started to rant. "I've been waiting for the day I would take over Huerta Cigars. Fuck the rest of the companies. I've worked with Father, sat by his side, talked with other cigar families, and discussed the possibility of merging to make Huerta Cigars even bigger."

"Bullshit. You never talked to him about anything but money."

RJ raised his hand as if he was going to backhand her, but she didn't falter. He might knock his wife around, but if he thought he was going to lay a hand on her she'd shred it and he wouldn't be left with enough to work his Johnson.

"You forget I'm the one who turned the rum business around when it was swirling the bowl, Sister. I brought in the big boys and signed the contracts. Not you." He leaned forward.

"You're right, so you deserve the rum holdings. Take them. I don't care."

"I'm not settling for a pittance when I deserve to run Huerta Cigars and all its holdings. It's mine. I have big plans for Huerta."

"Well I guess you should discuss your plans with me, RJ. Because now, I have two-thirds share and I'm the CEO of Huerta Holdings, including Huerta Cigars. Tío Manny has the other third." Sofia raised her hand and squished her fingers together, then separated them by a mere quarter of an inch. "He has this much interest in Huerta Cigars." Sofia stood, opened the simple humidor on her father's desk, and pulled out a cigar. She ran the delicate finger of tobacco under her nose, sniffing it before she clipped the end. Picking up the lighter, she turned the cigar around and leaned against the desk as she toasted the end. The smell of roasted tobacco filled her nostrils. Blowing on the end of the cigar, it started to burn bright red with each breath. She looked over at her brother, who was seething in his anger, his hands clenched into fists and his jaw set in a tight line as he returned her stare.

"You know, RJ, all you had to do was be a Huerta," Sofia said, puffing on the end of the cigar as she completed lighting it. "But you thought just having the name was your passkey into the business. You never sat with Father, you never talked about cigars with him, and you never wormed your way in enough to understand what the business meant to him. How he built this company with his bare hands, with no education above the sixth grade. You went to college, you drive fast cars, and you sleep with women as if they are disposable enjoyment made just for your pleasure. And now it all comes home to roost, my brother."

Someone cleared his throat in the room, pulling Sofia from her anger.

"If it's okay with you, Señorita, we should get these documents signed and I will take my leave."

Suddenly, Sofia was embarrassed that she'd gone on a tirade in front of the Huerta family lawyer.

"Of course, Señor Gomez. Let me get my Tío Manny."

A knock on the door precluded Sofia from going any farther. "Come in."

Manny Huerta, a taller version of her father, appeared between the open double doors.

"Lo siento, mija." He smiled at Sofia and nodded at RJ, who stood and beckoned his uncle.

"Tío, tell you me you weren't a part of all of this…" RJ swept his hands toward Sofia and the lawyer.

"My brother asked me for my advice, and I gave

it to him, RJ." He clasped RJ's shoulder and whispered in his ear. "Sofia is the perfect person to run Huerta Cigars. She has the head for it, mijo."

Sofia smiled at the comradery they shared. RJ and Manny, *compadres*. Cut from the same swatch of cloth. Both good-looking men who loved the ladies, except Tío Manny, a couple of years her father's junior, knew where business ended and pleasure started and never mixed the two. He had his own cigar factory—it was a hereditary Huerta trait, miniscule in comparison to his brother's estate. However, it kept him busy, happy, and with enough money to enjoy good Nicaraguan rum, fine cigars, and beautiful women.

"Tío, you've got to be kidding me. You know it's my birthright to be the CEO of Huerta cigars." RJ jerked away from Manny's touch.

RJ was acting like a kid in a candy shop who'd just been told he couldn't have the giant jawbreaker that he lusted after. That was his problem—he wanted for nothing. Her father had indulged his every whim and now he couldn't have the sweets. Don Roberto carried the guilt of their mother's death every day, putting it on like he did a pair of pants. Her death from complications of having RJ had thrown their father into a tailspin. Roberto had adored his wife. Like him, she was a simple woman who didn't need much to make her happy. Her death came as a crushing blow to the man who would do anything for her. Sofia remembered the many days after he spent drinking and smoking in his office, only leaving there and returning to life after her grandmother had gone in and set him straight. Her mother's name was never to be spoken again in his presence. Sofia had learned that the hard way one afternoon when she'd thrown a temper tantrum, screaming her mother's name and how she wished her father was dead, too. He'd fanned her behind and sent her to her room without lunch or dinner.

The Huerta family was familiar with hard times—they were the stones that built the foundation of their lives. Don Roberto's family in Cuba had seen their share of tragedy. His father had lost everything and sent his son, Sofia's grandfather, to work for the man who'd taken everything from them.

One day, Sofia, feeling especially sorry for herself, asked her grandmother how her father's family had survived in Cuba raising six children with barely enough food to eat.

"You mean they had options, mija?"

"Well, no. I guess not."

"Exactly, you get up every day. You do what you have to do to keep the family together, and you ask god to forgive you for whatever you did to make him angry."

"What did he say?" a young Sofia asked.

"Nothing."

It was her first lesson on being a strong woman. A dirt farmer's salary didn't go far, hence her grandfather's venture into the tobacco fields. Little did they know it would create the empire that would support a village.

"RJ, I know this has come as a blow, especially since you're the one who was with your father when he died. It was a blessing you were there and that he didn't lay in the field for hours or days."

Did she just hear her Tío right? Was RJ with their father?

Why was she just now hearing this?

"You were with Father when he died? What

happened, RJ?" Sofia was suddenly suspicious.

"Father wanted to go for a ride. You know how he gets when he's got something on his mind. So he asked me to go with him. I'm so thankful I was there when the horse reared." RJ slammed another glass of rum.

If Sofia were counting, that was his fourth or fifth glass. Not unusual for RJ. However, it was her father's funeral and she didn't feel like babysitting her brother.

RJ was clearly hurting, and with that she sympathized, but something under his anger belied simple mourning. What was even stranger was why RJ and her father were out in the fields on horseback together. RJ hated to ride.

She gave RJ a hard look. "No, I don't know how he gets, so why don't you explain it to me? What happened?"

Suspicion tightened around her gut as it clenched tighter. It would take work to try to wrap her head around the fact that RJ went riding with Papa. He didn't just hate riding, his hatred for horses started as a young child. An incident with a trusted breeding mare had spooked RJ so badly that he never went to the stables, but now here he was, riding with her father.

Bullshit.

"When did you grow a set of balls and get back on horses, RJ?"

"What do you mean, Sofía? I love the animals. I even bought a pony for Carolina." He refilled his tumbler and gulped it down. "Father and I have been riding a lot lately." He refused to make eye contact with her as he spoke to Manny.

"I don't believe you, RJ. I don't know what game you're playing, but I'm going to find out." Sofía stepped between him and Manny and drilled her finger into his chest. "If I find out you've done something stupid, RJ, you're going to be sorry." She pushed him back. "Do you hear me?"

"Sofía, he said Roberto's horse reared. You know how that stallion gets. I would never get on that black bastard. RJ did everything to save your father. You should be thankful he was there." Manny gently pushed her aside and pulled RJ away. "RJ, let's talk."

⁂

RJ stared at his beloved Tío Manny. How could the bastard betray him like that? He would have told Sofía...eventually. Well, maybe. But now the man had let the fact that he was with his father accidentally slip out. Maybe it wasn't accidental at all.

Asshole.

He'd confided in the man when Lina was first pregnant. Had Manny been the one to spill RJ's secrets to his father, thereby sealing his fate with the old man? Hadn't he provided his father with an heir? Granted, it wasn't his sperm that built the child, but it was his hand that was raising both him and his little sister. He'd had a vasectomy for a reason. However, his wife being the good little Catholic girl she was, she refused to get an abortion. He should have just beat it out of her. The bitch. Now she'd cost him his inheritance, his way of life, everything.

"I'm going to have that beast put down. He's too dangerous."

"The hell you are," Sofia stepped up.

"He's a fucking monster and he's responsible for Father's death. I see no other way, Sofia."

"I'm not going to let you put down Father's horse. He loved him."

"RJ, let's not speak of this now." A stinging slap on his back brought him around. "It's a bad time for everyone." Manny poured himself and RJ a liberal dose of truth and handed it to him. "Come, let's remember the good times. My brother was a good man, a good father, and he taught us all everything we know about tobacco. Sofia, here."

His sister took a glass and raised it. "To Don Roberto."

"To Don Roberto," the three said in unison.

"So, Tío, what will you do with your share of Huerta Cigars?" RJ probed before he swallowed a mouthful of his Flor de Cana. The taste of betrayal burned on its way down.

"Nothing, RJ. Roberto only left me a small piece." Manny enjoyed the rum before offering an answer. "I'm only on as an adviser. Sofia has my complete trust." Manny picked up Sofia's hand and kissed it.

"Hmm."

"Thank you, Tío." Sofia smiled at RJ, locking a petulant gaze with him.

Bitch.

"I'm just glad it's staying in the family," RJ lied.

"You should be. There are vultures out there, RJ. Circling, ready to pick your father's bones clean, leaving nothing for you and the family."

"It's true, Tío. I've seen them circling already. In fact, there are a few just outside this door, eating our food and feigning sympathy for the death of our father," Sofia said, walking away from the men.

God, he wanted to throttle the arrogant bitch. Every word she spoke now was like a knife stabbing him in the ears. Her voice grated on him. Huerta was his. He was the only son. He deserved to be the head of the family.

His gaze roamed around the office. It was the most ornate room in the house for a reason, as his father had explained to him one night when they'd been drinking and smoking cigars.

"This is what gringos want to see when they visit Huerta Cigars, RJ."

Artifacts from the cigar industry were objets d'art. A large antique cigar press contained wooden molds still holding the remnants of rolled cigars nested between the slats, the shaggy foot sticking out. A few were missing ends from people poking at the molds. The only thing they lacked was the wrapper, but these cigars would never be smoked. These were decorations, conversation pieces that his father used to show how cigars were pressed without having to venture out to the factory. A relic from the early years of Huerta cigars. A *chavetas,* a knife used to trim tobacco leaves used for trimming the wrappers—and still being used in the factory today—sat on a wooden base of a star cutter. It combined a thick wooden rolling surface and cutter all in one unit. RJ ran his fingers over the lines someone had scribed into the iron cutter, designating the lengths for particular cigars. While the unit came with a ruler, someone had etched their own lines. *Of course,* RJ thought. He was always amazed how workers had to mark "their" equipment. In the farthest corner of the office sat a huge, wooden cigar Indian, a throwback to cigar Americana. A gift to his father from a patron. He hated the thing. Its grotesque features were the subject of many a nightmare for him. As a child, he never went near it, and today he'd rather see the thing burned. His aversion to it was fresh in his mind. In fact, when he took over Huerta that was the first thing on the bonfire he planned to have in his father's honor.

Finally, several boxes of cigars sat out on display. They were set in a humidity-controlled Lucite display case. His father would always express great agitation when he offered a few sticks to a prospective client who he hoped would carry Huerta cigars in their cigar lounges, and they would ask for just "a couple of boxes" to see how they'd do in their market. These kinds of people often made the rounds of the cigar factories in Nicaragua, snatching up whatever freebies they could get, dissecting them in hopes of emulating them when they started their own boutique cigar. Boutique cigars owners were becoming the new fad. Men with too much money were looking for some prestige and gravitas, and the mystique of the cigar industry did that for them. A man with enough money could buy his way into a line of cigars, and he didn't need to know how they were made, how much a worker was paid— often only three cents a cigar—or worry about weather, pests, or droughts, a shortcut with little exposure or actual work. Then again, they got the last of the leaves, with the cigar manufacture saving the best for their own sticks. If supplies ran short, the boutique felt it, not the tobacco farmer.

In one particular incident, Don Roberto had lost his temper with a man who'd pushed his buttons just a little too far.

"Do you think people go to a microbrewery or winery and ask for a couple of cases to see how they'd do in their bars and restaurant? Because if you do, please tell me so that next time I'm in the States, I'll make sure to visit." His snarky remark was met with defiance as the man reminded Don Roberto that Huerta wasn't the only cigar company in Nicaragua. A quick phone call to the other factories shortened the man's trip considerably and lost him any opportunity to start his line of boutique cigars. Poor slob. He needed a lesson in the cultural differences between Americans and the Nicaraguan cigar industry. However, money talked, so RJ doubted he would go begging for long.

To help promote Huerta Cigars, RJ had launched the idea to set up cigar tours, bringing in average Joes and a few Janes to experience the cigar business complete with tours of the fields, the fermenting rooms, and the factories where they sorted, bundled, and rolled cigars. Most left with a renewed awe of the cigar industry while others saw it as an opportunity to exploit the Huertas and Nicaraguan generosity. Seeing the large warehouse full of cigar bundles was often overwhelming for some, but that didn't last long before some asked for handfuls of cigars "to try," of course. It got to the point that Don Roberto built a small aging room that only held about twenty-thousand sticks. Enough to be impressive, but small enough to keep event opportunists from over-indulging. RJ had convinced his father that it would be good PR if they purchased a small compound where the visitor could stay, eat, and relax, all the while smoking an unlimited amount of Huerta cigars for three to four days. Clubs along the beach never closed, but potential danger hid in the clubs. Young girls, fourteen and older, frequented the clubs, offering themselves as part of the night's entertainment. If they got into trouble, that wasn't his problem, but with a little grease, he could get just about anyone out of hot water. His reputation preceded him with the local police. It turned out the trips were a huge success, and Huerta Cigars enjoyed a moderate increase in sales and return guests, who forked over good money to have the ultimate cigar experience.

Well, he didn't have to worry about his father's disapproving glare as he partied the night away with the foreigners that came on the tours. He wouldn't have to worry about convincing him as he ran another idea past the old man just to have him shut him down.

No, he was glad the bastard was dead.

Chapter Four

The room was a beehive buzzing with conversation, but as soon as the doors to the office opened, everything stirred to a low hum. Several men from competing cigar companies and families stood together, heads bent deep in conversation. Most stopped what they were doing and turned toward RJ and his family as they walked out.

Silence.

Offering a half-hearted smile, RJ shook the hand of a man who walked toward him offering his condolences.

An American in the back caught RJ's attention when he nodded his head toward the doors. RJ looked at Sofia and remarked, "Don't start without me. I need to take care of something."

He walked away just as she was starting to admonish him. God, when was his sister going to get a clue? He didn't give a shit what she thought or said.

"RJ, I'm so sorry to hear about your father."

"Thanks, Chuck." RJ shook the hand offered and got a hearty slap on the back for his trouble. He had to check himself, wanting to slug the bastard. He doubted Chuck's sincerity, but then again, he wasn't very sincere himself.

Chuck Henson was one of the few *gringos* who lived full-time in Nicaragua and a completely hands-on boss in his boutique cigar factory. RJ had talked to several men about selling Huerta, Chuck being one of them. His small label would benefit from the purchase of Huerta, and he knew Chuck would pay handsomely for the Huerta name alone. With Huerta's built-in following and instant credentials, it could move him above the other well-established cigar companies.

How did one get rid of the competition? You bought them, seized their assets, and sold off the parts that you didn't need. Eventually, if you wanted to obliterate them completely, you retired the labels. However, that took years, not months. Several men in the room wanted to do just that, which was why they were at the bottom of the sell list, but RJ had to be honest—money talked and RJ was in a listening mood. At least he was up until twenty minutes ago, but he would figure out a way to change all of that.

"Chuck, we definitely need to talk about the future." RJ shook his hand and returned the hearty slap on the back. "Give me some time to get past the grief and get my father's affairs in order and I'll be in a better place to talk about the future," RJ lied, trying to buy himself some time to figure out what options he did have.

"Of course. What a shock to hear about Don Roberto. He was a great man."

"He was, Chuck. He sure was." RJ was practically choking on the words as they left his throat. He was going to have to get better at the subversive, or give up talking all together.

"Well look, I won't take up any more of your time. Again, my deepest condolences to you and your family, RJ."

His mind raced watching Chuck go back into the house. He was going to have to come up with a plan now. He didn't have the luxury of time on his side. Pacing the courtyard, he ran different scenarios in his head. Walking back into the room, he grabbed a glass off a tray being passed around. He offered a simple smile to a few who offered condolences.

A sideways glance alerted RJ to three men who'd been huddled in a circle when he'd come out of his father's office.

"RJ we're so sorry to hear about Don Roberto. Can we talk?"

RJ searched the room for his sister and Manny. He didn't want them seeing him meet with the men and raise their suspicions. Spotting Sofia sitting with their abuela, her attention focused on her made him relax a little more. Manny, as usual, was flirting with a few young women who'd gathered around the handsome, distinguished Latino. Lucky bastard was all RJ could think as he watched Manny kiss the hand of one of the young women, who gushed at the display.

"Sure, I need some fresh air." RJ passed each of the men a glass and followed the pack outside.

When they were finally out of ear shot of a few people who'd gathered in the courtyard, the group stopped near the fountain and circled around RJ

"To Don Roberto." The group raised their glasses in salute.

"To Don Roberto." RJ gritted his teeth.

The motley crew standing around RJ was made up of some of the most prominent families in the cigar business in Nicaragua. While there were other cigar businesses in the Dominican Republic, Cuba, and the US, in his opinion Nicaragua had become the leader in tobacco leaf quality, many of their plants coming directly from Cuba before, and some after, the embargo. His father had bred some fantastic tobacco, if he did say so himself. The fact that most cigars that were acquired for the American White House came from Nicaragua spoke for itself.

"*Compañero*, I hear that Don Roberto didn't leave you in a very good position in the company." Julio Torres looked around the group, most nodding in acknowledgement of the news. How did Julio find out? Was there a mole inside the company? It was that damn lawyer, he'd bet good money on it. He'd fix that as soon as he could get his hands on the bastard.

"Don't believe everything you hear, *mis hermanos*. I've got a stake in Huerta and Sofia won't run me out of my birthright."

"So, you do have the authority to combine Huerta Cigars with our companies? We need Huerta's long reach and contacts to do what we want to do. We've got some people waiting for our answer. So, time is money."

RJ's foul mood wasn't helping him form answers that the group would find acceptable, so he'd need to stall them until he weighed all of his options. On the one hand, he could preserve Huerta for himself, keeping it intact. On the other, RJ would be part of a bigger conglomerate that would have more power, influences, and money, but he might be squeezed out of any decision-making and still not have access to the kind of cash he wanted, or needed.

Decisions, decisions.

"I need time to grieve my father's death, my friends. Then there is the reading of the will. So, everything will come out then. Be patient, my friends. Be patient."

Esteban stepped forward. "We understand it

must have come as quite a surprise when your father died." He looked around at the men. "We were all shocked by the news. So, I can only imagine how you and Sofia feel."

RJ would wallow in their words of condolences and play his part. To do anything else would seem heartless. He hung his head and wiped at non-existent tears. "Thank you, my friends. Don Roberto wasn't just my father, he was a great role model and my friend. He was always there to pass on his wisdom and..." RJ choked, not because he was sorrowful, but he didn't think he could continue to craft the lie further. His hate was palpable. He surprised himself how quickly he'd gone from loving son to a hate-filled, vengeful man.

He didn't need to worry about finishing the sentence as a round of, "There but the by the grace of god..." Or, "Don't worry. You know he's with god," each man crossing himself as he said it. They were all words meant to comfort. However, RJ had damned his father's soul to hell, earlier when the will was read.

Ever the actor, RJ nodded his thanks and then mumbled, "Let's go in and have a drink for my father and smoke a cigar. I think Sofia has pulled some of Huerta Reserves to celebrate Don Roberto's life. Join me, my friends, and let's talk of business another day."

"Agreed." Esteban slapped RJ on the back. "There will be time for business later."

The group walked ahead of RJ. He wanted to let them go in first again, trying to avoid suspicion.

"Are you coming?" someone in the group quipped.

"I'm coming." RJ waved them off.

"Give the man a minute, amigo."

RJ sat on the edge of the fountain and rocked

back and forth. He was seething. He prayed he could hold his tongue once inside. Sofia and Manny would be standing there acting as if they hadn't just ruined his life. He was right when he told the group he needed time. Mulling over his options, there *was* only one thing he needed—a lawyer, a New York barracuda to challenge the will. He knew just the man who owed him a favor.

A big favor.

Chapter Five

Sofia and Manny walked through the house, escorting her grandmother outside to the inner courtyard. The heat was starting to get to the frail woman. Sofia had offered to walk her to her room where it was much cooler, but she told Sofia it was her duty to play hostess regardless of how hard Sofia protested. The constant stream of condolences was almost more than Sofia could bear, and she wondered how her grandmother kept offering a smile and a kind word to everyone who stopped to speak to her.

Even out in the open area of the courtyard, the noise was deafening. The energy was low but expected, the crowd made up mostly of workers from the factories and the fields. They rarely socialized together except for the annual holiday party and the big Huerta picnic that Don Roberto insisted on throwing every year. He pushed the idea that they weren't just a team, they were family, and he treated them as such. So, it was a rare occasion that the factory was completely closed other than the regular holidays.

Sofia smiled at the crowd and was getting ready to pass out cigars when RJ walked up beside her, put his arm around her shoulders.

"Everyone, if I could have a moment of your time…" RJ held his glass out to one of the house staff with a wine bottle, waiting until all glasses were filled to continue. "My sister, my abuela, my Tío Manny, and

I would like to thank you all for coming to celebrate the life of Don Roberto. Right Sofia?"

What the hell game was RJ playing? All eyes were on Sophia and RJ, so she didn't have a choice but to play along. Shrugging out of his grasp, she handed boxes of cigars to Julian, Manny, and a few other staff, asking them to pass them to the people in attendance.

Sofia reached down and helped her grandmother up. "My grandmother and I would like you to help us celebrate my father's life by enjoying one of his special reserve cigars. He was set to release these this year, but after some serious consideration we've decided to hold on to these for a little while longer before deciding what to do with them. So, please enjoy." Sofia held one out for her grandmother, who nodded in acceptance. Cellophane wrappers crinkling, the sharp snaps of cutters closing, and lighters and matches being struck echoed in the room as everyone started to light their sticks. Sofía extracted a cigar cutter, snipped the cap, toasted the other end, then handed it to her grandmother who finished lighting the stick. Her indulgences were rare, but it wasn't uncommon for Sofia and her grandmother to sit in her private courtyard and exchange stories while enjoying a cigar, Sofia telling her about her day, her grandmother sharing snippets of her childhood, or of her grandfather's life in Cuba. He'd died helping the Sandinistas fight the government, but that fact wasn't out for public consumption. That's why the family didn't have anything from early in Don Roberto's life. When you had nothing, it was easy to risk everything.

"Just like we will never see a man like Don Roberto again, it seems fitting to enjoy something no one else may ever have the pleasure of enjoying." Sofia raised her cigar. "To Don Roberto."

"Don Roberto." The crowd raised their cigars, or glasses, in salute to her father.

A sideways glance at RJ and Sofia could see he was struggling with a decision. Should he put his glass down to light his cigar or... Instead, he bit the end, avoiding the decision. He spit the tip on the ground and called out to someone who was lighting another.

"Amigo." He motioned his cigar toward their lighter. "Por favor, eh?"

"Of course. Allow me, Don Roberto."

The smile that split RJ's face sickened her. Stepping toward the ass-kisser she recognized from the sorting room, she corrected the arrogant statement.

"There was only one Don Roberto, so don't make that mistake again. ¿*Comprende?*"

"Lo siento, Señorita Sofia. I meant no disrespect."

RJ jumped in a little too quickly for her taste. "Excuse my sister, her grief over the loss of Don Roberto is making her overly sensitive. Thank you for the compliment. My father was an amazing man. I can only hope I can measure up to his stature. Gracias."

Sofia's utter contempt for her brother was at its boiling point. She not only wanted to set him straight, but she wanted everyone here to know that there would be a change to the organizational structure at Huerta Cigars.

"It's funny you should say that, RJ—"

"Sofia, may I have a word?" Manny pulled Sofia away from the men that had gathered around RJ.

Sofia yanked her arm from Manny's grasp, incensed that he would stop her from clearing up any misconceptions RJ might be spreading around.

"What the hell, Tío?"

"Calm yourself. I know you're upset—"

"Don't even use the excuse that because I'm a woman, I'm being irrational. I'm not. You see what RJ is doing. He's pretending he's the heir apparent of Huerta and the men are treating him as if he *is* the heir apparent."

"I do know what he's doing, but look around mija," Manny said in a hushed tone. "What do you see?" Before she had a chance to answer, he continued. "Those vultures I was talking about in your father's office are in this room. Look…"

She followed his gaze as it lit on several men belonging to various cigar factories. They were all standing around RJ like sentinels.

"You must not show your hand, yet."

"But Tío—"

"We know. He knows. Nevertheless, he's up to something, so watch and learn. This is a game, and you can either run the table or chase the rabbit. RJ is trying to back you into a corner. Don't bite back." Manny kissed Sofia's head. "Trust me."

"But—"

He put his finger on her lips. "Trust me."

She was torn between trusting her uncle or going with her gut.

Gut it was.

༄ ༄ ༄ ༄

Don Pablo stood next to the heads of the other cigar families as he felt Sofia and Manny's gaze light on him and the crowd he was with as he lifted his cigar in salute to Don Roberto. Ignoring them, he whispered to Enrigue Marquez who stood next to him. "Pretty soon, we'll be toasting bigger things."

"To bigger things, my friend."

"To bigger things," Pablo said. His own gaze roamed the room and couldn't help but see the anguish on Sofia's face as she had words with someone at the front of the room. He suspected RJ was behind whatever had happened, if his wide smile was any indication.

"Is it me or does there seem to be something going on between brother and sister?" Esteban said, raising his glass.

"There is definitely something going on, Father," Don Pablo said, mimicking his father's gesture.

"Find out what, and see that gringo over there? Find out what that he wants, too." He downed his rum and slapped his portly son on the back. "I'm not about to get into bed with someone who still pisses when he sleeps. And check out Sofia and see if that lawyer I saw her with earlier is talking. Grease his palm if you need to."

"And if he doesn't want to talk?"

Esteban shrugged. "Don't do anything to him, Son. Not everything has to be handled with violence. Set up the meeting and let's see if we can get Manny and RJ on board before we meet with the Americans. I don't want any loose ends."

"Of course, Father. I'll see you back at the house?"

"Later. I've got business I have to take care of before I go home. Tell your mother not to wait up."

Pablo saw his father pocket a few extra Huerta Reserves from a box on the table near the door before Esteban left. He wondered why his old man did that when he had all the cigars he could ever smoke aging in their factory. Poverty had a way of touching people, but his father had never been impoverished, not even close, so there had to be another reason for the man's gluttony.

"Enrique, set up the meeting at your restaurant. That way no one will suspect anything if they see us all together."

"Sure. My wife will love the business."

Don Pablo didn't say anything about paying for it, but he'd let the man find out later. Besides, he had a thing for Pipa, Enrique's wife. Hopefully, Enrique didn't know that. He smiled. Some men were just asking to be taken advantage of, weren't they?

"Okay, I'm out of here. I've got shit to do."

"I'm going to stay a little longer," Enrique said, shaking his hand.

"You do that. If you hear anything, let me know. If you see that lawyer, find out if he's sharing anything about the will. I'm thinking something happened in the office while we were all out here paying our respects to María."

"You want me to bend him?"

Pablo's eyebrows knitted together. "Esteban said no violence."

"Oh, right. Okay. I'll see what I can find out."

No one disobeyed Esteban, not even him. "You do that and let me know. See you guys later." A chorus of "laters" murmured behind him as he shut the door behind him.

Suddenly, he wondered if RJ could be trusted.

❦❦❦❦❦

RJ paced the spacious bedroom he shared with his wife, Lina. They wanted for nothing living at the Huerta compound. The colorful paint scheme had been Lina's doing. Local artisans' work covered their walls, and the tile floors were a welcome relief when the heat was unbearable. Windows from floor to ceiling lined the wall that looked out to their own private courtyard. The sound of the constantly running fountain was a soothing respite on the few nights RJ spent in his own bed. Only today, it would provide no relief.

There was no way he was going to let his sister get control of Huerta Cigars. She had practically embarrassed him when one of the workers called him Don Roberto. He was the new Don and she just needed to accept it. He'd worked hard to get this opportunity. Damn his father to hell. He clenched his fists, popping his knuckles. His anger was just like his passion, and he needed release.

"RJ, do you know what your sister just said to me? You need to get that bitch under control." Lina flew into the room with a flurry, dumping her purse and veil onto the bed.

Funny how opportunity presented itself, RJ thought. Open it to the universe and it will provide.

RJ jerked his wife by the arm and flung her against the wall rattling all the family pictures she'd insisted on putting everywhere. Sliding his hand around her throat, he pressed his body against Lina's, pinning her.

"What the fuck?"

"Shut up. You're the fucking reason we're in this situation, *mi cariño* ," he said, his teeth grinding as he spit the dagger-like words at her.

"Me?"

"My father knew those bastards aren't mine."

Lina couldn't hide her contempt. "So…"

"You are a fucking whore."

"You're an impotent freak," she said, trading insults.

"He's left everything in Sofia's hands. All because

of your slutty ways."

"Oh, I'm sure your father knew all about your trips to New York to see that little home-wrecker you've been supporting all of these years." Lina laughed.

RJ couldn't conceal his shock before dropping his mask of deception. He'd gotten good at the deceit, but obviously not good enough. How did she know about Jessica? It didn't matter. It wasn't Jessica who'd cost him his inheritance, it was Lina.

RJ's hand tightened around Lina's neck, his thumb rubbing against the small bones in her throat.

"If you weren't fucking around, he wouldn't know the kids aren't mine."

"If you weren't barren, I wouldn't be sleeping around, *pendejo*."

He squeezed just hard enough, but not so much that she couldn't breathe. He hadn't wanted kids, ever, so he'd taken steps to eliminate any mistakes that might come along and stop his enjoyment of the fairer sex. Somehow it didn't matter now.

"You fucking *cabróna*. I could snap your neck. I get nothing, unless I want to work for it. I'm sure my sister is going to cut me off and if she cuts me off, she cuts you off." He squeezed tighter. "But I guess you can put those skills you're spreading around to work and put food on the table for those brats of yours."

A sharp pain charged though his body. Lina smiled as she had a vise grip on his nuts and wouldn't release them. He felt himself getting hard as she tightened and then released his sack. He might have a hard time getting it up sometimes, but he loved it rough.

"You're going to threaten me, RJ? You forget, I know where all the bodies are buried in this little charade you're playing."

Chapter Six

Sofia's head lay in her lap just as it had many times when she was a child. María ran her gnarled fingers lovingly through her brown hair, nails gently massaging her head as they traveled back and forth over her scalp. When she was troubled, Sofía would find herself in María's room unburdening her troubles. This afternoon was no different. María knew her granddaughter was troubled. She suspected her mind was flooded with questions about her father, his death, and the family that needed to survive and thrive. They were practically drowning her as well as she watched her only grandson and granddaughter fight at the funeral.

"Nana?"

"Yes, mija?"

"Did you know RJ was with Papa when he died?"

The mindless stroking stopped. "I did. I told him he should talk to his father. Fighting only divides a family and...well, you and RJ are only going to have each other when I'm gone. So, I think you should try and understand what RJ is going through right now, mija. His father has just died and he just found out that Roberto has left everything to you and Manny. How would you feel, mija, if your father did that to you? He's a man, and it's different for men."

Her heart ached for her grandson. He had battled so hard for his father's affection. Knowing that his mother died just after giving birth was a lot to carry for a man, especially a man like RJ. He had constantly worked to prove to his father that his mother's death wasn't in vain. She had told Roberto that while he had lost a wife, he had gained a son who would carry on the Huerta legacy. However, María understood her son's hesitancy as the young boy grew into a man who respected little and demanded much.

Sofía closed her eyes, tears seeping out. "I've worked hard, Nana. I've earned my place, but I see that you think RJ should get everything."

"That's not what I'm saying, Sofía. You're smart, hardworking, and you've earned everything you've worked for, too, but RJ...he's different. He is like a boat with no rudder. He seems to be searching for something, but I don't know what that is, do you?"

Sofia shook her head and buried it in her lap. María had a difficult time distinguishing the little girl with the grown, successful woman weeping on her lap. Her own tears would wait until she was alone before they fell. Another hard-learned lesson courtesy of her own mother.

As a young child, she had lost her prized puppy. Devastated, she sought out her mother for comfort.

"María, it's only a dog. Please, you're making a scene. Want me to give you something to really cry over?" Her mother grabbed her shoulders and shook her. "You're a Ferro, pull yourself together. We are strong and don't weep over a pet."

"Yes, Mother."

A handkerchief was thrust into her hand. "Wipe your face, now."

This lesson would be repeated only a few more times before María understood her place as a child.

Seen and never heard. Weakness was never rewarded like strength and determination, qualities that were reinforced in her house on a daily basis.

"I want to know what happened to Papa, Nana. Is there something you aren't telling me?"

María hesitated. What she did know wouldn't help right the situation at hand, so it was better to leave it where it belonged—in the past.

"Sofía, family is the only thing that matters. Your father has passed and now is not the time to hold grudges. We must be united. I hear that there are those that would like to see Huerta fail. RJ is the only brother you have, he's the only family. Remember, family will always be there for you, no matter what." At least she hoped that was the case with her two grandchildren. They would need each other if she was right about those that wanted to see Huerta fall.

The overhead fan beat off-kilter, doing its best to move the air, but it wasn't enough to cool the thick layer of sweat that covered him and his lover. RJ lay in the crumpled sheets of their lovemaking with Estrella lying beside him trying to revive his spent cock, tracing imaginary patterns on his thigh, strokes moving closer to his dick with each pass. It wasn't having the intended result his lover was hoping it would.

Stopping her hand, RJ drew it up to his lips and kissed each knuckle.

"What's wrong, mi amor?" She hoisted herself on top of his body. Bracing her chin on his chest, she tried to look as seductive as she could, hair flying out of the ponytail, framing her face.

"Lo siento." He always seemed to be apologizing to Estrella. She was the one he should have married, not Lina. However, he married with his head and not his heart. Mentally, he'd already divorced Lina. Emotionally, she was dead to him. Now, if only she would truly die, he could marry Estrella and they could leave Nicaragua. Maybe move to the Dominican Republic. Cigar businesses were plenty, and with his knowledge he could easily take over a small farm and build it as his father had done. Fuck, who was he kidding? If he wasn't given Huerta, he'd take it from his sister by force.

"What are you thinking about, lover?" Estrella pushed his chin down and playfully scratched his stubble.

He wasn't in the mood for conversation. Pushing off his chest, she straddled his hips, the weight of her hitting him just right. Positioning herself over his cock, she rested her hands on his chest again. Leaning over, she pulled the hair tie and let her hair cascade over his head, the black curtain surrounding their faces. Her hips rolled back and forth, rocking on him.

He pushed her up and wrapped his hands around her breasts, squeezing the supple flesh. He pinched her nipples between his thumb and index finger, a squeal slipping past her still red lips. How her lipstick never rubbed off was one of those secrets he was sure only women knew. Her head lobbed back and she threaded her fingers through her hair, grinding hard on his hips. She always got off faster than he did, which made her more appreciative later and she showed that appreciation by going down on him, working him until he could drill rock with his hard cock.

"Oh, baby." She moaned, lifting herself just

enough so he could slip inside her. She brushed his hand away as she buried him as deep as she could. "God damn, baby. You're like a…oh god." She groaned, wiggling back and forth. "Ay papi, Oh shit, oh…"

RJ just sat back and watched. Estrella was on cruise control and he didn't need to take the wheel or push the gas pedal. She did it all on her own. Her body jerked and shuddered as she bounced harder until he was sure she was about to break him. Sweat beaded across his body as his own orgasm pulsed out in waves. Grabbing her hips, he shoved himself in as far as he could, holding her shaking torso steady.

Just as fast as it had started it was over and Estrella rolled of him, huffing. "I like it when you're mad, lover. You fuck better." She wiped the plastered strands of black hair out of her face and then curled into him.

He rolled around her, holding her tight. Yep, he should have married Estrella. She knew him better than anyone. They'd grown up together, played together, and then drifted apart, her going to the US for college, him staying home to learn the family business.

"So, what happens how?" she said, tucking his hands between her breasts. He moved his hips between her ass cheeks and rubbed his limp dick against her. He told her everything. Being left out of the will, his father's betrayal. Well, he told her almost everything, but he hadn't shared his plans, and he'd need her to help him put those plans in motion.

Leaning back, he stared at the wobbling fan. His brain felt like it was churning at the same off-kilter speed.

"Someone owes me a favor and I think it's time I called it in."

"He's going to help you get Huerta Cigars?"

"Oh, he's going help all right. He's going to break that will or all his little secrets are going fall out like garbage when the sack splits open."

"What are you cooking up, lover?"

"Nothing you need to worry about, mi amor."

Turning around, she gathered the sheets around them, and kissed him. "And what about Lina? When are you going to get rid of the *puta*?"

He pinched her chin and kissed the tip of her nose. There was no reason he needed to be married to Lina now that she had cost him everything, so she was expendable. That didn't mean he was going to jump back on the hamster wheel of marriage with Estrella. While he recognized she should have been the one he married, he was still young and he had a few things he wanted to do before another union, if marriage was ever in the cards again.

"I need to take care of stuff with Huerta first, but since the little bastards aren't mine, she isn't going to get shit from me. I'll take a paternity test and find out no judge would make me pay for kids that aren't mine."

"Soon, RJ?"

"Soon my little, star." He pulled her in closer and smiled. Women were so easy, he thought, stroking her back. "I'm going have to lay low until I get this lawyer from San Francisco down here and on the case. So, I might not be back here in Managua for a couple of weeks. Think you can live without me that long?" He stood and walked over to his jacket and pulled out a slender box, then sat on the edge of the bed twisting the box between his hands.

"Do you think you can miss me for a few weeks?" He smiled, looking at the box and then back at her.

She was practically drooling, eyeing the blue velvet jewelry box. "Oh, I think I can be convinced to be a good girl, depending, of course..." She bounced on the bed as she reached for the box, but he lifted it over his head out of reach.

"Depending on what?"

Sheepishly, she smiled and met his gaze with a lusty one of her own. "Depending on what's in the box, lover, of course." She spread her hands out, palms up.

RJ snickered. Yep, women were so predictable. Now, all he needed to do was figure out what Sofia's weakness was.

Estrella let out a childish squeal and bounced on the bed again as she opened the box and peered at the sparkly baubles inside.

Yep, easy and predictable. He smiled. Picking up his phone, he slipped on his pants and took advantage of Estrella's distraction.

"Lewis, my friend. I've been trying to get a hold of you. Where the fuck have you been?" RJ said, closing the slider behind him. "I'm calling in that favor."

The line was quiet as the implication sunk in.

"Now?"

"Yes, now. If this isn't a good time, I can send over those papers I've been holding. I'm sure the police would be happy to handle that little problem."

"Fine," the stressed voice on the other end agreed. "What do you need?"

☙☙☙☙

RJ rolled the edge of the tumbler on the table. His swagger was only matched by the jerkish grin he flashed at the curvy woman who made the mistake of crossing his path. A quick slap on the ass, her reward for her unknown error of merely being beautiful around RJ. The audacity. Before he could react, the stinging red handprint was already rising on his face by the time her boyfriend ran to her rescue.

"What the fuck, asshole?"

RJ stopped and stared the man down. "What?"

As the man stepped forward, RJ reached in his pocket as he said, "Pendejo, go for it." RJ's hand stayed in his pants as he checked the woman out and then looked back at the man. His face was on fire, and it was a good thing the woman's companion had showed up. She needed a lesson on how to treat a man who showed her some attention.

Bitch.

The man gruffed, looked at the bulge in RJ's pocket, then grabbed his girlfriend's arm and walked away.

"That's right asshole. You don't want to screw with a Huerta."

The man turned and flipped RJ the bird, spouting, "Good to know whose ass I'm gonna take pleasure in kicking. You better watch your back, asshole."

RJ chuckled as he heard the woman chastise the man, asking him what he was waiting for as he dragged her down the street.

"RJ, mijo. What are you getting yourself into?" Manny clamped his shoulder and pushed him into a chair.

RJ shrugged out of his grasp and backed away from his uncle.

"What are you doing here, Tío?"

"Looking for you, Nephew. You left so quickly, I wanted to make sure you were okay."

RJ was once again pushed back into a seat at one of the outside tables at the bar. The music bounced off the walls inside and ricocheted out of the doorless structure. The drinking establishments popped up on the beach as quickly as they closed. The cheap cost of a liquor license and the endless stream of tourists meant there was always plenty of money and somewhere to drink, regardless of the time of day or night. The other thing he could count on were plenty of young girls trolling the bar scene. With the legal age to drink more of a suggestion than a law, the clubs were filled with pretty, nubile girls hovering around older gringos like flies.

"Two Flor de Cañas," Manny said, flashing two fingers. "With a couple of colas between them."

"Anything else?" the waitress asked suggestively.

"Yeah." RJ pulled the woman onto his lap. "Let's talk about whatever pops—"

"RJ." Manny cut him off. "Have some respect." He shot RJ a coarse look.

The woman quickly dislodged herself. "I'll get those drinks."

"Thanks, Lupe."

She winked at Manny and disappeared.

"What are you doing, Nephew?"

RJ inspected his nails, bit the tip of one, and pulled the nail back to the quick. It bled instantly, but he covered it with his lips and laved at it. He'd always had the nervous habit of biting his nails, to the point that his father had put hot sauce on them as a child to keep him from biting them. It didn't work, the evidence his clean, neat nails trimmed to the quick.

"RJ." Manny tapped the table to get his attention.

"What?"

"Why aren't you with your abuela?"

RJ shot him a glare. "I have business to take care of."

"What business? Your father just died. You need to be with your family. Appearances—"

"Fuck appearances, Tío." RJ avoided his uncle's stare. "My sister is the one who needs to worry about appearances. She's the head of Huerta, remember?"

"RJ—"

RJ slammed the table and stood. "What? I don't owe anyone anything. So get the fuck off my back."

He'd had enough of Manny's bullshit. "When I want your opinion, Tío, I'll yank your chain. You always were my father's lap dog."

Within seconds, RJ was crushed under the weight of his uncle's arm against his chest, pinning him against the wall. His other hand was around RJ's throat.

"Know your place, Nephew. You are not your father and I'm not one of your bitches that run around you in heat. You'll show me some respect, or I'll take those little brass nuts you're hanging onto and shove them down your throat."

RJ gasped for breath, grabbing at the hand tightening around his throat. His heartbeat thumped out a rapid dance in his ears and his vision tunneled. He was passing out. He slapped at Manny's wrist as he tried to mouth an apology. Manny finally eased his grip around his neck, but didn't release him.

"Grow your little boy-ass up. If you want to get a chance at leading Huerta Cigars, get your shit together. You can't afford any more enemies, RJ, so don't make the mistake of making me one in a long line of people waiting to knock your shit out. That guy who you just threatened? He's a cop and I'm sure he doesn't appreciate you putting your hands on his wife. Your daddy isn't around to bail your ass out anymore, so tread lightly now. I doubt Sofia would do you the same kindness."

"My sister, she's the reason I'm cut out of the will. She made Don Roberto proud with that bullshit line of cigars she's producing. We all know she doesn't have the stones to run Huerta. It's still an old boys' club, Tío. You know that, and the fact that she's gone as far as she's going to take Huerta. So, don't dismiss me, yet."

Manny practically picked him up and sat him in the chair, his hand still controlling him as he pushed on RJ's shoulder. "Your father's charity event is in San Francisco next week and you need to be there."

RJ jerked out of his uncle's grip. He rubbed his neck and coughed. "I'm not going. I have business here."

RJ knew what was more important: his meeting with the other cigar families and planning a takeover of Huerta. While his sister and uncle basked in the limelight, he'd be putting his plan in place. Besides, Lewis would be here to help. He owed RJ big, and RJ had to make sure Lewis complied. He'd faxed all the documents, foregoing an email trail. He hated the trace digital technology left. His paranoia was well placed, especially after he'd gotten wind of Lina's newest fling via a little snooping on her laptop. The pictures weren't only disgusting, but he'd seen a side of his wife she never shared with him. Photos, lots of them, of her being tied up and a remarkable variety of bondage. Hell, if he knew the bitch liked to be spanked, he could accommodate that and so much more. He'd forwarded the pictures to himself and then cleared her browser history and email files so it couldn't be traced back to him. He would use those in the coming divorce. Now that his father was gone, there was no use holding onto dead weight.

Besides, while everyone was away it would give him the time and space he needed to bug Sofia's office, the house, and the factory. He needed to know who was doing what and be able to counter any action Sofia took. He was building an empire, and he needed soldiers for that kingdom. The easiest way to bring people to his side might involve a little blackmail.

"Let's have a drink and put all of this nonsense behind us, RJ. I'm not the enemy. Besides, I have Sofia's ear."

Manny poured them both a liberal drink and motioned for RJ to take his.

Lifting his glass, Manny said, "To everything Don Roberto built. To Huerta Cigars."

"To Don Roberto, may he rest in peace." RJ wanted to choke on his words, but he forced them down with a swallow of Nicaragua's finest rum.

"Now, tell me what could be more important than paying respect to your father's memory and some serious facetime at a Huerta event?"

"Business, Tío. Business."

Chapter Seven

Lewis, to what do I owe this honor?"
Lewis Worthington was a man of distinction.
His classic Greek features, achieved through a little
nip here, tuck there, and a nose job to fix what a
few fistfights couldn't, accentuated graying temples
and provided him an air of respectability he didn't
deserve. Even though he'd started Worthington,
Bennett, and Schuler, he spent more time womanizing
than practicing law lately. However, none of the
partners had the guts to call him out for his behavior.
Unfortunately, he brought in more business than the
other two partners combined, so they knew which
side was face up when they put butter on their toast
in the morning. It was also the reason Laura called her
father by his given name. She was constantly trying to
distance herself from her father. Hard to do in a firm
that carried her name, but she knew it rubbed him raw
when she did it. It was her way of pulling the scab off
every time she saw him.

He patted the leg of his typical Armani pants
with a folder before tossing it to the stack of growing
work she already had for the week.

"Honey, you really need to get a paralegal to help
you with these," he said, tapping the pile.

His daughter, Laura, responded with dry sarcasm.
"Gee, I do, but she always seems to be busy in your
office, sir."

He ignored the implication. Everyone at the firm knew he was philandering with Gemma Slaughter, and watercooler gossip had Gemma working overtime most nights, which explained why Laura's mother had been calling for dinner dates more often.

"What's this?" Laura moved things around on her desk so she could lay out the hefty file.

"A big client from Nicaragua."

"I don't do international law, Lewis." Laura Worthington was every bit her father's daughter. The mounds of paperwork that covered her desk were a testament to Worthington fervor. Her firm tone had a hint of her father's casual arrogance. A Worthington did not quibble, cajole, or whine.

She pushed the file back toward her father. "Besides, it's all in Spanish and my high school Spanish is rusty."

Lewis eyed the folder and tossed a displeasing glance at his daughter. While he was an asshole and she might be his daughter, he didn't tolerate insubordination from anyone in the firm. His mouth contorted itself into something akin to a frown. She suspected the Botox was keeping him from executing it fully. He pushed the folder back across the desk, practically into her lap.

"This isn't exactly international law. This is a client whose father just died. The will was read and he just found out that Daddy left it all to his sibling. I figured you could relate with your brother and all."

"Sounds like a smart man, that father." The inflection of her use of "father" wasn't lost on Lewis as he blanched then recovered, spearing her with a look that meant don't-even-go-there. "So, what's the problem?"

"You need to find a loophole."

"I already told you, I don't do family law and this isn't even in English or in the US courts. I'm swamped, Lewis."

"You need to handle this and keep it off the company books. It's a favor to this client."

Lewis sat down in the utilitarian guest chair. Her office wasn't as ornate as some of the partners' offices, probably because she hadn't earned partner yet. Eight years at the firm and there were still two men ahead of her and several had hopscotched over them all. Corporate politics were like chess—you studied your opponent, in this case your corporate peers, and moved your knights and bishops accordingly. High-dollar clients were bishops and moved you up and diagonally. Corporate clients were knights who could be positioned to take out another corporation. Those were fewer and far between, so the fact that Lewis was tossing her a knight meant that he had something up his corporate sleeve, but what?

"Why me?" She eyed him suspiciously.

She was his daughter, so sexual favors were off the table. He never did anything without procuring something in return, or you ended up owing him a favor that he would call in at a later date.

"Laura…" he said as he contemplated the nails on his pudgy digits. She often wondered if he was her true biological contributor. They were polar opposites, and the only thing he passed down was her drive to succeed and master her environment. "It's time you earned partner. Don't you think?" He stood and twisted. "If for nothing else, it will get you better office furniture." He walked over to the window and pulled the vertical blinds sideways, peering down at the bustling San

Francisco street below.

"But you just said I needed to keep it off the corporate books. So, there are no billable hours in it for me, so no partner."

"Take the fucking case, Laura," he said, the vein in his face popping out as it did when he was pissed.

Laura studied her father. He was more of a corporate extortionist than a lawyer. Early in her career, she had sat second chair on a few cases he was litigating. The soulless way he had approached the cases almost made her want to quit the profession altogether. The only problem was she liked to eat, have a roof over her head, and drive a nice car. So, to ease her corporate guilt she did pro bono on the side, which probably helped account for her lack of a personal life. Subsequently, while she wanted to laugh in Lewis's face, she had to admit her drive to make partner was all she had left in her career. Then, maybe, she could think about a career change, or at least a personal life.

"What's in this for you, Lewis? It seems like small potatoes compared to some of the corporate accounts you handle. I'm kind of surprised that you want to take on a simple contested will."

"Let's just say I…" Lewis rubbed the bristle starting to form on his chin and gave Laura a sideways glance. "I might just have a vested interest in seeing this will negated."

Why wasn't she surprised?

Laura wanted to open the folder, but she needed to establish boundaries with her father, of all people.

"Okay, so give me the Reader's Digest version of the will."

She owed Lewis her lucrative legal career in the bay area. True, she didn't have to start at the bottom with all the newbie lawyers since her father owned the firm, but he didn't cut her any slack, either. She'd thought about leaving a lot lately, but a small part of her was loyal to her family and the firm, even if Lewis was a Class A bastard. The few times she'd toyed with starting her own firm also left her a little less enthusiastic when she considered the late hours, long days, and working weekends again. Then there was all of the ass kissing she would have to do to get a solid, reputable client list. Getting slimy was easy; getting respectable was a little more difficult. No, staying where she was planted worked for her, for now.

Lewis sat back down and pulled on the tie that was cutting his neck in half. He steepled his fingers in front of his face and rested his lips against them in contemplation as he stared at Laura.

"It's simple, if he contests the will, he gets one dollar for his troubles."

"Case closed. That was the easiest case I worked on. There isn't anything to do, Lewis."

Lewis's tie must have been doing its job. As his jaw bunched, a blood vessel on his head popped up and his face was starting to turn a nice reddish hue, all signs that he was getting pissed. No one ever dismissed Lewis or a case he brought to you personally. However, the stack of cases on her desk took precedence over one that made it very clear that if contested, the heir would only receive one dollar of the inheritance.

Lewis placed his elbows on the Lucite desk and leaned forward, closing the distance between himself and Laura, and whispered, "Take the fucking case. You're a good lawyer. I don't care what you have to do to break this will, but find a way." Lewis stood, snatched the file, and pulled on his tie again, straightening it.

Clearly, it was cutting off the blood supply to his brain. She was certain he knew that most wills were iron-clad and written by lawyers, or did her father forget that little addendum? "I'll be back when you're ready to take my advice." He looked back at her. "You *will* take the case, Laura. I'll be back tomorrow and we'll discuss it again."

"Tomorrow's Saturday," she corrected her father. He'd be out on the golf course early and then at his mistress's late and of course he'd miss their traditional Sunday family dinner, citing work as his excuse. Why her mother put up with his shit was beyond Laura.

"Fine, I'll be back on fucking Monday and your answer had better change between now and then, or else. Oh, and by the way, it seems you and his sister have something in common. Maybe you can use that to our advantage."

The large pane of glass next to the door vibrated in protest as he slammed the door behind him, leaving without another word between them. She hated when he talked in code, but she wasn't interested in him or the case. When he called on Monday, she'd remind him of it again and they would do this little waltz around the desk then, too.

"Are you okay? What was that all about?" Gemma rushed into the room, steno pad in hand.

Laura raised her hand, stopping the prattle from her assistant. "Leave, please."

"Ms. Worthington are you—"

"Leave, now."

"Yes, Ms. Worthington."

Laura could see Gemma running after her father as soon as the door shut.

"I think I need a new assistant."

Laura walked over and straightened the painting her father had skewed when he slammed the door. Laura's office was a far cry from the tobacco field in Nicaragua. Its stark white walls held a few pieces of art—if color splashed in random patterns and a famous person's signature qualified it to be called art. White leather couches and two identical white leather chairs positioned in front of her clear Lucite desk completed the office ensemble. She'd often witnessed a client or two slipping their shoes off during a meeting, and was surprised more than once to see a toe peeking through a hole in a golden toast sock. While the rich wore expensive suits, sometimes what was hidden underneath was disgusting.

She turned off the warbling fluorescence to try to stave off what was starting to be the mind-bender of all migraines. She slid off her stilettos and ran her manicured toes through the short wool shag. She threaded her fingers behind her head and closed her eyes. Her lunch hour was her time, and the implied giant, flashing do-not-disturb sign that should be outside her door was on for all to see.

Laura picked up a folder and tapped the Manila case file against her palm. Like anything, be it a new case or hobby, she threw herself into it whole hog. It wasn't like her father was leaving her with any options. He'd be back as promised, and Lewis always got what he wanted. Being his daughter was irrelevant.

Rubbing her forehead, she thought she might as well get started on something. What she knew about the cigar industry, let alone cigars in general, could fit on the cigar label. So, she did what she always did and booted up her tablet, and typed "cigars" into the internet search engine with one hand while still rubbing her neck with the other. Pictures of fields, cigars, and men standing hip-deep in plants splashed across her screen.

Her ass slid across the slick leather of her high-back office chair. Settling in, she studied the photos. Pictures of workers in the tobacco fields. A warehouse of some type with big wheels covered in wire netting and what looked to be tobacco leaves tied to it. Workers posed in front of the pallets of tobacco. Women standing behind tables of tobacco leaves— none smiling, their focus on the leaves they held in their hands. Another picture showed workers sitting at tables behind stacks of rolled cigars. It was clear this product was produced by hand. Peppered throughout the pictures was an assortment of men in Panama hats, cigars wedged between their lips, toasting each other with glasses full of what she could only surmise was liquor.

Tahiti. I need to be on a beach with an adult beverage that carries one of those paper umbrellas that says, "I'm on vacation" *all over it,* she thought, running her toes through the carpet of sand.

The photos were stark, but she still faced the reality that she didn't know anything about the cigar industry. She needed to fix that. Pulling her phone from her purse, she dialed the one person who would indulge and nurture her newfound "hobby."

"Hey, Lala. How are you?" Her brother's voice boomed through the speaker.

"Michael. How are you, Brother?"

"I'm good. So, what do I owe this call to? I suppose Mother asked you to intercede regarding her dinner invitation for Sunday?"

Michael hated their father but adored their

mother. Why she stayed with Lewis Worthington was beyond anything he could fathom, and he often told her that. Michael had told his sister repeatedly it would be a cold day in hell before he sat at a table to break bread with Lewis.

"Hey, Michael. Busy?"

"For you Lala, never. What's up?"

"Are you still smoking cigars?"

"Sure, why?"

"I need a favor."

"Don't tell me you need help picking out a gift for Lewis?"

"No, Michael." She knew better than to ask Michael for help when it came to their father. "No, I have a new client and I need a lesson in cigarology. Got time for me?"

"Sure, how about dinner tomorrow night and then we can do cigars after?"

"Huh, I don't know."

"Trust me Lala, you want to have dinner before you smoke your first cigar. I mean, unless you just want me to come over and talk about cigars?"

Laura wasn't a voyeur in anything. She experienced life and did her research, so just talking about cigars wouldn't do. She really needed to get the whole experience if she was going to be forced to represent a cigar client. Besides, it wasn't as if Lewis had given her any option about taking the case.

"I'll pick you up at your place?"

"Sure, I'll be waiting downstairs."

"Around seven, okay?"

"What, you don't want me to see your new digs?"

Michael had just purchased a condo in the city. He said the commute into town from his country house was a bitch on a daily basis, but when he was off he wanted to be out of the city and out of reach. So, his home in the country was strictly his alone after working all week in the city, but she had yet to see his city condo.

"Hey, you can come by anytime, Sis. I just smoke out on the balcony, but the fourteenth floor gets a little chilly in the winter. But hey, if you're game…"

"No, no. I was hoping you'd take me to that cigar lounge you belong to."

"Sure, we can get something to eat there and then smoke our little hearts out."

"It has a restaurant? What kind of place is this?"

"Just pick me up, Lala, and you can get the full experience yourself."

"Okay, see you tomorrow at seven."

"Paging Dr. Worthington, paging Dr.—"

The line went dead before she could confirm their plans. Did she need to make reservations? She didn't know the name of the lounge or even where the place was, so that was an impossibility. They were going to dinner. Did that mean she should dress up, or was her office drag enough? Shoot! She should have asked more questions, but Michael was busy beyond belief, she was sure. Good thing they weren't meeting today. Her watch said 3:30 but the clock on the wall read 3:15. She had an obsession with time. It was all billable in her world and it didn't pay to be late, regardless of the time of day or day of the week, even at home.

A day would give her time to do more research, but where to start? At the beginning, of course.

❧❧❧❧❧

Laura swung the SUV in front of the high-rise. Lit

up, it looked like it was right out of the fifties' Rat Pack era. Art deco revival was in full swing in the city, As well as its attempt to save some of the older high-rises. The spotlights on palm trees was out of touch with the cold day. Fog always eased its way in by 3:00 p.m. She had a love-hate relationship with the city. She'd grown up in the "Snob Hill" area, as her friends called it. She'd graduated high school and went to university at Santa Clara College of Law. Gallivanting around Europe with a backpack strapped to her back wasn't in her future. No Europe and no tripping through the vineyards of France as her best friend Trudy had done after graduating high school. To this day, Trudy talked about some Italian guy she'd *bumped* into. Her reward for her quick fling was an STD—nothing glamorous about it. Trudy, what a piece of work. Laura had lived vicariously through her best friend's letters, emails, and the few pictures she had time to send Laura. Now she was a mom, and had 2.5 kids and an executive hubby, living in a townhouse off Lombard Street. Trudy hadn't exactly settled into family life easily. She was still looking for adventure in any way she could find it.

Michael stood on the sidewalk. The suit jacket paired with a button-down shirt, tie, jeans, and loafers.

"Hey, Lala. Right on time." He looked down at his watch, tapping the face of it.

What did he expect? She was always on time, hence the reason she insisted on picking him up. His penchant for being late was almost legendary. She wondered how she juggled all the women he entertained in his professional life as well as his personal life.

"Did you expect less?"

"Nope," he said, reaching over and offering a

kiss on her cheek. Before stepping in, he stood back and marveled at her wheels. "Wow, this is nice." He caressed the dash as if it was a woman. "Woohoo, she's solid. When did you get this?"

"Couple of months ago. She's a tank, perfect for city driving." Laura laughed.

"Perfect." He looked adoring at the interior of the SUV.

"Covet much, Michael?"

"All the time, you know me little sis. I like a girl with curves."

"Hey, is that a stab at my weight?"

Michael laughed. "Are you kidding me? You look great."

Laura had been trying to lose a few pounds lately, but it wasn't working. With the amount of work her father had thrust upon her lately, she didn't have time to hit the corporate gym. A great perk for the company, but one she wouldn't be able to take advantage of anytime soon. So pizza, pasta, and a glass of wine were her best friends lately, and not necessarily in that order. Sometimes a glass of wine was the best she could muster up as a meal replacement.

"Well, I still love the SUV." Michael strapped himself into the seat, patted his thighs, looked over Laura, and said, "Let's go, baby."

"Well, she isn't a Benz or that nice little Porsche you have stored in your garage."

Michael was a good-looking guy. He rarely lacked for female companionship and always had a beautiful woman on his arm. Settling down was like trying to catch a feral cat. They were beautiful to look at, they came around when they wanted, but as soon as you got too close, BAM! They darted off never to be seen again.

Unless, of course, they wanted an audience, a mouse or two left as a peace offering. In Michael's case, a dozen roses, a piece of jewelry, or something equally bright and shiny was his entree back into a woman's life. Laura couldn't figure out why he didn't settle down, but he didn't.

As for family get-togethers, he never spent the holidays alone, but always with her and her mother. However, Sunday was family dinner night regardless of whether Lewis would be in attendance or not. Michael often opted to forego family dinner night on the off-chance Lewis might make an appearance. Their rift had been long and deep, beginning when Lewis had stepped over the line with one of Michael's dates. He'd found his date for the evening wrapped around his father in a bed upstairs as Lewis plied her with promises of high-rise dreams, sparkly jewelry, and weekends in Carmel. It wasn't that Michael even liked the girl that much, but his father…that was another thing. That night only fueled his hatred for his father, like throwing more logs on an already out of control bonfire. Michael had stormed out of the house that evening with Laura fast on his heels. Their brief conversation told Laura everything she needed to know, and the fire shooting off from Michael would have burnt the whole house down if she hadn't interceded. God, Lewis had a way of sparking anger, pissing people off, and not giving a damn who he left burning in his wake.

"Oh, come on, don't be jealous. You can have one if you want to make the payments."

"That's just it. I'd rather keep a few bucks in my pocket rather than a fast piece of metal under my ass. Besides, you know I'm saving up to renovate my place in Napa."

"Ever the frugal legal eagle."

"Anyway. So, where's the cigar lounge you belong to?"

"The Banker Building."

"Ah, I should have guessed."

"What?" Michael patted her leg. "It's been too long, Lala. How are you?"

"Good."

"How's Mom?"

"Good." Laura focused on the traffic. Bumper-to-bumper, San Francisco style. People crowded the old antiquated freeways and the Bay Area Rapid Transit System, trying to get out of the city and to homes where high-rises didn't exist. Open spaces meant nothing higher than a two-story house. Eventually, she'd leave the grind and hustle of the cement cowboy cab and move to her place in Napa. That's why she had few trappings of her profession, unlike many of her peers who seemed to have them all. She saved it for an early retirement, where she could grow a few grapes, sow some seeds, and relax where people were kind and respectful. A side benefit, the air didn't smell like poisonous, noxious gas, plants didn't come in containers hanging off balconies, and shopping meant more than schlepping a few bags to your apartment.

"So, are we down to one word?"

"Sorry, I was just thinking."

"Turn here, we can valet this beast."

"Valet?"

"Another one-word answer. Good. You're going to be great dinner conversation tonight, Lala."

"Michael."

She couldn't help it; she had a lot on her mind. She didn't like not knowing what she didn't know. Her world revolved around facts. She wanted everything on the table before she decided to represent a client. She'd represented a client before that not only blindsided her at the litigation table, but the opposing counsel took great pride in being the one to present the fraudulent evidence. That not only lost her the case, but also besmirched her honor and put her ethics in question.

"Hey...You in there?" Michael snapped his fingers in front of her face.

"Turn in here." Michael pointed to the round driveway in front of the Banker Building. Well-dressed men ran around the arch, popping in and out of and between the cars, passing little bits of paper to waiting patrons and tossing keys to runners who had to pick up and dash back with said patron's vehicles. A uniformed lad opened Michael's door and shook his hand furiously.

"Dr. W. How are you this evening?"

"Good, Taryn. How's the wife?"

"Oh, she's big as a house now. Ready to pop."

"Good. Now remember, she needs to stay off her feet until it's time."

"Yes, sir."

Taryn barely looked old enough to have graduated from high school, let alone ready to be a father.

"How's school going?"

"Meh," Taryn said sheepishly, then looked at Michael. Clearly, the men had a relationship of some sort. Michael was always there to help someone out, regardless of their station in life. Another genetic marker they inherited from their mother.

"Don't quit. Promise me you won't quit." Michael arched an eyebrow then bent down to whisper something in the young man's ear.

Taryn nodded his head and wiped at his eyes, then ran over to Laura's side of the vehicle. "Ma'am?" His palm up, he waited for the keys. She slung her jacket on and tucked her purse under her arm, walking around the vehicle.

Her car raced off as another quickly took its place. The Banker Building was a busy place with boutiques on the lower levels, condos in the middle, and high-end restaurants and lounges at the top of the building. The penthouse had been taken over by the VIP cigar lounge and bar, and what would now be the most luxurious, high-dollar view in the city.

She hadn't been in the building since the remodel. Long hours combined with hating to shop prevented a foray into it. The remodeled building looked great. Having seen it now in all its grandeur, she would be remiss if she didn't bring her mom into town to do some shopping. Now, shopping was the only contact sport her mother participated in. At least, at her level, it would be considered a contact sport. If Saks or Neiman Marcus had a team, she'd be on it.

"Wow," she said, looking up.

"Nice, huh?"

"Very."

"Let's go eat and smoke some sticks and learn about cigars."

"Lead on." Laura slapped him on the back. "You're a good man."

"Huh." Michael shot her a confused look, the earlier conversation clearly already forgotten.

"How you encourage Taryn to finish school and take care of his wife."

"He's a good kid. Has a whole future ahead of him and I'd hate to see him stuck in some dead-end job trying to support a wife and kid." Michael brushed off the compliment and waved Laura into the elevator. "Come on, let's get a drink before this gets too mushy."

"Yeah, we wouldn't want you to get all girly on me." Laura laughed, following her brother into the elevator.

Pulling a Platinum card from his breast pocket, he slid it into the penthouse slot and pushed the button.

"Wow, they really don't want the average Joe up here, do they?"

Michael pulled the corners of his mouth up and shrugged. He cast her a sideways glance. "VIP has its privileges, Lala," he whispered, then winked at her.

Laura looked around the elevator, its polished brass finishes exactly what one expected in a VIP penthouse lounge and restaurant. From her vantage point in the back, the passengers who'd entered with them looked more like an off-the-rack sale at Gucci and the other high-end stores that littered the lobby. Mink coats, Coach bags, and lots of platinum and diamonds mixed with suits and briefcases rode up with them on the elevator.

At each floor the elevator lightened until finally there were only three left on the ride to the penthouse. Without ceremony, the door swished open and all Laura could do was stand in awe as she looked out into the entryway to the VIP lounge.

᷍᷍᷍᷍

She was greeted by marble travertine tiles, black with gold veins running through them. The dark mahogany walls with intricate crown molding rose up to the twelve-foot ceilings. Beautiful accent lighting highlighted expensive etched glasswork, and signed artwork hung on the walls. The foyer opened out into a much larger room that had leather couches and tall, wingback leather chairs clustered in groups of two, four, and six, with larger groups of couches around marble tables.

"Wow, so this is how the nouveau riche live." Laura looked around in amazement.

"Not what you expected?"

"No, no it's exactly what I expected for a penthouse VIP cigar lounge."

"Don't forget a kick-ass restaurant." Michael smiled at her, then fixed his tie. "How do I look?"

She laughed at his metrosexual appearance. "You look fine. I guess the bigger question is, am I dressed appropriately?"

Michael kept silent, extending his arm so she could take it.

"Really?"

"Don't say I didn't warn you."

Laura's heels clicked on the expensive black Italian tiles, the gentle tap-tap-tap of her heels announcing their arrival. She didn't have time to be afraid it would draw attention as they moved down the long hallway. She was right, eyes turning toward them as they spilt out into a much larger room. The small square groups were designed to be intimate, most likely so that you couldn't overhear somebody talking at the next table. Looking around the room, she couldn't help but notice the mostly male clientele. A cork popping caught her attention. To her left was a mahogany bar, the wood identical to the timber used throughout the club. Behind it, a young man in a black suit and red tie poured what she was sure was expensive champagne and top-shelf drinks. Putting them on the tray and the champagne in a bucket, he handed it to a female server who was dressed similarly.

"You look fantastic, Lala," Michael said, smiling back at her. Extending his arm, he waited again.

"Really?" She protested again and he put his arm back down.

"Okay. Again, don't say I didn't warn you."

No sooner had they entered the lounge than a rather paunchy man walked over to them.

"Michael, how are you?" the man said, looking at Laura, practically drooling as he completely ignored Michael. "Who do we have here?" Before a word could slip past Michael's lips, the man continued. "Good evening. Allow me to introduce myself. Dr. Stein, head of cardiothoracic surgery."

"Laura, Dr. Stein. My boss."

"Actually, Michael, I'm not technically your boss."

Laura took the hand that was extended.

The man raised Laura's hand to his pudgy lips and practically sucked it into his mouth.

Oh gross.

"It's a pleasure to meet you, Dr. Stein." Laura looked at Michael and then back at the doctor.

"The pleasure is all mine, I assure you. If this handsome rogue doesn't take care of you, please don't hesitate to look me up."

Without another word, he turned on his heel and went back to an older woman who was clearly his wife, if the displeasured look she gave was any indication. He sat next to a younger version of his wife—probably his daughter—and continued talking without taking a breath. Oh, he was one of *those* men. He loved to hear himself speak and relished a captive audience. *Lovely.*

Michael extended his arm again, and said, "I told you so. If you're with me, chances are you won't be hit on as much. This is a VIP meat market of sorts. Look around, do you see very many women in here?"

Before she could answer, Michael rubbed his stomach. "Are you hungry?"

"Starved."

"That's my Lala. Let's go get something to eat and then we can smoke a few sticks afterward. Then, I can impart all of the knowledge I have of cigars, which is very little, but I suspect a little more than what you know." He strolled into the main lounge.

Searching the larger room, it looked as though it had smaller rooms that spoked off the main hub past the bar and outward. To her left, past the bar, huge French doors ran floor to ceiling. They were open and Laura could see the beautiful skyline peeking against the darkening sky. She loved that view, and from up here she suddenly wished she could afford a penthouse with a million-dollar view of the city.

"So, tell me, Michael, what's the cost to belong to a VIP lounge like this? Surely, we're talking high dollar."

"I won't lie, it costs a few bucks. However, this is my sanctuary and well worth the price of admission. I can come, have a few drinks, smoke a few good cigars, and relax away from the prying eyes of the public, my patients, and anyone else I'm hiding from."

"Well at least you're honest," Laura said, taking her jacket off and handing it to the coat check. Pulling her phone from her purse, she checked it for any missed messages from her office.

"Lala, you're not going to sit glued to that thing

all night, are you?"

"Where's yours?"

He tapped the breast pocket of his jacket. "Right here. Although, I only answer when I get an emergency call ring. Then I know it truly is in an emergency."

"Oh, don't tell me we're going to play *that* game again are we?"

"What?"

"You know, my job's more important than your job?" Laura gave Michael a sideways glance. "Look, Dr. Badass, I would never say my job as a lawyer is more important than your job as an ER doctor." Laura smiled at her brother as they weaved their way through the clusters of chairs and cigar smoke.

The restaurant was tucked away in the back of the lounge. If the decadent smells emanating from the front door were any indication of the kind of meal that was in store, she knew she was in for a treat. Michael opened the door, ushering Laura through to the maître d' station.

"Welcome Dr. W. Good to see you again."

"Good evening, Peter. How are you?"

"Fine, sir. Thank you for asking. Your usual table?"

"That would be great, Peter. Thank you."

Laura cast a sideways glance at Peter and said, "Your usual table, really?"

"What? I told you this is my sanctuary. Besides, you know I hate to cook."

"Yes, I quite remember how many meals you've had at your house."

"Yeah—zero."

"Well, I guess we didn't get our cooking genes from Mother, now did we?

Their mother wasn't known for her cooking

abilities, and the few Thanksgivings she had attempted cooking a turkey has been a disaster.

"Quite right," Michael said.

They chuckled at the memories they shared from their childhood.

"How would we ever have survived if it wasn't for Francine?" Laura said.

She had such great memories of their old cook Francine. Her passing had been a blow to both her and Michael, and especially to her mother, who was often Francine's dinner companion at night when her father "worked" late. Her mother had often told her how Francine had been her sounding board, been the one to hear her cries at night over her frustrations with Lewis, and helped her deal with her own demons.

"Francine was wonderful. I miss her every day," Michael said as they stopped at their table. "Ladies first."

Michael pointed to the plush, dimly lit booth. Barely able to see anything, Laura sank into the buttery soft leather. "I think I might need a booster seat." The maître d' pulled the napkin from the plate and placed it on Laura's lap.

"Dr. W, your usual? Would the lady like to see a menu?"

Before Michael could even open his mouth, Laura responded, "Yes, *the lady* would like to see a menu. Thank you, Peter." Her tone was rather abrupt. Being referred to in the third person pissed her off. It was as if she couldn't speak for herself and harkened back to a time when women, much like children, were seen and not heard.

"Of course, madam." Peter left in a huff.

"I'm sorry, Michael, but this is really kind of old

school don't you think?"

"What do you mean, Laura? This is what you pay for when you join a VIP club. It's what most of the membership expects. Many of the people that come here are well-paid executive types, there are all kinds of deals being made here, and the last thing they want is to play Twenty Questions with the staff."

"So, like that backroom club men belonged to in the forties, fifties, and sixties that were done away with decades ago. They didn't let women like me be a part of their little inner circle."

"Lala—"

"I feel like I'm an interloper. That somehow I don't belong in this world."

"Don't be ridiculous, Lala. This is how people work nowadays. They have a couple of drinks, smoke a few cigars, connect with other people of a like mind, and do business. It's casual, and it's the way the world works now, Lala."

"You mean *still*, right?"

Laura knew he was right. This was the kind of world she didn't circle in. Backroom deals felt dirty to her. She was used to being upfront about her business dealings. Facing them head-on and taking a face-to-face approach in a business setting. She couldn't ignore all the high-powered suits sitting around having a bourbon, or a scotch, talking business. Maybe she was the one out of touch with how the world worked in the executive class.

"Your menu, madam," Peter said, opening it and putting it on the plate in front of her. "Shall I get you a drink, madam?"

Michael was clearly in his element here. He had an established routine, a usual drink, a usual meal, and he was clearly a regular at the VIP Club.

"Can I get a rum and coke, please?" Laura perused the menu. "What do you usually order Michael? What do you recommend?"

Peter spoke up quickly. "We have a wonderful filet with a bordelaise sauce with mushrooms and Yukon Gold mashed potatoes. Would that be to the lady's liking?"

"That sounds perfect, Peter. Thank you." Passing the menu back, she ignored the sudden nose-out-of-joint Peter was sniffing the air with.

❧❧❧❧

Peter pulled the table away from them, then extended a hand toward Laura.

"Madam."

Scooting, she grabbed his hand and pulled herself up. Michael fell out from the other side and adjusted his coat and tie. She wasn't used to this kind of service. To be fair, she didn't dine on junk food, she just didn't spend a load of time in pretentious restaurants.

"Peter, as usual." Michael slipped his hand against Peter's, slipping him a large bill.

"Thank you, sir. It's always a pleasure. Don't forget the benefit tomorrow."

"Benefit?" Laura's interest was piqued.

She loved charity events, especially when it was for a good cause.

Peter faced Laura. "Black-tie event for a hospital in Nicaragua and remembrance for the founder of the charity, Don Roberto Huerta. He recently passed. Tragic accident, I hear." Michael handed Laura her purse. "Huh, I hadn't thought about going, but perhaps." Michael glanced at Laura and shrugged. "Ready to smoke your first cigar?"

Apprehensive, Laura nodded. The room suddenly felt hot. Maybe she needed some air first. The wine seemed to be going right to her head.

"You okay?" Michael grabbed her shoulder, steadying her. "Let's get you out of here and get you home and we can save Cigar 101 for another night."

"No, no I'm good. I think I had one too many glasses of wine. I'm not used to having a drink during the week." She brushed Michael's hands away. "I'll be fine. Let's go smoke a cigar." She pasted on a smile sure the feeling would pass.

"Follow me. This place has one of the biggest humidors on the west coast."

"Lead the way."

The path to the lounge wasn't a direct one, but more of a circuitous path around the main floor of the lounge. It was even more packed, if that were possible, in the hour it had taken to finish dinner. Raucous laughter filled pockets of the room, while in the quieter corners smoke wafted toward the ceiling, the only display that anyone was occupying that domain.

Domain.

Funny, Laura thought. *That's exactly what parts of the lounge feel like—someone's domain. Like a piece of real estate that the respective lounge member held court in.*

"Are there regulars here?"

"What do you mean?"

"Well, are you a regular?"

Michael cocked his head, thinking about the question. "I have a locker here."

"Do you come on a regular basis?'

"Yeah, I suppose, if you put it that way, I'm a regular."

"Do you have a place where you like to sit? I see lots of people fluttering here and there. Do they always sit there?" Her hands motion around pointing to no one in place in particular.

"Oh, yeah. There are definitely guys for whom this is a second home."

"Interesting. Is there a pecking order?"

"Where are you going with this, Lala?"

"Oh, I don't know. I just know how men are, and wonder if there is a place where you all go and measure your penises and see who's at the top of the pecking order?" Laura laughed. "I'm just kidding, Michael. Relax."

"Wow, and you thought that the idea of a VIP lounge was antiquated. I think you need to check that viewpoint at the door, sister." Michael slapped her on the back harder than required, she was sure.

"So...is there a pecking order?"

Michael looked out the door and studied the room intently.

"Sure, I suppose. The fireplace is valuable real estate. The back corners are usually taken by the judge and his court, so to speak." Michael made air quotes around *court*. "A few city council members and the mayor are off talking all the time."

"Really? How many?"

"Why?"

"Because they could be breaking the law if they are meeting to discuss business for the city."

"Come on." Michael turned his back on her.

"See what I mean about an old boys' club? I doubt the women who sit on the council are here. So,

by extension, they could be making back-room deals."
Laura held up her hands when Michael turned to
glare at her. "Hey, don't shoot the messenger. I'm just
saying."

"Well, should we just leave, or can I trust that
you'll use your better judgement before outing what
you see in here?"

"Relax. I'm just here to learn about cigars."

"Hmm."

Without thinking, she walked through the door
Michael had been holding open and found herself dead
center of the humidor before she finally stopped.

Notes of cedar and tobacco mixed with the
coolness of the air in the humidor. The room was
bathed in gold tones from the overhead lights, with
some lights accenting what Laura imagined was where
the high-priced cigars resided. It was exactly opposite
of the room they'd just left. Its simple shelves of bare,
untreated wood lacked the opulence of the lounge.
Interesting. The ceiling was at least ten feet high with
shelves going up at least eight feet, and atop those
shelves were boxes of cigars still wrapped in cellophane,
stacked to the ceiling. Moving closer, she noticed some
cigars were in boxes while others were in trays.

"What's the difference?" Laura pointed to the
cigars.

"Good evening, Dr W. How are you this evening?"
A curvy, caramel-skinned woman with jet-black hair
that framed her face walked into the humidor. Her
name badge said Yessenia.

"Yessenia, how are you?" Michael exchanged
air-kisses on each side of her face. "This is my sister,
Laura. Laura, this is Yessenia, and she is the foremost
expert on cigars here at the Club. Her grandparents

emigrated to the US from Cuba. Her grandfather was a cigar roller and passed his love for cigars to her father, and he passed it on down to his children." Looking at Yessenia he asked, "How did I do?"

"Great. So how can I help you tonight?"

"What can you recommend to a new cigar smoker, such as myself?" Laura pointed to herself for emphasis.

"Hmm...since you're a new smoker, you don't know what your tastes are yet and you haven't developed your palate. So, a mild cigar is probably a good place to start."

Laura watched the beautiful woman as she picked up a cigar, ran it under her nose, and then offered it to Laura to smell.

"Have you had dinner yet?"

"I have." Laura returned the smile.

"Good to know. I'd hate for you to get smoke-sick your first time."

"Smoke-sick, oh god."

Michael chuckled, his hand on Laura's lower back for reassurance. "Relax. It would only happen if you inhaled, or picked a bold cigar. You won't be doing any of those things, so relax."

Suddenly, Laura wondered what she got herself into as she eyed the cigars. The look on her face must have been obvious because Yessenia giggled a little and grabbed both of Laura's hands.

"You'll be okay. I'll start you with something very mild. We want this to be a relaxing and enjoyable experience. If it isn't, you won't come back." Yessenia frowned and knitted her brows together, then batted her long eyelashes at Laura.

God, she's good. I bet she sells men boxes of cigars on a regular basis with that look.

"Why don't we try this one? It's mild with a Connecticut wrapper, so it's going to have a little peppery note to it when you start, but it will mellow out after the first half- to one-inch. Then there are going to be some mellow tones like toast, or various creamy notes. Someone recently said they thought it had a toasted marshmallow taste. Now, I don't know about that, but it is a mellow cigar."

"How many of these things have you smoked?" Laura held her hands out and did a turn, looking at all of the cigars. There had to be a thousand in the room, easily. Different sizes, colors, lengths. Who knew there were so many Makers and brands? The colorful labels, boxes, and styles surprised her. Luckily, she only had to deal with one.

"Hmm, almost all of them."

"All of them?"

"Well, I have my favorites. I tend to like a medium stick. Something with leathery but buttery creamy tones."

Did she just say leathery, seriously? Laura was in a world that didn't register with her, either in its language or its words. Laura wondered how those things could be found in tobacco, considering she'd tried cigarettes when she was younger and all she tasted was an ashtray. At least that's what it felt like. Blech.

"Stick?"

"Oh, sometimes we call cigars 'sticks.' Never call a cigar a stogie—that's for the amateurs and people in the movies. If you're a true cigar smoker, you call it a stick or a cigar." Yessenia handed Laura another cigar.

"This is a smaller ring gauge, and a little shorter in length." Yessenia held the cigar up, smelled it, and handed it to Laura.

"Ring gauge, what does that mean?"

"Ring gauge is the circumference of the cigar. It means how big it is, based on how large the circumference is instead of the length." Yessenia held up a fatter cigar. "This one is a fifty-five ring gauge." She held up another one. "This one is a sixty. Some men like to get these big fat ones between their lips. And yes, it's very phallic, but some of the best sticks have a large ring gauge." She tossed Laura a knowing look and then smiled at Michael. "No offense, Michael. I just see some of these men with these big fat sticks hanging out of their mouths and think, are you really enjoying that?"

"None taken." Michael threw up his hands. "I tend to like a robusto or a corona myself."

"Well, why don't you pick something out for a newbie like myself?"

"Sure. You trust me?" Yessenia winked at Laura, then smiled.

Yep. Yessenia could empty this room of its product in a matter of minutes, Laura concluded.

"You're the expert."

"Great, let's try a mild- to medium-body—"

"Won't I get sick if it's too strong?" Laura felt the beginnings of panic.

"You said you'd trust me."

"I'm sorry, you're right, I did. Lead on, please." Laura moved with Yessenia as she described the different wrappers, fillers, and lengths.

"I think this should be perfect." Yessenia handed Laura a rather small cigar.

"This is a corona size, perfect for a short smoke, but not too short."

"So, size doesn't matter?" She spared a glance at

Michael, who blanched at the joke.

"Seriously?"

Laura shrugged and said, "I'm just kidding, calm down."

"Well, it does if you want to take some time and enjoy a good cigar." Yessenia patted Laura's hand and walked her to the door. "We'll light it outside. My manager doesn't like anyone smoking in the humidor. He thinks it corrupts the rest of the cigars."

"Oh, I didn't know that," Michael said, killing his lighter.

"Does she treat everyone like this? She's a little giddy if you ask me," Laura whispered over her shoulder to Michael.

Yessenia stopped at the edge of the bar where a mixed assortment of cutters and lighters sat in a tray. Pulling one, she held it up for Laura's inspection.

"I'll show you how to cut the cap, toast the end, and light the cigar, then we can pair it with something to drink." Yessenia smiled.

Yep, she could sell an acre of snow and call it clear liquid sunshine and no one would care. Laura marveled at the woman's ability to give the "feel-goods."

Laura gave Michael a sideways glance. His own glee was off the chart as he practically leaned over Laura to watch Yessenia.

"A little excited, are we?" She gently launched her shoulder at his chest as she poked fun at his excitement. "What gives?"

He shrugged. "I'm kinda excited to be the one you're sharing your first cigar with."

So, this is what a rite of passage feels like. A dad gives his son his first sip of beer, his first driving lesson, his first smoke, his first prostitute—wait, where did that come from? Laura mentally slapped herself.

"This is a guillotine cutter, it cuts the cap off." Depositing it back on to the tray, she held up another. "This is a 'V' cutter. See the little V when it opens?" Her long manicured nail pointed out the sharp V when she slid the cigar into the cutter's hole. She picked up another and held it up. A round circle was all Laura could see.

"What's that?" she asked, confused at the design.

"It's a punch. It literally punches a hole into the cap of the cigar. Lots of men love this type. Me, I like a V cut. It keeps more of the cap in place and reduces some of the nicotine."

"Let's go with that one then." Laura smiled at Yessenia, the perfect saleswoman.

"You got it."

Yessenia cut the end of the cigar, which was lucky for Laura as she probably would have snipped the wrong end and looked stupid. She grabbed a lighter and snapped it open. The flame jetted out with unexpected power.

"This is a three-flame torch lighter," she said, closing it and then sparking it again to life. "Personally, if I have matches, I go with them. I think the gas flame gives it a little different taste and I have to backdraft the cigar." Laura must have looked confused. "I have to blow out the cigar to try to get rid of the aftereffect flavor of the butane from the lighter. When I'm in a pinch, though, I use my lighter." She pulled out an elegantly slim lighter wrapped in leather. "I always have something with me, just in case." She winked at Laura, pocketed the lighter, and picked up a box of matches. Even the box screamed elegance. The black-

and-gold writing mirrored the travertine tiles she had walked in on. Nothing cheap here. Yessenia struck two matches, picked up the cigar, and instructed Laura on what she was doing. "I'm toasting the end to heat up the cigar before lighting it."

"What does that do?" Fascinated, Laura watched the flames licking the bottom of the cigar as Yessenia twisted it around.

"It starts to open up the tobacco, releasing the oils and gently gets it ready to burn."

"Interesting. So, you just can't put it in your mouth and light it up like a cigarette?"

Yessenia's shocked look surprised Laura.

"Heaven's no! You'll ruin a good cigar that way. I guess if you're in a hurry you could. We don't want to do that." She pointed to a man whose cigar end looked like it was on fire. "We aren't trying to burn a barn down. We are coaxing the flame to light the end." Yessenia blew on the tip of the cigar, lighting the end to a red glow. "Now, it's ready. There are some lighters that give you a flame and not that torch, so if you have one of those you go about lighting your cigar the same way."

Laura watched as Yessenia blew the end red again, then handed it to Laura with instructions to gently suck on the end, but not inhale.

"Now, take a puff. Hold it in your mouth and then gently force the smoke out."

Yessenia pouted her lips and expanded her cheeks. "Like that."

Laura pulled on the cigar gently and then gazed down at it. She held the smoke. Who knew breathing exercises would be part of the process?

"Now, let it out."

Pursing her lips together, she blew the stream of smoke above her head, not wanting to offend anyone.

"How was that?"

"Good, that's perfect." Yessenia's smile of encouragement was contagious. She looked over at Michael, who nodded and puffed on his own lit cigar.

"Now take another puff and hold it in your mouth and taste it."

Laura did as instructed. She was nothing if not a good student. Easing the smoke out, it glided up and past her nose where she caught a whiff, and more smells and flavors hit her palate.

"I tend to move my tongue forward pushing the air out through pursed lips. That's just me. Now, let just a little bit flow through your nose. You get some flavor that way, too."

Immediately, Laura's eyes watered as she forced smoke through her nostrils, but Yessenia was right, she could taste and smell different notes of coffee, cedar, and something else she couldn't quite put her finger on. Her tongue clicked as she tried to taste the cigar smoke.

"Wow, you were right. I could definitely taste pepper on my lips and cedar, or is it coffee, on my tongue?" Laura smacked her lips together again and gently forced air through her nose.

Yessenia patted Laura's hand. "Now pair it with something to drink and you have the perfect start, or ending, to a night."

"What do you recommend?"

"Hmm, a whiskey or a bourbon. My personal preference is a chocolate Port or root beer. If it's morning, coffee or hot chocolate."

"Really? Root beer?"

"Uh-huh. The flavors of the root beer work really well with the cigar." She held up her hands. "Don't ask me why, I just like it when I don't want something alcoholic. Well, my work here is done." She gave Michael a once-over. "I leave her in your capable hands." She air-kissed his cheeks and spotted a group of men entering the humidor. "Oops, duty calls."

"Thank you again," Laura said, offering an appreciative smile.

"Go and sit outside and enjoy your cigar. I love to people watch when I smoke. A small vice. The fresh air will enhance your smoking experience."

"Thanks, I'll do that."

"Have a great evening."

"Thanks again."

"Let me know if you need anything."

All Laura could do was follow the shapely ass and stilettos as they sent Yessenia on her way to the next clients.

"I think she likes you," Michael joked.

"Oh, please. She's got great people skills."

Michael and Laura both looked wistfully as Yessenia's hands covered her ass, catching the glass door of the humidor. "Yes, yes, she does," he said, smiling.

"I'm betting she could sell cigars to a tobacco farmer and he buys more than he even needed just because of her wonderful temperament."

"Are you saying that because she's a woman? Or because she was flirting with you?"

"I'm shocked. That is such a sexist statement, Michael."

He raised his hands in defense. "I'm just saying."

"I bet if you were in that humidor right now, she would be just as nice to those men who walked in."

"Maybe." Michael motioned for the bartender.

"Hi, Michael. What'll it be?"

He looked down at Laura and nodded toward the bartender.

She gazed at the back of the bar. The bottles all were in their own separate cubbies with lights shining on them. They look more like expensive jewels in a bracelet than expensive liquor.

"What do you have that would go with this?" Laura held up her smoldering cigar.

The bartender shot her of a look of, *Really?*, before explaining everything that would go with her stick.

"I'll have the chocolate Port. It sounds wonderful." Laura smiled.

Michael chimed in. "Yeah, I can't think of anything better than chocolate and alcohol combined into a yummy drink."

"Did you just say yummy?"

"I did." He face-palmed. "You're such a wonderful influence on me, Lala."

"Well, we do have the same genetic bios. So, it stands to reason we might sound alike in some ways."

Two drinks were deposited on the bar next to them. "Thanks, Tim." He raised his glass in salute.

"You got it, Bro."

"Come on, let's go sit down and enjoy these." Michael clinked his glass against Laura's and then raised his cigar to his lips and pulled, the red ball at the end of the cigar squealing to life.

"Lead the way," she said, her hands full.

Laura had to stop at the open French doors and marvel at the skyline. She could see the Golden Gate to her left, Sausalito in the middle, and the Bay Bridge to the right. The terrace wound around the lounge and she could only imagine the view on the other side. The coolness of the fog made her shiver. Suddenly, she wished she'd kept her coat. She spotted Michael waving at her as he patted the seat next to him. He picked one around a fire pit filled with colored glass, flames licking against the glass walls. Not only did it look inviting, but it was perfect for a night like tonight.

The terrace, like the lounge, was divided into intimate groups, including cabanas with their walls down, only a whisper of an opening in the front allowing a peek into the inside of the privacy chamber. That was the only thought that came to Laura's mind— she could only imagine what was happening behind those curtains that hid the occupants, involved in backroom deals or romantic trysts.

Michael called to her again, and Laura started in his direction but stopped at the sight of a slender foot peeking out from the side of a wing back chair. A shiny black stiletto balanced precariously on the tips of toes, swinging back and forth trying to dislodge itself from its owner. It was mesmerizing as the shoe did a delicate arc back and forth. Occasionally the toe snapped the shoe back on the foot and then let it drop as it began working its hypnotic magic, undulating back and forth.

"Laura."

Thank god Michael knew enough not to use her nickname in public. It would be very embarrassing if it got out.

"Excuse me," Laura said, walking around the weaving stiletto. Trying not to let her gaze move up the slender calf and the woman connected to the shoe, she sat next to Michael and set her Port on the marble ledge surrounding the fire pit. Her lit cigar dangled between her thumb and two fingers. Still trying not to look at the woman, she couldn't help but cast a sideways glance at her.

Before she could take in the full beauty of the woman, Michael interrupted. "What was that all about?"

"What are you talking about?"

"You put on a full-stop like that woman's leg was keeping you from moving forward."

Laura blushed. It had been a while since a woman vexed her. Instead, she focused on her work and her goal to move to Napa.

"It was nothing."

"Ha." Michael pulled on the cigar. He closed his eye and let the smoke push out over his head. "She's quite beautiful," he said, nodding in the direction of the black stilettos.

"I hadn't noticed." Laura raised the cigar to her lips and took a small puff, watching the end glow just a bit.

"Well, that's interesting, because she is staring at us."

"She's probably staring at my handsome brother. I'm surprised you aren't over there trying to make small talk.'

"I would've if she didn't have a hulk of a man on her shoulder talking her ear off. She's fucking gorgeous."

"Gosh, little brother, I can practically see you fucking her with your eyes. Just your type, and she smoke cigars, too."

"How do you know what she looks like? I thought you didn't notice."

"I make my living paying attention to details without being obvious."

Laura turned her back to the woman and focused on the dusky skyline. Pretty soon it would be drizzling on the terrace and she would again wish she had her jacket. She released the small bit of smoke she held in her mouth and leaned back against the cushion.

The dark Port mesmerized her as it swirled in her glass. She was fighting hard to avoid looking at the woman behind her. Curiosity was eating away at her resolve in the same way alcohol ate away at a person's good judgement. Lifting the dark liquid to her lips, she took a sip and let it linger on her tongue. Essence of chocolate danced on her taste buds before she swallowed. *God, that is heaven in a bottle.* Chocolate and wine, the only thing that would make it better was a warm bath incorporated in the concoction. Ecstasy flooded from her pores as her brother touched her hand.

"That good, huh?"

"Oh, yeah." She closed her eyes and took another sip and slipped farther down on the cushions, resting her head against the headrest. "It's that good. Want to try?"

Michael wrinkled his nose at the offer. "I'm not much for sweet stuff, but give me something musky and sweaty and I'm all over that like a hawk."

"Now really. Do you have to go there?" She could fill in the innuendo.

Michael let a chuckle barely rumble past his lips. As he tossed her a sloppy grin.

"Hey, I was only saying—"

"I know what you were saying. Knock it off." She backhanded his stomach.

"Lemme try it." He snatched the glass from her hand before she could offer up a protest.

"That is yummy."

"Yummy?" She followed his gaze when she realized he wasn't talking about the Port.

Laura tried not to stare at the woman, who was still trying to lose her stiletto as it swung precariously from her toes. Her mouth was agape as smoke gently eased its way past red lips that were like a neon sign screaming, "Kiss me, kiss me." Before she could divert her gaze, they locked eyes and the woman quirked a smile at Laura.

Shit.

Laura's face flamed with the embarrassment of being caught staring. Or was it the heat of the gas pit in front of her? Either way, she needed to cool off.

"You know what? I think I need some air. Save my spot." She stood and smoothed her dress.

"What? We're outside. There's fresh air everywhere." Michael looked up from her to the woman and back to Laura. "I got you. I'll save you a seat, Lala."

Laura, still holding her cigar, frowned at Michael for using her nickname. He mouthed an apology and put up his hands. She put the Port on the low table that circled the fire pit and walked to the edge of the balcony where no one was standing. Centering herself, she took a long, deep breath and searched the only thing she recognized, the skyline of San Francisco.

"It looks like your cigar's out. May I?" The woman who'd been sitting behind her presented a lighter and flicked it between them. The flame lit up her features, casting a golden glow on her caramel skin and her lush lips as she pressed them together in a pout. God, she was even more beautiful up close.

"I'm sorry?"

"No need to apologize. I just noticed you were out

and I thought perhaps I'd offer you some assistance."

Laura shot her a puzzled look.

"Your cigar. I mean your cigar seems to be out."

"Oh, thank you." Without thinking, Laura handed her the cigar.

The woman offered up a soft laugh and tilted her head. "May I?" She tossed Laura a seductive look, and, without waiting for an answer, took the cigar. As she placed it between her lips, Laura's body felt like one of those kid drinks where you drop a fizz tab into it and it started bubbling. She couldn't help but stare. The woman looked like she was making love to the cigar, the way she gently rolled it between her ruby-red lips as she puffed on it. The hypnotic flame cast a warm glow on the woman's face as it danced around the cigar as she coaxed it back to life.

"There you go." The woman twisted the cigar around toward Laura, hints of red lipstick still on the tip. Laura hesitated as she thought about putting it to her lips and rolling it around in the same way the woman did. Taking a puff, she let it linger a bit before she cocked her head back and blew the smoke above their heads.

She felt like she was in an old forties' movie where the man lit the woman's cigarette for her in a show of chivalry and handed it back to her, then lit his own. The electricity that passed between the couple was almost Tesla-esque. Anyone standing next to them might get burned if they could feel what Laura was feeling, or perhaps it was all in her head. She inhaled slowly, held the smoke in her mouth, and then blew it out up over their heads.

"You don't have to do that." The woman's breathless words were whispered next to Laura's ear.

A hint of a Spanish accent registered in her mind. Laura could feel her warm breath as it tickled her ear. God, if she didn't know better, she'd think she was on hypersexual overdrive. There wasn't anything about the way this woman looked that didn't excite her.

"What do you mean?" Laura said, puzzled.

"It's a cigar lounge. I don't mind the smell of cigar smoke."

"Oh, I didn't want to be rude. This is my first time smoking a cigar."

She didn't know why she offered up that little tidbit of information, but when she got nervous, she babbled like an idiot. Moreover, this woman was making her nervous.

"Really, I couldn't tell. You're such a natural."

"You think so?" Laura doubted the woman.

"Trust me, I've seen some interesting ways people 'smoke' cigars, and you don't seem out of place here."

"Thanks." Laura tried not to make eye contact, turning slightly away. She was sure she was blushing, if the sudden warmth crawling up her neck was any indication.

"So, you decided to come with your husband to see if he really comes to the cigar lounge all the times he's not home with you?" Her sensual laugh drifted past Laura.

God, is this woman flirting with me?

Pointing at Michael, Laura shook her head. "Him? Oh, he's not my husband, he's my brother."

"Really?" The woman stared at Michael. Laura was sure she just green-lighted the highway for the woman to pursue Michael.

In her younger years, Laura had friends who'd tried to get to her brother through her, friending her and then worming their way into an invite to a party or family function. One particular incident had caused such a row between her and Michael that he didn't speak to her for over a year. She'd learned crazy came in all body types, dye jobs and social statuses. Why should this woman be any different? Before she could shove off, the woman asked her another question, even more curious than the last.

"So, your husband doesn't mind you coming down here with your brother to smoke cigars?"

Laura practically choked, coughing on the mouth full of smoke. She waved her hand in front of her face trying to clear the air so she could breathe.

"Oh, are you all right? Tio, agua por favor," she seemed to command to the man chatting up what had to be the only other two hot women in the club.

"Si, si." He ran over with a glass and handed it to the woman, who handed it to Laura.

A big swallow made her choke even more; the water turned out to be champagne. At least that's what she thought, sputtering as it burned on the way down.

The slap on her back practically put her on her ass. She had to grab the rail to prevent her knees from hitting the tile.

"I'm so sorry. Tío what was that?"

"Champagne. Sorry, mija. It's what was close."

"Aye." The woman muttered a few words in Spanish Laura didn't understand. "Here, let me help you sit." She grabbed Laura's elbow, guiding her to a seat.

"Thank you." Laura half inhaled and then choked again trying to regain her composure.

As they sat, Laura noticed Michael had found someone to keep her seat warm while she was choking.

Some doctor you are.

"Are you okay now?"

Laura blushed. "How embarrassing. Yes, I'm fine now, thank you."

"Perhaps a glass of water?"

"No, no, I'm fine, really." Laura coughed again, waving her off.

"Are you sure?"

Laura smiled at the woman. She couldn't help but feel like she was getting lost in those brown eyes the longer she stared.

"So, your husband…"

"Oh, I'm not married."

"Oh, what a pity. A beautiful woman such as yourself. My name is Sofía, by the way." Sofía offered her hand to Laura, who stared at it. A heat crawled up her neck before she took Sofia's hand and shook it. She felt as if she were battling a fever each time the woman was near her. Christ, she wasn't used to being thrown off this easily.

"Pleasure to meet you, Sofía. I'm Laura." Nodding her head toward her brother, she wanted to cut to the chase. "That good-looking man over there is my brother, Michael. He's very single, but I have to warn you, he is quite the charmer under the right circumstances."

Sofía cocked her head toward Laura. A puzzled look flashed and then disappeared as she answered. "I imagine he is. So…"

Michael rushed over to Laura as she waved him off. "She saved my life while you were otherwise occupied."

"Oh please, I did no such thing. Your sister was choking, so I offered her something to drink. Unfortunately, my uncle handed me champagne, which I'm afraid made matters worse."

"Well, Laura, you seem to be none the worse for wear."

"Is that your professional medical opinion?"

"Oh, a doctor. How fortunate for you, Laura." Sofía smiled.

The hook was baited and set. Now it was only a matter of time before the woman reeled Michael in hook, line, and plunger.

"This is my brother, Michael. I'm sorry what did you say your name was again?"

"Sofía."

The Spanish accent hit all the right notes as Laura looked back at Sofía. God, she was beautiful.

"How do you do, Sofía?" Michael said her name with the same inflection she had said it. Laura watched as he took Sofía's hand and raised it delicately to his lips, just as Dr. Stein had done to Laura.

Oh brother. Laura rolled her eyes and looked away. *Not you too, Michael.*

"It's a pleasure. So, I understand this is your sister's first time at the lounge. Are you a regular?" Sofía said, looking at Laura.

"I am. It's my sanctuary, so to speak." Michael led Sofía to where he'd been sitting and patted the seat next to him. "Please..." He motioned for the waitress. "Please bring whatever she's having and another for my sister, too. Laura?" He nodded to the other side of him and patted the seat.

Christ, she didn't want to sit and watch as Michael hooked another stray. Taking a puff of her cigar, she turned and looked out at the jeweled city below her. The stars met the hills as the fog eased its misty tendrils up them. Ready to gobble them up just like Michael was with his new friend.

"Laura, won't you join us?" Sofía patted the seat next to her.

Laura hesitated, and then said, "You know what…" She looked down at her watch. *Billable time.* "I have some work to finish up before I start tomorrow. I really should be going."

☙ ☙ ☙ ☙ ☙

Sofia had caught sight of the pair the moment they'd entered the lounge from the restaurant. After they'd left the humidor, she beelined it into the humidor to speak with Yessenia.

"Yessenia."

"Sofia, how are you?" She gave Sofia a gentle hug. "I was so sorry to her about Don Roberto. You have my deepest condolences. How are you doing?"

"Thank you, that's very sweet of you to ask. I'm doing okay."

"And RJ, how is that brother of yours?"

"Same as always. He's family, but we don't get to pick our family now, do we. Anyway, he is very upset that Father didn't leave him anything of the company."

Yessenia sucked in a breath. "No. Why?" Raising her hands, she stopped Sofia. "I'm sorry. It's none of my business. So, did you bring me anything for the humidor?"

Sofia walked over to where her father's cigars were on display and noticed hers on the shelf right next to the long line of Huertas. "How do you like the new line?"

"Oh, the Angel Blanca and the Negrilla Diabla? They're wonderful, and selling well. You did a great job mixing the tobaccos for those."

The Conundrums sat next to her others. She pulled one from the box and smiled. "This one," she said, raising it to her nose and inhaling. "This one is my favorite."

"The name fits it perfectly. Everyone has a different experience smoking it." Yessenia smiled. "When are you releasing it to a wider audience?"

"After Vegas. I wanted to roll it out sooner, but now with my father's death, I don't think it's the right time. November and the big conference there will be perfect. Sí?"

"Oh, sí."

"So…" Sofia looked around the humidor to make sure they were alone. "That gringo couple that came into the lounger earlier…did you see them? Tall, dark-haired man and a shorter woman with blond hair. Do you know them?"

"Oh, you must mean Dr. W. He's a regular. Her, I don't know. She's probably his girlfriend, but she has a different vibe than the others. He's always coming in with a new lady every once in a while. He's super cute, right?"

"I just noticed them. I thought I would invite them to the benefit we're having for my father's charity. You know, the children's hospital we're building in Nicaragua?"

"Your whole family is amazing. I'll be there. Anything I can do to help kids, you know?"

"Thanks, we can always use some beautiful women at the event." Sofia smiled and patted Yessenia's arm.

Yessenia smiled. "So, you like the gringo, huh?"

Sofia shrugged. She wasn't going to confirm

anything. Cigar lounges were like gossip mills—too much grist for the mill and it ran forever. She liked keeping her personal life separate from her professional life, but the woman intrigued her.

"He's regular here. I see him all the time." She threw her hands down, dismissing him. "He's a doctor, specialist I think." The pressure in the humidor changed slightly as someone came in. "Give me a minute and we can talk more."

Before she knew it, several more men came into the humidor and tried to chat up Sofia. She politely rebuffed their advances, but some persisted. It didn't look like the steady stream of guys were going to let up anytime soon, and she didn't want to miss her chance to invite the handsome doctor and his girlfriend to the benefit. It was a perfect fit for the doctor—a children's hospital with his name written all over it.

"Hey, Yessenia, I'm going to get a drink and have a cigar. We'll catch up later."

"Sorry." Yessenia pouted. "I'll come find you later. Bye."

With that, Sofia had found out enough info to satisfy her curiosity. Now, she had to track down her uncle and make sure he was behaving himself. God, her feet were killing her. Maybe she'd let him fend for himself while she enjoyed a glass of wine and a smoke.

How fortuitous that after seizing the opportunity to light the intriguing woman's cigar, she now was seated at the same fire pit as Laura and Michael.

"Your brother has just ordered another round of drinks. Please, Laura, stay and have a drink."

"Laura, come on, it's still early. We don't have a curfew anymore and you don't have to worry about Dad waiting up. Come on. At least finish your cigar, then you can go."

"Yes, please don't let me ruin your first cigar. I will go. I don't want to intrude on family time. My apologies." Sofia stood. She hadn't wanted to make the woman bolt for the door. She only wanted to find out her name and…well…clearly Laura wasn't in the mood for talking.

"No." Laura raised her hand, stopping Sofia. "Please stay. I apologize for my rudeness. Of course I'll finish my cigar. Besides, I have a *yummy* Port to finish," she said, eyeing her brother. "I'd hate to see good chocolate go to waste."

"Chocolate?" Sofia was intrigued.

Michael stood and handed Laura's Port to her just as the waitress brought the next round of drinks. Setting another Port next to her first one, she was glad the drink came in a rather small serving. After two glasses of wine she'd be buzzing, but the Port seemed innocent enough.

"Would you like to try it?" Laura offered her fresh glass to Sofia.

"You don't mind?" Sofia let her eyes flash across Laura's business attire. A well-fitting suit accented the curves Sofia found sexy. She loved business suits on the right person.

"Not at all. Please, I insist." Laura handed her the glass.

As she focused on Laura, she slowly raised the glass to her lips. A small sip was all it took as the essence of chocolate danced on her tongue.

"Hmm, it's very good." Sofia handed the glass back to Laura, who'd taken the seat between Michael and herself. Her hand consciously brushed against Laura's as they transferred the glass between them.

Sparks shot through her at the touch. Sofia didn't believe in love at first sight, but lust? *Oh yes.* She definitely believed that one could want someone the first time they met.

"Where is your friend?" Michael asked, breaking the connection and searching for the hulk of a man.

"Oh, my Tío Manny. He's over there, wrapped around a woman, I'm sure."

Everyone turned to see Manny in fact doing just that, or was the woman wrapped around him? It was hard to tell, but Sofia knew her uncle well. He never went home alone, ever. Huerta men were as sexy as they came. Where her father wasn't handsome, Manny had stolen all of the looks in the family. In return, her father was gifted the loyalty and honor genes between the pair, and was a good family man.

As if he knew all eyes were on him, he turned and raised his glass to his niece and waggled his eyebrows. Sofia giggled, raised her wrist, and tapped her watch. One hour, he mouthed to her as he diverted his attention back to his date, waving her off.

"See, he never lacks for company. My father often said Tío Manny never met a stranger in his life. I think he was referring to women, but I can't be sure."

"So, Doctor, will you be coming to the benefit tomorrow? It's to raise money for a children's hospital. I hope I can count on you to attend?" Sofia smiled and then glanced at Laura. "Perhaps, your sister will join us?"

Before Laura could answer, Michael chimed in. "We'd love to be there. I'm a sucker for kids."

Laura scoffed. "You are? Since when?"

"Might I remind you of our encounter downstairs? Taryn?"

"Oh, right, true. Michael does love a good cause." Laura offered a generous smile to her brother that lit up her face.

Sofia couldn't help but stare as Laura wrapped her lips around the cigar and gently pulled on it. Everything about her was polished, from her classy business suit to her hair tucked up in a bun. A few errant hairs added to the charm she exuded. A self-assurance bubbled off Laura, that quiet confidence a woman who had power, but didn't abuse it, had. Another sip of the Port and Laura seemed to be relaxing a bit.

"So, Laura what do you do?"

"No shop talk Lala. You promised," Michael said.

"Lala?" Sofia asked, intrigued by the pet name.

Laura shot him a stern look before looking back at Sofia. "It's a childhood nickname that he's not supposed to use in public."

"It's cute," Sofia said, trying to diffuse what was obviously a term of endearment Michael had for his sister. It beat what her brother often called her. His vocabulary wasn't as heartwarming.

"Okay, no shop talk. How about those Niners. Will they go to the Super Bowl this year?"

"Oh, I have no idea who's the best. It's been a while since I've watched football."

"You like football?" Laura acted surprised.

"Oh my god, I love football. I played in high school and then in college. However, I wasn't good enough at Stanford so they cut me. Meh, their loss." Sofia shrugged it off and waved her hand.

"You played football?" Laura's shocked look surprised Sofia.

"What, do you not think that women can play football?"

"No, I think women can do anything they set their mind to, but I was just surprised. You definitely look like you can handle a linebacker."

"Oh, you thought I meant American football." Sofia belly laughed so loud the terrace went almost silent. "Oh…" She cringed, then whispered, "Sorry, I didn't mean to laugh at you. I just thought we were talking about soccer. I'm so sorry, I got football in my head and then I meant soccer."

"You went to Stanford?" Michael asked.

"Don't look so surprised, Michael. Money can buy a lot of things." She offered another smile, then slapped his leg.

"Maybe, but it can't buy your way into Stanford."

"True, so I had to rely on good grades *and* money. My father wanted me to come to the United States to learn business, and I did." She shrugged again. "Besides, my mother had dual citizenship and I was born in the US when she came to visit her family. That's why I'm here, to see my mother's family and do some charity work. They're also the reason I came to Stanford. I wanted to get to know my mother's family." Sofia was tired of talking about herself. She wanted to learn more about the beautiful woman who'd caught her eye the minute she walked out of the restaurant. "So, please, Laura, do you have any hobbies, since work is off the table?"

Laura pressed her finger to her mouth. Sofia watched as the finger slid back and forth over the pouting lips. She knew what *she* was thinking and it wasn't a pure thought, at least that's what her mother would have called it.

"I'm remodeling a place I have in Napa. Actually, it's on the outskirts of Calistoga, but close enough."

"I love Napa, mostly the wines, but I've always wanted a place there. It's so beautiful, nestled in the foothills. Don't you think?" She leaned forward and let her gaze wander. "I mean it doesn't lack for beauty, I should say."

Laura's fever was back, as was evident as it warmed her pale face. Her expression didn't change as Sofia held her gaze. A strong woman who wasn't intimidated by a stealth compliment. Sofia was definitely going to have to get to know this woman much better. While they had an agreement to leave careers out of the conversation, Sofia could deduce by the Coach bag and Vera Wang pantsuit that definitely wasn't off the rack, that Laura was corporate or at least white collar. Her gaze was drawn to well-manicured nails that begged to be dragged over bare skin. She rubbed the goosebumps on her arm.

"Have you been to Napa?" Laura yanked Sofia from her not-so-innocent daydream.

"Of course, several times. I spent a week at the most fabulous spa there. Auberge du Soleil, have you heard of it? It's adults only and well, not that I don't love children, my brother has two, I just want to relax and enjoy a small bit of sanctuary when I vacation." Sofia smiled, but still couldn't shake the feeling she'd struck a nerve somehow with Laura as she continued to roll the stem of her Port glass back and forth. "Is your cigar not to your liking? Perhaps I can recommend something more pleasing."

⚘⚘⚘⚘

Laura felt as if she was in a continuous state of, for lack of a better word, arousal. The more Sofia said, the more she read into. She *was* construing them to be sexual innuendos, wasn't she?

"Auberge, I've heard talk of it, but with a place in Calistoga, I don't get to try the local flavors much."

"Of course. How wonderful it must be to enjoy the grapes and leisurely life."

"Laura, enjoy a leisurely life? I think you're referring to someone else. My poor sister is a workaholic. Thanks to my father, of course. He keeps her quite busy."

"Really?"

Laura backhanded Michael. "We're not talking work here. Remember?"

Michael offered a fake grimace as he rubbed his stomach. "Ouch." He laughed and then kissed Laura's hand. "Sorry, I just don't want you pretending you're not a hard worker, Lala."

"Lala? I think that's the second or third time I've heard you call her that, Michael."

"Lala..." Michael reached over and slipped his arms around her shoulders, pulling her in closer. All that was missing was the noogie that he often scrubbed across her head when he got like this. "Is a name that—"

"Michael." Laura's warning tone stopped him dead.

"I was just going to relay the cute story that got you the nickname."

Laura shook her head. "Over my dead body."

"Now I am intrigued. However, I'll respect your boundaries, Laura. I have a brother, so I know your pain."

Before Michael, and by default Sofia, could embarrass her more, she turned the tables. "So do you have any hobbies?" Laura said, then took a puff of her cigar hoping she didn't have to revive it. She wasn't sure she was proficient enough yet to restart a dead stick. Perhaps she could coax Sofia to relight it, again. A shiver sliced through her as she remembered Sofia's lips around her cigar. Sexy as hell didn't quite cover it, but it was a start. "Anything you mind sharing?"

Laura could give as good as she got, and she was starting to get her flirting legs back under her. It had been a while since someone had been so overt, but she found Sofia intriguing. From the dark brown hair, to her curvy-in-all-the-right-places body, and that to-die-for accent, it was all working into a system overload for Laura, but even the best attorney rarely pushed her off her game.

Sofia tossed her head to the side, offered a smile, and then ran her tongue over her top lip.

Zing, she's good.

"Hmm, I love fast cars."

"Really, do you own any?" Michael's interest reignited.

Sofia tossed a sheepish look toward Michael and then looked at Laura as she answered. "I have a sports car. I like to drive way too fast. My father always is admonishing me about my driving. Seems I have a few tickets."

The way Sofia's eye widened when she talked about her car was similar to the way Michael acted when talking about his metal stallion. Laura didn't understand all the fuss about a hunk of metal, but then again, she didn't get why people sat around watching men chase a little white ball, or how people could sit for hours watching cars go 'round and 'round for 500 laps.

"A few?" Laura smiled at the almost gleeful look

on Sofia's face.

"Well, I haven't been a very good girl when it comes to my car." Sofia pouted. "It seems I have become very familiar with the local police."

"I see, so you like to drive fast?" Michael interjected.

"I do, it gives me a feeling of freedom. I get in my Jaguar and I..." Sofia closed her eyes and tilted her head back. Laura was captivated at the sight. "I'm flying. The top's down, the breeze is flowing through my hair, and it's almost as good as—"

Sofia stopped cold. Laura found herself leaning in waiting for her to continue.

"Sex," Michael shouted out. Everyone in close vicinity turned, looked at them, and some started to laugh as Michael blushed. "I know exactly what you mean." Michael slapped his thigh. "It's like sex." He finished her sentence for her, completely oblivious of the eyes watching him.

If she hadn't known her brother as well as she did, she would have looked for the biggest sofa and crawled under it just to get away from the smirks and laughter. As soon as the conversations turned to sex, that was her cue. Time to go home.

"Well, I hate to be a wet blanket, but I need to get home. I have a ton of work." Laura rose and patted Michael on the shoulder. "Need a ride, or shall I assume you still want to stay and you have enough bread crumbs laid out that you can find a way home."

"Oh, come on, Laura. I was just kidding."

"I know, but I really am tired. I've been working all day and I have another full day of research tomorrow. You know how Dad is. He's breathing down my neck with this new case."

"I can get a ride home, no worries. Besides, I'm sure I can find something to entertain me until I'm ready to leave."

Laura couldn't help but notice the way Michael practically devoured Sofia with his eyes. A pang of jealousy poked her. She was used to her brother's charm luring in beautiful women of all sorts, but she was consistently irritated when she and Michael were attracted to the same woman. She hated feeling like they were in competition.

"Well," Laura said, her hand jutted out at Sofia, who stood. "It was a pleasure to meet you. I hope we meet again someday."

Sofia stared at her hand, seeming to fumble with her words, then gently grasped Laura's shoulders, pulling her closer and kissing each cheek. "This is how we say good-bye in my family." Sofia whispered. "Oh, I think we can make that happen. Right?"

Laura's face flamed instantly. "I'm…I mean, yes, I'm sure we can make anything happen…if we want."

"Exactly," Sofia said, still clutching her hands.

Chapter Eight

Sofia wished at that moment she were a man. If she was, she would pick up Laura's hand and kiss it. A simple pleasure men always seemed to indulge in with a beautiful woman. The gesture seemed to be used as a prelude, or an ending of sorts. She couldn't even begin to crawl into the mind of a man, but she suddenly wanted to find out what it felt like to at least kiss her hand.

"Laura," It lingered on her tongue like the subtleties of a fine wine, like a kiss on the lips. She wanted to say it repeatedly, in the same way she wanted to pull her close and kiss her.

Laura returned her gaze at the mention of her name and offered a slight, nervous smile. She didn't get a sense Laura was timid, not if the lively conversation they'd shared with Laura's brother was any indication. Clearly, it seemed as if Michael had other ideas on what might happen when Laura left. Unfortunately, they weren't Sofia's idea of a great ending to an evening.

"Well, I'm sorry we must say good night, Laura," she said, wishing she could stay the night talking to the engaging woman, but she would blame her departure on Manny, saying he was restless. Damn. Lucky for her he was still engrossed with the comely brunette he'd chatted up earlier in the night. They'd been in a clinch most of the evening. She caught sight of him out of the corner of her eye. Her uncle definitely had good taste in women. She often joked with him about the fact that they couldn't go out together, since they had the same palate for women. His timing was impeccable. He walked up, his arm pulling the woman closer. He was impatiently stomping his foot like a pubescent school boy wanting to get his prize home to play with before she turned into a pumpkin at midnight.

"Good night, Sofia. Thank you for the lesson on lighting my cigar."

Sofia flushed. She'd been flirting with Laura at that point and she was optimistic it wasn't lost on Laura that she found her...interesting, to say the least.

"Well, I hope I see you at the charity event. I hear the benefit will be extraordinary. Good food, wine, and great cigars. Perhaps you'll allow me to light your next cigar as well?"

Why she didn't tell Laura the benefit was for her father was simple: they'd agreed not to talk shop. Cigars and the charity benefit were shoptalk for Sofia. She hadn't made the rules, but she was happy to follow them if it meant a little extra time with her new friends. She'd been happy to settle for talk of San Francisco, wine, soccer, and the latest reality shows that never seemed to end. She was sure she'd have time to explain things at the event. Assuming Laura came, of course.

"Michael, I hope you can convince your sister to come. It's for a good cause."

Michael winked at her and said, "I'll do my best, if it means getting a chance to see you again." Before she could say anything to stop him, he continued. "It was a pleasure to meet you, Sofia." He raised her hand to his lips again and kissed it softly.

"Laura," Sofia offered her hand. "It was a pleasure to make a new friend tonight." She cradled Laura's hands between hers and smiled. The warmth between them spread through her like a raging fire.

"Sofia." Manny's voice was insistent as he tried to get his niece's attention.

"Yes, yes, Tío. Thank you both for a delightful evening. Again, I hope to see you at the benefit. Good night." Sofia stepped closer, kissing each side of Laura's face. Clearly, she was surprised at the action as Sofía begrudgingly released Laura's hand and gave Michael a quick kiss on each cheek.

"Hasta luego." Sofía retreated with her uncle into the elevator and continued to watch Laura until the doors swished closed.

"What was that all about?" Manny reached around his date to push the elevator button, the brunette still ensconced on his hip.

"Nothing, just making new friends, Tío."

"Uh-huh. Careful, mija, she's an American."

"Meaning?"

"Your home is in Nicaragua and I have never known you to be one to just love them and leave them like me. Besides, look at what happened with your mama. She was American and it almost killed her when her family disowned her for moving to Nicaragua." Manny tried to soften the blow with a smile, but he was right. Her mother's family never forgave her father for stealing her away to Nicaragua.

Manny smiled at the woman on his arm and kissed her neck. She nodded her head and playfully slapped at his arm.

"I don't expect anything. I'm just here for the ride. I hear Latin men are wonderful lovers."

Sofia rolled her eyes. *Did she just say that?* Manny's flirting was legendary and shameless all at the same time, but he never apologized for it. On the contrary, he engaged in it with a wild abandon Sofia wished she had. The fact that he practically just told the woman he was getting ready to bed her and that he wasn't the type for long-term relationships put him in a whole other class of asshole, but he was *her* uncle asshole.

"Yes, well I can handle my own personal life, Tío."

"I'm just saying. Remember why we're here, Sofia. RJ has sent a shot over the bow of Huerta Cigars. While we're here, he's down there planning something. I know it. I've seen it in his eyes and he's not playing around, mija."

"I know, Tio. I know." She ran her fingers through her curls, a genetic gift from her mother, and sighed. The length of the day was wearing on her like a wet coat dragging her down. Suddenly, all she wanted to do was kick off her shoes, peel her dress off, and wade down into a hot bubble bath, replete with soft music and wine and perhaps a thought or two of Laura.

Her uncle was behind her in full snuggle mode with his date. Thank god for that little blue pill he was always picking up at the airport pharmacia when they left. Otherwise, he'd be dragging his ass around in a wheelbarrow, too. Lucky for Sofia, buying a condo in the Banker Building meant she only had to endure the gushing a few more minutes. The only problem was, she didn't know if she could wait four more floors until she put a sizable distance between the amorous lovebirds.

Ding.

Luck was on her side.

"Night, Tio. Don't forget to set the alarm when

you get home."

Silence.

Sofia pulled loose the slim titanium keycard from the keyring. A quick wave and the lock clicked. Pushing the massive ten-foot, black lacquer door open, she waved the card in front of the alarm, shutting it down.

"Lights." The lights in the front room popped on and then throughout the condo. "Dim, one, two, three. Perfect." The mood lighting glowed in the house. She tossed her small handbag on the table, extracted her earrings and watch, and tossed them into the dish that held her keys. Sofia leaned against the cream leather couch and yanked one shoe off and then the other, letting them remain where they fell. Reaching around she unzipped and shimmied off her dress, allowing it to join the shoes on the floor. God, she was more tired than she realized. How she'd lasted through the flight from Managua, a day of meetings and a few visits to local cigar shops, and then ending the night at the cigar lounge, was beyond her. Well, perhaps not. Meeting Laura had been a shot of adrenaline for the evening. She couldn't put her finger on why she was so attracted to the woman. Digging her toes into the deep pile of the carpet, she ran her feet back and forth over the soft crush of wool as she thought about Laura, trying to figure out what drew her to the woman. Perhaps it was the self-confidence that she exuded, or the way she held herself. If she were a guessing woman, she suspected Laura was probably a CEO of a tech company or something. Hell, everyone in San Francisco seemed to be connected to tech in some way. Their conversation had been short, but it looked as if they had a few things in common—Napa, good wine, and perhaps cigars. At least she hoped she wasn't creating phantom commonalities to justify her sudden interest in the woman.

Twisting her head around and reaching up, she pulled at the muscles in her shoulders. A hot bath was beckoning to her. Passing her office, she stopped and noticed the blinking light on her tech hub. Only a few people had her San Francisco number, mostly family and a few friends. Unless she transferred her calls from the office to the unit, there shouldn't be work calls, and she hadn't transferred her number. It could be home, or...well she wouldn't relax until she eased her mind. Her abuela was all she had left of her father's parentage, and she didn't want to be away if something happened to her. It had taken all she had to get on the plane to come to San Francisco. Her grandmother eased her fears, telling her she wasn't going anywhere. Besides, she was only in her late seventies, and she still had plenty of life left in her, she assured Sofia.

Pressing the button on her answering machine, she heard a familiar voice pop on. "Sofia, honey. It's Grandma Shirley. I was so sorry to hear about your father. I hope you got the flowers George and I sent down. I know they won't replace your dad, but we wanted you to know we were thinking about you and your family." Her voice crackled a bit as she said that. "I know you're in town for the Huerta benefit, and your grandfather and I were wondering if you'd like to do dinner? Well, I'm sure you're super busy, but I just wanted to see if we could see you while you were in town. Love you, honey. Bye."

Sofia flopped into the office chair, and the cold leather made her gasp as it made contact with her overheated body. Christ, she'd completely forgot about visiting her grandparents. Her shoulders sagged at the weight of family obligation. It was a good family obligation, and it was a duty she would be glad to take on, especially now that her father and mother were both gone.

Shit.

Part of the reason she'd come to Stanford to go to school had been to spend time and get to know the other side of her family. Her grandparents, Shirley and George, were wonderful people, kindhearted, warm, and loving. They'd had three daughters, her mom, her aunt Margaret—Peg for short—and her aunt Elizabeth. Every time she saw her aunt Peg the resemblance to her mom shook her. While she'd only had a few years with her before she died, she still remembered her gentle smile, a family trait, and her soft, sweet smell. She'd slept with her mother's pillow for years after her death, just cuddling it at night. Her scent only lingered for a few months, but she could swear she could smell it years later. It still sat on her bed, even now. Like an artifact from the distant past, she kept it close to remind her that she'd had a mother, once.

Sofia wiped at her eyes. Memories were like the yin and yang of life. They brought you comfort, but they also brought pain. Lately, it had been the pain she'd been pricked with. Her father would be in that yang of life now. She missed her mother even more for what could have been. Her father, she would miss for what had been.

Yin and yang.

Pushing herself from the chair, she noticed the time. It was her excuse not to call tonight. Tomorrow, she'd do it tomorrow. She walked to the door, hit the frame, and stopped. She didn't have tomorrow. Her father's death taught her that.

Walking back out to the front room, she pulled her cell phone from her purse and tapped the screen.

"Dial grandma Shirley."

The phone went through its machinations and started the ring. As several rings went by, Sofia considered hanging up. It was late, but not too late, she hoped.

"Hello?" a frail voice answered.

"Grandma? It's Sofia. I hope it's not too late?"

"Oh, sweetheart. Nope, not too late at all. We're just watching the news. Honey, it's Sofia. How are you, sweetie?"

Sofia smiled. It was like a balm to her soul to hear her grandmother's voice. While she loved her abuela, her mother's family was so far away that seeing them had become a treat unto itself, a phone call uplifting when she needed something of her mother.

"I'm good, Grandma. I did get your flowers. Thank you so much, it meant a lot that you sent them."

"Oh honey, I'm so sorry about your dad. He was a good man and your mother loved him a lot."

"I know. I know." Sofia wiped at the wetness on her cheeks. "So, I'd love to have dinner with you and Grandpa. I have the benefit later this week, but I'd love to see you before. Maybe you and grandpa would like to come to the benefit?"

"Oh, you're so sweet. I'll talk to George. I'm sure he can help, too. I mean, if you want."

Her grandparents had done well in the tech industry. Her grandfather had been one of the first employees at Apple. At that time, they didn't pay well, but they did offer stock options and he'd taken whatever they'd given because he believed that computers were the wave of the future. Those early stock options had netted them millions. Who knew a fruit could be worth so much? Her grandfather, that's who. He'd become a venture capitalist after he'd cashed in his stocks a decade later. He and Shirley had traveled, raised their girls, and, now retired, lived well and quietly.

"That would be nice. How does lunch sound?"

"Oh, that sounds wonderful. I'll talk to your grandfather and aunts and I'll see who can join us. Is that okay?"

Sofia wasn't sure she was ready to see the whole family, but why not? She didn't know when she'd be back up here after the benefit.

"Sure, I'd like to see everyone."

"Why don't I call you tomorrow and we can set a time?"

"Okay."

"Sofia? How's RJ? I tried to call him but it went to voice mail. How's he handling Don Roberto's death?"

"I don't think he's very happy, Grandma."

"No, I don't guess he is. It's tough losing both your parents. I'm so sorry, sweetie. I truly am." Shirley's frail voice cracked again.

"I know, Grandma, and I love you for it."

"I love you too, honey. Tell you what ,why don't you come over here for lunch? Might be easier."

"Whatever's easiest, Grandma. Everything all right?"

"Oh sure. I just don't want us to be a bother."

"You're not a bother, Grandma. We'll talk tomorrow and work out the details."

"Sounds good, honey. Talk to you tomorrow."

"Love you," Sofia whispered into the phone.

"I love you too, honey. Hang in there, it'll be

okay."

The connection dropped as the pop echoed in her ear. Sofia leaned back in the chair and looked at the picture she had of her grandmother. She imagined it would have been what her mother would have looked like had she lived. She noticed three missed calls from her, hence the reason she'd called the condo.

Yeah, she was due some family time with her grandparents. She missed them and wished she visited more, but lately it just wasn't in the cards. She'd make it up to them, somehow.

Waving her hand over the light switch, she turned off the lights behind her as she dragged herself to the bathroom. Keying the control pad, she started the bath, set the temperature, and turned on the essential oils steam. She'd take a sauna and then dip her weary body into the bath. She was a routine kind of gal, and even if it killed her she'd enjoy the steam room and her nightly hot bath.

Peeling off her panties and bra, she tossed them into the hamper. Her hand splayed, she ran her it down the ugly scar that bisected her stomach. The remnants of a simple surgery gone horribly wrong. Thanks to a severe infection, she lost her ovaries, uterus, and gallbladder. That meant children were out of the picture. While clothed she felt invincible, strong and ready to take on the world, the minute she peeled away the façade clothes provided, she was immediately reminded that she was less than perfect. As she'd done every night, she traced a finger down the long, raised, brown scar. It was dark pink on the top where it was smooth and wide. She was lucky to be alive. Quite fortunate for her, her father had put her on a medical plane and entrusted her care to her grandparents. She owed them her life. They had been with her through one of the darkest times, second only to her mother's death. A month in the hospital with only two visits from her father, who was in the middle of a drought and trying to save his business, they'd sat by her bedside morning, noon, and night.

She loved them beyond words.

Taping the music button, she was hit with a face full of lavender-scented steam. Taking a deep breath, she relaxed onto the cedar bench. Even though she didn't need to, she poured a ladle full of water onto the hot stones. She liked the sound of the water as it sizzled on the rocks. Positioning a towel under her head, she threw her arm over her eyes and thought about the only thing that had caught her attention today.

Laura.

While she often reflected on her day while she took a sauna, it was more about analyzing business dealings or planting schedules or new marketing plans for her cigar line. Sofia smiled as visions of Laura clouded her mind. Sofia wondered what Laura's parents looked like. Laura was the polar opposite of her brother, Michael, with his tall angular features, dark hair, and drop-dead good looks. Laura was pale with dirty blond hair. It didn't look like the sun had kissed that skin in a while, so clearly she spent her days cooped up in an office. Her soft brown eyes were cautious and inquiring. Sofia liked that about her. She was reserved, not loud and brash like some of the women she'd gone out with. Well, it wasn't like she dated a whole lot, but enough to know what she liked and what she hated.

She stroked her reminder, flicking the sweat off her stomach.

Rolling onto her stomach, she wondered if the

feeling she was getting from Laura was accurate. Did she bat for the same team? Surely, the stolen glances, the quick smile, and the nervousness wasn't just an act, cute as it might be. Sofia's gaydar was never wrong. Well, there was that one time in Havana, but the woman had been intoxicated and to quote the old trope, two drinks away and every girl is gay. That was a quick lesson to never take a straight woman to dinner, definitely not anyone in the cigar business. Her father had to live that one down the hard way. Not something Sofia planned on repeating, that was for sure.

So, was she, or wasn't she?

Chapter Nine

The small airport at Managua was more like a giant mercado, vendors selling coffee, touristy knickknacks, leather goods, and the most important thing: the last chance pharmacia where people could buy their drugs at a reduced price, and even some they couldn't get in America. The line was two-deep, mostly gringos with the most coveted thing in Nicaragua—American dollars.

RJ, followed closely by one of the workers from the estate that was loyal to him, weaved his way through the small throng of deplaning passengers. He'd almost missed the flight. Estrella had needs he felt obligated to fulfill and he took his obligations seriously. He inhaled deeply; her smell still lingered on him. It was almost euphoric. By the time he realized the hour there wasn't time for a shower, so he half-heartedly washed around Estrella still wrapped around him. She'd made it clear they weren't spending enough time together. Christ, he practically felt as if he had a side-wife. Lina wasn't nearly as demanding or needy.

No, Lina had her own side-ass that she spent her days with while the kids were in school. The nanny had been a necessity when they both decided home wasn't where the heart was anymore. Hell, it was more like a torture palace and now that he wanted a divorce, it would be ground zero for the war that was imminent.

Spotting Lewis Hollingsworth, he waved his

hand and motioned him over. He had a car waiting at the curb and he didn't need to be hassled by the local police, so time was ticking.

"Lewis, how was your flight?"

A good-looking man for his age, Lewis Hollingsworth was a buttoned-down, uptight, and smug prick—just the way RJ liked his frenemies.

"Long." Sweat was wearing Lewis like a cheap shirt. The wet pits and beads dripping down his neck where his repeated wiping was missed by the pocket square he'd pulled to mop up his face and it wasn't even daylight. The sun had set an hour ago, but the heat was like the ever-present person in the room you couldn't run away from even if you wanted.

"Couldn't have been that bad, Lewis. You have your own plane and I'm sure you had a little diversion on the way down."

"Yeah, well it's going to take more than a little diversion to—"

"Relax, after this little jaunt, you'll be free of me for good. Consider your debt paid once this is all over."

"I'll believe it when I have those photos and negatives."

RJ tapped his chest. "Got 'em right here." He looked down at his cubavera shirt. "Oh wait, I must have left them in my other suit." He patted the linen shirt's chest pockets and then the lower pockets on the shirt again. "Yep, must have left them at home."

"I'm sure you think this is funny, but I'm not laughing, RJ."

"Why don't you let me take your coat, Lewis?" RJ *helped* Lewis shrug out of his sport coat. Unfortunately, his shirt was worse for wearing. He was soaked from head to…well, RJ didn't want to know. Lewis avoided

RJ's gaze and tugged at his tie. "Lighten up, Lewis."

"What do you want, RJ? Why couldn't we do this over the phone or in the States? I already told you I put my best lawyer on the case. I don't think it's wise that I be the one handling your dispute of the will."

"Well, I needed you here. I need a set of documents and I don't need a paper trail or an email trail. So…" RJ raised his hands and looked around. "Besides, my sister is in San Francisco and what I need help with can only be handled here. So pull yourself together and try to relax. You look like a tourist."

RJ nodded to his man to pick up Lewis's luggage.

"I am a tourist, asshole."

"That's what I love about you, Lewis, your acerbic wit. I've missed you, my friend." RJ put his arms around Lewis's shoulders and jerked him closer. "I know you'll handle this, Lewis. Besides, I've arranged for some fun later," RJ whispered in Lewis's ear. He was already getting on RJ's nerves and the bastard wasn't here twenty minutes.

Lewis threw his arm off his shoulder and jerked away, but not before it caught the attention of a cop walking through the crowded airport.

"Everything okay?"

"Fine, my friend here just got in from America and is a little tired." RJ looked over at Lewis. His face blanched of color. "Right, amigo?"

Without missing a beat, Lewis slapped RJ on the back. "Yeah, it's been a long day. I'm ready for some cigars and rum."

"Hmm, passport?" The cop motioned to Lewis.

RJ waited as Lewis looked at him and then back to the cop. He nodded toward RJ. "It's in my jacket."

"Oh, allow me." RJ fished through the pockets.

"Aw, here it is. Right here." RJ handed the passport over to the officer. "See, we're all good."

"Business or pleasure."

"Pleasure, my friend. Isn't it always pleasure with these Americanos?" RJ patted the officer on the shoulder.

The cop passed the passport back to Lewis with a disgusted look and walked past RJ. "Get him out of here and make sure he doesn't get in trouble."

"Yes, sir."

RJ jerked Lewis's arm. "Let's get the fuck out of here before you get thrown in jail and I can't get your ass out."

"What, you can't pull strings down here? I'm shocked. Guess Don Roberto's influence didn't trickle down to you, huh Junior?"

The comment pricked and RJ bristled. All he could think about was decking the smug bastard, but he needed him. So, that would come later.

"Don't worry about how far my reach is within Nicaragua. It was long enough to keep you out of jail, or did you forget?"

RJ must have struck a chord. Lewis yanked at his collar, widened his tie, unbuttoned his shirt, and dabbed at the sweat that seemed to coat his face.

"I'm here aren't I?"

RJ threw his hands wide and flashed a cheesy smile. "Truce, Lewis. Come on, let's lay down the hatchets and get down to business. Relax, man, it's going to be fine. I have faith in you, buddy." RJ opened the passenger door to the SUV and swept his hand wide. "Come on. I have a meeting we need to get to and then we can get a drink, smoke a cigar, and relax before we dive headfirst into the paperwork."

Slamming the door behind Lewis, RJ flipped him the bird just low enough that Lewis couldn't see it.

"Bastard," he said, walking around to the back of the SUV.

"You okay, jefe?"

"Yeah fine. Let's get this shit on the road."

"Yes, sir."

"Let's get to the restaurant; the guys are waiting for us." RJ offered Lewis a glass of rum.

"Ice?" Lewis held the glass out.

"Of course."

The ice pinged off the side of the glass and then splashed into the brown liquid. RJ touched his glass against Lewis's. "Salud."

"Salud."

"So, Lewis, you've seen the will. What's the plan for me to get my business back?"

"I've looked it over. I think you might have a small problem, RJ. However, I've passed it on to an associate of mine. She's on it. That's why I don't know why you insisted that I get my ass down here, right this minute."

"I don't want an associate working on my case. I want someone who's got a vested interest in my case, and that's you, Lewis." RJ pointed at Lewis. "You, my friend, have a lot of reasons to make sure I get the cigar business." RJ was indignant that he was being passed on to a lower peon. He didn't want just anyone salvaging his family fortune, he wanted someone like Lewis. Someone who liked to get dirty, and Lewis crawled in the mud with the best of them on a regular basis. "What small problem?" He peered over his crystal tumbler.

"Your father incorporated Huerta in the US, so you also fall under US law."

"What? That's bullshit."

"Your mother was American, was she not?"

"Yes, but…"

"So, your father took every precaution that the business would be protected both here and in the US." Lewis shrugged. "Not uncommon, especially if he didn't want to pay import tax. It opens him up to other things like US taxes and restrictions, but it also seems there are some assets in the United States."

"What assets?"

Lewis shrugged. "Don't know if they are Sofia's or Roberto's, but I'm thinking he did it to protect the business from you."

"Bastard." RJ scratched his head. "I want you to get on this right now, Lewis. I don't want someone else handling this. I trust you and only you."

"Look, the woman who's on it is an international law specialist. She's very capable, RJ. I trust her with my life." Lewis repositioned the air vent right at his face, turning his face back and forth. Americans seemed to have a tough time with the jungle humidity and Lewis was no different.

"Hmm." RJ leaned back, his arms spread across the seat. "Well, just in case you need some ammunition, I've taken a few steps that I think will help with the case."

"What have you done RJ? I hope you haven't done anything illegal. It will only make matters worse."

"I would never jeopardize my case. Be assured it has more to do with my sister's proclivities than it does anything else."

"Stop talking in code and tell me what you mean?" Lewis wiped at his ruddy face.

"My sister likes the ladies just as much as I do, so

I've taken some steps to make sure she falls in line. If you know what I mean." He elbowed Lewis and patted the slight bulge in his shirt pocket, sure he was getting his meaning.

"Who are these men we're meeting?" Lewis's disgusted, judgmental look pissed him off. Who was Lewis to judge him? Wasn't he the one who liked the young ladies? Very young ladies.

"Possible business associates."

"We're here, boss."

"Perfect."

"Lewis, I need you all-in tonight. We're meeting a couple of the local families with cigar companies. They want Huerta to join them and form one of the biggest cigar cartels in the world and run it as one big business. Or they want to buy me out."

Lewis sat staring out the window, looking more like a hood ornament, back straight, his eyes did not blink. RJ smacked him on the back. "Did you hear me?"

"Yeah, I got it."

"So, take mental notes. I'll do the talking you just sit back and listen. Pay attention to anything these guys might be saying quietly. Sometimes it's what they aren't saying that's important."

"I get paid to pay attention to the little details, RJ."

"Good, so we are on the same page, then."

"Same page, same notebook, same class." Lewis pushed RJ's hand off his shoulder.

❧ ❧ ❧ ❧

María stood at the door of the office. It was packed with so many memories. It was originally

Alejandro's office and when he turned the business over to Roberto, Alejandro had taken a back seat and let Roberto run the business. He trusted his son implicitly. Roberto had worked side by side with his father, from the fields, to the rolling rooms, to the boardroom. Roberto had been a faithful student. He idolized his father and wanted to make him proud at every turn. She hesitated at the door. The memories flooded her mind and she staggered, grabbing the door handle for support. Spying the humidor, her hand hovered over the lid. It was something that she hoped would be handed down the line of Huertas until there were no more Huertas alive. María ran her fingers over the engraved nameplate. It was one of the few things of their former life together. Roberto had made sure he'd kept it in a place of prominence. Just seeing it now, she recognized it was her lifeline to her husband and their life together. It was made out of wood from the simple shanty he'd built when they first arrived. Their early days in Nicaragua had been tough. They weren't prepared for the loneliness, and the lack of friends and family, so they clung to each other. A small plot of land had slowly grown to the estate that they had now, but the early days had been tough and several times they found themselves on the verge of divorce. But, children had come, the glue that kept them together and focused on what really mattered.

Alejandro had taken great pride in two things: the new compound he'd built to house their family and growing business, and the day he could finally bulldoze that house. He hated it. It reminded him of his own simple house back in Cuba. It represented poverty, and it was a constant reminder of what he'd left behind. His parents still lived in the broken-down shack and no matter how many times he'd asked his father to come to Nicaragua, his answer was still the same: "I was born to the soil and I'll die on the soil, Son."

That simple plot of land had poisoned every memory Alejandro had of Cuba. It represented everything his father had lost during the war, and he couldn't fathom why his father insisted on staying, clinging to it. No matter how hard his father worked the soil, it would only produce a handful of tobacco plants, which María's father bought from him each year. She wondered if Alejandro knew that her father torched those plants, never to use them for anything. He considered them sub-standard and often said he didn't want them corrupting his cigars. If Alejandro didn't know, she wasn't going to be the one to tell him. As for Alejandro's father, she knew it pained him the few times they'd talked about him rejecting Alejandro's offer to move him to Nicaragua, but Alejandro had come by his stubborn streak honestly—he'd inherited it. She'd reminded him that it wasn't easy for an old man to change, just look at her own father, she'd say.

"Change isn't a bad thing, María. If we don't grow, we die."

He had been right about that. Alejandro's father was exactly where he was when they'd left. While he didn't hold it against them when they'd left Cuba, the same couldn't be said for her own mother. She refused to speak to her when she'd gone home for her father's funeral. It had been strained at best. But Fernando had only made things worse at the funeral. He'd never forgiven her for not marrying him and he made it known after a few beers.

She stroked the humidor lovingly, remembering the day he rode the bulldozer right through the structure. A wicked smile of delight split his face. He was almost juvenile as he smashed it to the ground. Picking up a few boards, he tossed them to the side and then lit the rubble on fire.

"What are you doing, Alejo?" She walked over to him and stroked his back.

He hugged her tight and kissed the top of her head. "I'm going to build a humidor from the wood," he said, pointing to the few pieces he'd tossed aside. "I don't want to forget how far we've come."

"Hmm." She reached down and picked up their youngest son, Roberto, who had been squealing with delight the whole time Alejandro had worked the dozer. "Shhh, Papa's talking, mijo."

"Ride." He wiggled back and forth on her hip and pointed to the bulldozer.

"Papa, want to take him for a ride?"

"Sure. Come here, mijo." He patted the seat of the bulldozer and placed him on it. Crawling in behind their son, Alejandro scooped buckets of dirt and surrounded the burning fire. It was symbolic of their lives rising from the ashes with a new company, a young family, and the bright future that lay before them.

María lifted the lid of the humidor and traced the inscription inside.

Huerta Cigars, established in 1959. Followed by Alejandro's signature.

The relic had been passed down to Roberto when he took over the business and now he had passed it on, not to his son, but to his daughter, Sofia. María smiled and wondered what Alejandro would say about his legacy being passed down to a daughter.

"It's in the blood, María. We Huertas are born

with tobacco flowing through our veins."

If he could only see how Sofia had turned a small plot of land into a thriving business, he would be proud. As for RJ...well, she wasn't so sure he would understand RJ. He was so much like Manny and not Roberto, but he was a Huerta and that was the only thing that mattered. Sophia and RJ were the only family she had left, and a grandmother's love didn't judge.

María lowered the lid on the humidor and sat in the chair opposite the large box, her hands still touching the humidor. She couldn't bring herself to break the only contact she had with Alejandro, not yet. Not when he felt so close.

Chapter Ten

The action around Don Pablo Vega was on overdrive as the table was set for dinner. He decided to have the little get-together at Rique's restaurant as a show of good faith and to throw the man a bone. He liked it when people owed him favors. It allowed him to keep a tight leash on the men he did business with. The inner courtyard of the restaurant kept the heat of the day at bay and provided enough shade that it kept the humidity down, too. He'd called the meeting to get a handle on his burgeoning cartel and to bring one more family into the fold. The only problem was he didn't trust RJ Huerta. Don Roberto's death had been a shock to everyone, including him, but he wasn't sad to see the bastard go. No, if he was honest, it was a blessing in disguise. He'd tried to talk to the old man and bring him into the cartel, but Don Roberto wasn't having any of it. He had high hopes for the cartel. With a new opportunity that had presented itself recently, they would be getting into the US market in record numbers. However, it wasn't without some risk, but nothing in life was without risk, right? They called it opportunity.

Don Pablo's family had been in the cigar business for decades and the Huertas had stumbled onto the scene relatively late. In his opinion they hadn't earned the respect they thought they were entitled to. Somehow they'd hit a home run with their other ventures and they'd been lucky with cigars, by accident as far as he was concerned. He suspected the luck had more to do with Don Roberto's Cuban roots than anything. The word back then was Alejandro had squirreled away some of Cuba's finest tobacco seeds when he immigrated to Nicaragua. Cuban tobacco was prized for its quality, deep dark leaves, and heady aroma. What held Cuba back now was they hadn't had the benefit of bringing outside breeding to the line. While they still had the mystique of being Cuban, Don Pablo would put his cigars up against a Cuban any day. His cigars were that good. He'd stake his life on it.

Don Pablo pulled a fat stick from its leather case and rolled it under his nose and inhaled. The cedar notes were like a balm to a bad day. Before he could cut it, a woman stood next to him with an outstretched hand.

"Let me get that for you, Don Pablo." She smiled as he gently placed it in her palm.

"Gracias, Pipa."

Pipa winked at him and raised the cigar to her own nose, inhaling deeply. "Is this the Reserve?"

"Si."

"It seems very nice."

"It is."

Don Pablo ran his hand along her thigh and around to the back of her ass, giving it a gentle squeeze. She playfully swatted it away, but he knew she'd come around later and do more than light his cigar. While he was a large man, he never lacked for beautiful women. Why would he? He had one of the largest cigar factories in Esteli and it was only going to get bigger once he sealed the deal with the rest of the families.

"Here you go," she said, handing the lit cigar back. He took a long draw from the cigar and let the smoke linger in his mouth. *Heaven, that right there is heaven*, he thought as he eased it out of his mouth.

"Tequila, rum, or American whiskey?" Pipa pointed to the bottles at the bar.

"Rum, sweetheart. Always Nicaraguan rum."

She poured the dark liquid into a crystal tumbler and placed it in front of him.

"Leave the bottle." He winked at her and grabbed her ass again. "That way you don't have to keep running back and forth to fill my glass. Besides, I want you to save your energy for later."

"And what would my husband say about that?" she kidded, swatting his hand away.

Before he could say anything else, Rique Marquez yelled across the room, "Don Pablo, don't tell me you're starting without us?"

Rique slapped him on the back and bent over to give him a hug. "Compadre, how the hell are you?"

"Good, good, Rique. How's business?"

Julio Torres and his brother Armando followed Rique in slapping Don Pablo on the back and offering the portly man their hands.

"It's good, Don Pablo. It's good. How do you like the restaurant? Are they taking care of you?" Rique pulled Pipa in for a hug and kissed her cheek.

"Very good care, Rique." He smiled at Pipa. "Very good care."

"Good, we don't want you going hungry, my friend." Rique suddenly seemed peeved, but he really couldn't care less. A little innocent flirting never killed anyone.

"Armando, Julio, how are you?"

The two brothers were part of a large family of cigar manufactures who had a factory in the Dominican

Republic and one in Nicaragua. Like his family, theirs had been in the business for decades, too. So, joining forces made sense, at least it did to Pablo. It would be hard to take over their business if they were constantly battling for dominance in the large market. To take down a goliath sometimes you needed to infiltrate it and wound it from the inside.

"Good, Don Pablo. Thanks for the invite. Something smells good." Armando sniffed the air and took a seat. Julio sat down next to him.

"Where's Esteban? I thought he would be here, too." Enrique popped a few plantains into his mouth and smiled again at his wife, wiggling his eyebrows.

"I'm handling the meeting tonight. He's got his fingers in something else so he wants me to take care of things."

"Okay, cool." Rique swatted his wife's ass and poured himself a drink.

Don Pablo motioned for a round of drinks for the table as he puffed on his cigar. "I'm glad you're all here early. RJ is on his way, but I wanted to talk to all of you first."

"What's going on?" Rique clipped a cigar and looked like he was creating a bonfire as he lit the end.

There were certain things he could excuse when it came to the way people smoked cigars. He could even forgive those flavored cigars Americans seemed so intent on producing, but treating a fine smoke like junk food wasn't one of them. One needed to toast the end and then gently coax it to flame. Much like the way one had sex, in his opinion. Slow, deliberate, and with plenty of time to charm it to life.

"Remember Don Roberto's funeral?" There was a small chorus of yeses as he looked at each man.

"Anyone notice the gringo in the back of the room?"

"You mean the one RJ was talking to outside?" Armando piped up.

"Exactly."

"I just figured he was another cigar lover who knew Don Roberto. There were quite a few Americanos there that day."

Pablo shook his head. "I checked him out. He's got some deep pockets and word is he's looking to invest in, if not buy, a cigar company." Pablo popped a plantain in his mouth and waited for the revelation to take purchase in the group's collective hive brain.

Rique paused long enough to let the smoke clear, then answered, "You think he was there to talk business to RJ?"

Pablo slapped the table and hoisted his huge frame up. "Maybe, but I'm thinking RJ doesn't have a big enough stake in Huerta to say yes to any offer."

"Why do you think that?"

All the men in the room followed Pablo as he walked around the inner courtyard. He knew how to command their attention. Money. He chomped down on the end of the cigar and rubbed his hands together.

"Call me skeptical."

"I've known RJ a long time, Don Pablo, and he's next in line to head the company. Surely Don Roberto wouldn't leave it to that sister of his?" Rique was on his feet now, a drink in one hand and his cigar perilously close to dumping a load of ash on the floor in the other.

Pablo thought he was going to lose his mind at the rate Rique was pissing him off.

Cigar etiquette 101: mind your ash.

"Look, this is a huge deal and I just don't want anything standing in our way of collaborating with our friends in America. Besides, I've got a lot riding on this."

"We all have a lot riding on this, Don Pablo."

His rancor rose the more he was challenged. No one need to remind him of the stakes or who had more to risk. He'd put everything into this deal, and he wasn't about to let some gnat's ass tell him they had more on the line. Asshole.

He peered down his nose at the toad and took a puff of his cigar, watching as the man practically shriveled in his shoes.

"I mean, we've all got some skin in the game, Don Pablo."

Before he could say anything, he heard the sound of a car outside the restaurant.

"We'll talk later." He hoped the man's dick withered off as he waited for the impending hammer to be dropped on his head.

❧❧❧❧

The SUV pulled up in front of a small hotel of the main street. The dirt streets and old buildings that flanked each side of the hotel were in vast contradiction to the beautiful building they were going to enter. The bright paint job and ornamental iron work that decorated the building were beautiful and clearly costly. It always reminded RJ of a painted lady, too much makeup almost made it gaudy and ugly. A few coins had been spent on the hotel to make it beautiful, but in turn it also made it stick out like a throbbing thumb that had been hit with a hammer.

Three men were standing outside smoking cigars when the SUV pulled up.

"RJ glad you could join us," a slender man named Miguel Esparza said. He jerked on RJ's hand like he was milking a cow. His heavy gold bracelets clanging with each jerk.

"Likewise, mi amigo." RJ motioned for Lewis to join him. They'd spent the afternoon entertaining a few women at the Flying Pescado and then a short nap had been in order. Lewis needed it and RJ needed to get his new photo collection developed and in order.

"Mi amigo. There you are?" A short, stocky man who'd clearly had too much to drink already held the door open.

"Enrique, how are you?" RJ wiped his sweaty hand against his slacks and extended it.

"Starving, we've been waiting on you." He pushed the hand away and gave RJ a bear hugged, then spotted Lewis. "Who is this?"

RJ tried to help Lewis ease out of the SUV, but his friend slapped away the offered hand. So, he grabbed a box of cigars and walked with his compadre. "An old friend. He's visiting. You know, cigars, rum, and women." RJ slapped Enrique on the back and winked, walking away from Lewis.

"I might be old, but I'm not that old."

"Oh, and he's feisty. He'll fit right in, RJ. However, I'm not sure the group wants someone else at the table," Enrique said, opening the door.

The welcome rush of cool air hit RJ. He stood for a moment blocking the door, enjoying it.

"Hey, leave some for the rest of us, pendejo," someone from across the room yelled.

"Armando, how are you, you son-of-a-bitch?" RJ sauntered over to the man rising from the table. He didn't want to seem too anxious, but he was already ready for the meeting to be over.

RJ turned in a circle and looked around at the

courtyard of the restaurant. "Wow, this is beautiful. Who owns this?"

Enrique had already sat at the table stood and held out his arms and then pointed to himself as a beaming smile split his face.

"This is yours, Rique?"

"Yep, my wife was tired of cooking and so she made me buy this. She said, 'Rique,'" His voice went up in pitch. "'With all that money, you can at least get me a cook.' Fuck that, if I'm going to pay someone to cook, I'm going to make some damn money while I'm at it. So bam, she got a cook." He laughed, slapping his buddies on the back.

"Who do we have here," Armando said, nodding at Lewis.

"Everyone, this is a good friend, Lewis Worthington, an Americano."

"Lewis," one of the men still seated at the table said.

A heavyset man at the head of the table wiped his brow and then inquired, "I thought we were here to talk business, RJ. Why do you bring this gringo to the meeting?"

"Lewis, may I introduce Don Pablo Vega. Don Pablo, this is my lawyer, Lewis Worthington."

Don Pablo eyed Lewis suspiciously. "I didn't know we were bringing counsel to the table, RJ. I just thought this was a friendly discussion about Huerta Cigars."

RJ jumped as two of the men stood and reached into their waistbands. "No, no, he's here on another matter. I didn't want anyone thinking that I was hiding something if they found out who he was. It's a small country and well, you know how people like to gossip. It's the currency of the country, mi amigo."

"Hmm,"

"Besides, it would have been rude of me to leave him at the ranch, especially since he just arrived. Verdad?"

"Yes, yes, sit down then."

RJ sat at the far end of the table with Lewis right next to him. Pouring himself and Lewis a drink, he raised his glass in toast. "To cigars, may they be like women: hot and long burning."

"Salud," everyone said in unison.

"So, Lewis, what kind of law do you practice?" Don Pablo asked.

A quick kick from RJ and a sideways glance was a cautionary gesture.

"I mostly consult now. I'm at that stage in my career where my experience is better used in analyzing a situation and giving advice."

"I see." Don Pablo looked at RJ, casting a suspicious glance at him. Don Pablo was a smart man and did not suffer fools easily. He was one to take action and ask questions later, so RJ could feel the weight of his stare as it bore through him.

"So…" RJ slapped his hands together. "I'm starving. Are we eating first or talking?"

Enrique snapped his fingers and a simple meal of beans, rice, fish, chicken, and thin-sliced fried plantains were deposited on the table. All waited until Don Pablo filled his plate before the rest of the men ladled food onto their own. RJ scooped up some beans and rice with the flat plantain and shoveled it in his mouth while Lewis daintily sat spearing the chicken, chewing it until done and then scooping a mouthful of beans, repeating the process with each food type on his plate. He was methodical in the way he never let his food touch and never ate different foods at the same time. RJ wanted to laugh, but he didn't want to bring any further attention to the Americano.

"So, RJ, when can we expect you to join the cartel? We've been talking, and agree that adding your father's cigars to our collective will grow the market quite well." Don Pablo wiped at his mouth, pushed away from the table, and grabbed his glass of rum. "How long before you get your cut?"

"I'm working on it. As you know, my sister is out of the country, so she's dragging her feet. But I'm sure when she gets back, I can get my share of the company."

"I thought you were going to convince her to join the group," Enrique said, his mouth full of food. Clearly, manners were not in his wheelhouse.

"I'm still trying, but I wouldn't bet on her coming around." RJ pushed away from the table and stood. He pulled a cigar from his vest pocket, snipped the end, and wiped his mouth before he sucked on it making sure it was pulling enough air. Toasting the end, he walked to the center of the patio and let the warmth of the sun beat down on his face. "You know Sofia. She's hardheaded, but I'm working on her."

He caught Lewis looking at him. A dour look crossed his face before he lifted his glass and took a swallow of rum. He noticed Lewis scanning the room before he and RJ locked eyes again. He gently shook his head as he walked over to RJ.

"Have a cigar, Lewis." RJ opened the box and pushed it toward Lewis. "You'll have to tell me what you think of my father's reserve." He walked to everyone and passed them out. "We had these at the funeral, but I don't think we really had enough time to enjoy them. You know what I mean?" He nodded at Don Pablo.

"So, Don Pablo, let's talk about what Huerta gets if we join your little group."

"What do you get if you join our little group, RJ? Access. Access to some of the biggest money you're ever going to make, my friend." Pablo picked up his drink and took a swig. "But then again, perhaps I should be having this conversation with your sister. I mean—"

"Don't insult me. We can sit here and trade barbs or we can do some business. It's completely up to you, Don Pablo."

Who the hell did this little prick think he was? Pablo smiled, but inside he was thinking of a million places a body could be hid in Nicaragua. If RJ wasn't careful, Sofia was going to end up an only child and with everything that RJ prized. His father often said, a wise man knew when to shut his mouth and avoid looking like an idiot where a stupid man let everyone know of his impairment.

"How's your Tio Manny?"

"Why?"

"I like him. Besides, he's got a small factory. Maybe you can invite him into the deal. That way you and your Tío can convince Sofia that going with the cartel is worth her time. Unless of course you don't think you can persuade her."

Question a man's abilities and he usually stepped up to prove you wrong, but question his manhood and you had a fight on your hands. Pablo wondered if he was going to have to go that far to get RJ to commit to his offer.

"I can talk to him." RJ bristled as he answered.

Pablo slapped the table. "Good, let's eat. I'm starving."

Chapter Eleven

The rays of sun squeezed through the slim gaps between the slats of the wooden blinds. Laura turned away from the window, trying to will herself back to sleep. Six hours wasn't long enough, not after the night she'd had. Coming home, she'd made the premier mistake of checking her work email before taking a shower, which she desperately craved. In her inbox was an email from her father, demanding—no commanding—she take on the case of the contested will or consider looking for employment at another firm, which, he added without trying to hide the threat, might be hard to find without a good reference from him. Napa was looking better and better with each passing hour. She'd take on pro bono cases if she had to, but she wasn't about to be bullied into taking a case that was a waste of time.

She'd rung her mother late and talked about the issue with her. If she was going to be awake at an ungodly hour, the woman who'd birthed her and made him part of her gene pool was going swimming with her, regardless of the time.

"Christ, Mom. I don't know why he's so insistent that I take this case. It's a fucking will for Christ's sake."

"Laura…" Her mom's silence meant she'd strung together too many cuss words in one sentence, again. "Why don't you just take the case and show him that it's not winnable? He'll look like an ass and you'll have made your point."

"Because, I have a stack of work on my desk and adding one more stupid case is going to push my other clients further back. Besides, some of these cases already have court dates and I can't very well go into court and tell the judge, 'Hey, my dad has given me this bullshit case so I haven't been able to prepare anything for my client. Can I get an extension?'"

"I get it honey. I really do, but you know your father. He won't stop until he's got what he wants."

"Yep, I do know that—"

"Laura."

Her mother knew she was dangerously close to calling him a bastard.

"Is he there right now? Let me talk to him."

Laura suddenly wished she'd kept her mouth shut when her mother's voice softened, apologetically. "No, sorry honey. He said he had business out of the country. You know your father."

Laura knew exactly where her father was, and she just happened to work with the *new* client. The fact that her mother knew anything was surprising, if it hadn't been for the fact that she was almost positive her father had called her mother to put some pressure on Laura. Her mom probably wouldn't even have brought it up if it hadn't been for her getting pissed off at the email she'd received.

"Oh, I have news," her mom chirped up.

"Really, what?"

"I'm interviewing cooks-slash-housekeepers tomorrow. I think it's time I got someone to replace Francine. I'm not eating right, and the house needs a woman's touch, just not mine." Her mom laughed.

A surge of relief pumped through her. Or maybe

she was just releasing pent-up guilt she'd been holding because she hadn't seen her mom in a week. Who got guilty for not seeing their mom for a week? She did. "That's great, Mom. Did you need me to come over and help?"

"No, I think I can handle it. Besides, I contacted an agency that specializes in household staff."

Another shutter of guilt fell off the house she was building, and Laura was thankful that her mom was finding her sea legs, so to speak. She'd been so independent before, but after her father's umpteenth affair, she'd just become a shell of the woman who took her to girl scouts, soccer lessons, and to their traditional high tea on Sunday afternoons.

"Well, I'm glad you've decided to replace Francine. Not that she could be replaced, but at least you'll have help to take care of that monstrosity of a house."

"Yes, it will be nice to have someone around the house again."

A piece of her heart broke as her mother almost sounded forlorn.

"Well honey, I should let you go, it's getting late and you know how I like to watch my shows before bed."

"Okay, well if you need anything, Mom, call me."

"I will honey, and I want to you to think about taking that case and showing your father it's unwinnable."

Her shoulders sagged. "I will, mom. Night."

"Night, honey."

Laura sat staring at the computer screen. Her finger hovered over the delete button. God, she was tempted to send it to the trash file, but if she knew her father, he'd just resend it in the morning and pester her mother all over again, berating his wife for not convincing Laura to take the case. She wasn't fourteen anymore and it had barely worked then, and only because she didn't want to disappoint her mom.

Bastard.

She pulled the pillow over her face to completely cut the light. Just a few more minutes. Saturdays only came once a week and she tried to enjoy them when she could. Besides, it was looking like she'd be busy again tonight, which wasn't a bad thing considering it meant she'd see Sofia again. What kind of name is Sofia? Laura wondered. Pulling her phone from under the pillow she tapped the screen and pulled up the internet. Typing in "Sofia," she waited to see what it meant.

"Sofia means wisdom. It's Greek, American, German and Ancient Greek. Interesting, perhaps she's from ancient Greece sent to sweep me...what am I saying? Geez, I don't have time for daydreams." Laura flung her arm out from under the pillow and tossed the phone down on the bed. Rolling over onto her stomach, she pulled the pillow down over her head. She suddenly felt like a schoolgirl thinking about her first crush, only Sofia wasn't her first crush. Hell, she wasn't even a crush. Just someone she'd met last night and had a casual conversation with, who she might have liked, or wanted to spend more time with, or... Hell, it didn't matter. She didn't have time for that kind of stuff. Her self-imposed girl pact meant she had to stay focused on the end game. A move to Napa, out of the hill-climbing, fog-infested rat race. Survival of the fittest, San Francisco style.

Shit.

Squeezing her eyes tight, a few extra hours of sleep would do her outlook a ton of good. There was only one problem. Every time she closed her eyes, Sofia's sexy smile broke through. She had curves for days, not that boney model frame women were sporting these days, and that dark, almost black hair was something she could see herself running her fingers through and... God, what was she thinking? Laura tossed the pillow across the room and sat upright in bed.

"God." She slammed her fists onto the bed. Throwing the covers and duvet across to the floor, she swung her feet down and stalked to the window.

"You suck. I'm trying to sleep and the sunlight gets through you stupid things." Laura yanked on the strings, lowering the whole unit down to the floor.

"Great." The sun beamed its happy sunshine on her. Throwing her hands up, she almost felt like a vampire with an allergic reaction to vitamin D. "Fuck," she screamed.

She kicked the shades, and for her trouble she stubbed her toe. Cursing a blue streak, she flung herself on the bed.

"What the hell is wrong with me?"

A muffled ring stopped her from answering herself. The only problem was she didn't know where her phone was. Getting down on her hands and knees, she rooted around the sheets and covers she'd thrown on the floor, finally snatching it from the pile.

"What?"

"Well that answers my question. Who pissed in your cereal bowl this morning?" Michael said, the sounds of a bustling hospital his background music.

"Sorry. It's been a crappy morning. By the way, what question?" Laura almost tripped on the pile as she plodded to the bathroom.

"The question about a particular overnight guest."

She knew he was smiling on the other end and it perturbed her for no uncertain reason.

"No, I didn't have an overnight guest. Besides, I thought she was more into you with that whole car love affair thing you two had going on."

"Oh for the love of all that's holy. Are you screwing with me? No, I tried my suave, Mr. Doctor routine, but she wasn't having it. She had eyes for my big sister." He made kissing sounds over the phone.

"Can people see you acting like this? Or is this reserved for me? Why are you calling me?"

"Wow, you are in a pissy mood. What gives?"

"How long do you have?" Without waiting for his response, she laid it all out for him. "Dad sent me an email last night and practically told me if I didn't take this stupid case, he was going to fire me, and basically said I'd never work again in the city."

"What? What the hell is so big about this case?"

"I have no idea. It's a simple will. The client wants to contest it, but it's pretty iron clad. If the son fights it, he only gets a buck and his kids don't get their inheritance. Dad said something about using whatever it took to discredit the old man who died, and the heir apparent, but I didn't read any further. I deleted the whole thing."

"You know he's going to resend it, 'cause he knows you're going to delete it. Sounds like he's not taking no for an answer."

"Yep. So, I'm wondering what's so special about this case."

"You know the man better than I do, Lala. He's

always been an asshole to me, but he's your asshole now. So, tread lightly. He doesn't take no for an answer."

"Yep, I know. So, why'd you really call, because you know I'm not the kinda girl to take someone home the first night."

"So are you thinking about it."

"Stop. I'm not thinking about anyone. So…"

"I called to see what time you want me to pick you up for the benefit tonight."

"Oh, Michael. I don't want to go. Really…I mean it's just that…I don't…I mean I have nothing to wear and I've got all this work to do."

"Are you avoiding a certain Latina, with a killer body and eyes that just scream, 'Fuck me'?"

"Her eyes don't just scream fuck me. Besides, that's not very respectful. She wasn't some kinda hussy you're used to."

"Whoa, now wait. I date refined, schooled women."

"Yeah, the kind schooled in the finer pleasures of lovemaking, I'm sure."

"Hey, is that anyway to talk to your brother. What would your mother say?"

"You started it. I don't know let's call her and find out."

"Opps, paging Dr. Bickerson, paging Dr. Bickerson."

Michael laughed into the phone. "Oops, gotta go. Lala, I'll pick you up at five, be ready. I don't want to have to honk."

"Michael, I don't have anything to wear. Besides—"

A click was the only response as she tried to plead her case.

"Shit."

Hitting speed dial, she called him right back.

"You've reached Dr. Hollingsworth. If this is an emergency hang up and dial—"

Laura killed the message and tossed the phone on the rack of towels in the corner.

Crap, she knew he'd be at her house promptly at five whether she liked it or not and he wouldn't leave without her.

"Great, now I have to go buy a damn dress." She jerked on the water lever for the shower and hit herself in the face with the cold spray. Jerking back, she protested. "Can I get a break here?" she said to no one in particular. It was going to be one of those days.

❧❧❧❧

A strand of hair gently caressed her cheek with the breeze rolling in the light, moist lick of fog rolled in. Grasping at the errant lock, Laura tucked it behind her ear. She watched as the fog rolled over the hill, gobbling up the terrain like white fire, covering everything in its slow path. One could set their watch to the route as it rolled over the ocean and up the bay. It was the very reason she'd grown weary of the bay area and craved the unbridled sun of Napa. The dreary cold hand swept across the once warm terrace. She watched as fire pits, as if on cue, sparked to life like small bonfires. Pulling her wrap tighter around her, she suddenly wished she'd opted for a dress with sleeves. What had she been thinking, picking sexy over practicality? She knew why, and she had just spied the reason walking through the foyer.

As if on command, men turned and smiled

lecherously at Sofia's arrival. Her own brother, Michael, offered a typically male welcome as he straightened his bow tie and cracked a toothy grin. He'd stepped right out of a British spy movie, all the way down to his French cuffs and designer cuff links. He wouldn't be dateless for long. She, on the other hand, had spent a good twenty minutes restyling her hair in the women's lounge. Michael had brought his Porsche, with the top down, and all assemblage was demolished the minute he punched the gas. She'd barely been able to get her wrap over her head before every tucked and curled strand had come undone. He'd made some crack about her looking like a babushka or something. She couldn't hear him due to the over-bassed music spewing from the speakers. While the windswept look suited him, she on the other hand looked like a frizzed-out cat pulled ass backward through the bushes. A woman had taken pity on her and broke out some hair spray and a teasing comb, and within a few minutes she was almost as good as new. Who used those anymore? But a few shakes and she practically looked passable.

Returning her attention to the entrance to the lounge, Laura had the perfect vantage point for being a voyeur. Sofia smiled and returned the air-kisses, overly long handshakes, and compliments. Her uncle, tight on her hip, was running interference, never allowing anyone to get too, chummy. His look was more eighties chic—open collar, a few gold chains, and his blue tux was worn more like he was clubbing in New York's old Studio 54. Nevertheless, a few of the ultra-rich women were already eyeing him and his hip attire, licking their lips like he was a rare steak ready to be devoured. He popped a cocky grin and winked at someone off to his right, then moved a man out of the way so Sofia could move past.

Sofia looked like a skilled politician as she smiled, shook hands and air-kissed her way through the crowd. She spent time with each member who attended the event. Laura could imagine the simple yet efficient chats Sofia was having with the mostly male attendees. The few women who attended were treated exactly the same. Selfies abounded and Sofia offered a dazzling grin in each photo, leaning in to get that close, but not too close, picture that all the men wanted. Groups of men beckoned her to take group photos and she joked and slapped at their arms, the way a flirtatious woman does to make clear her would-be suitors know they weren't getting any further than the photo.

Michael suddenly appeared next to Laura. "Hey, she's good. Sofia sure knows how to work a crowd, doesn't she?"

"She does. Kind of reminds me of Yessenia in the humidor. Ice to Eskimos." Laura smiled at Michael, who was staring at Sofia. "Yep, ice to Eskimos."

"Should I show her my car?" Michael wasn't really asking her permission as much as he was letting her know he'd be showing off his baby.

"Why not? You two have that in common. I'm sure she'd love to see the Porsche."

A twinge of jealousy bit through her. The thought that Michael would try and, oh she didn't know, work his way into her bed using his car, made her angry. She'd seen him work his magic like that before and suddenly he was driving off with a new squeeze. It hadn't bothered her then, so why now? Because, because nothing.

"You won't be mad?" Michael said.

"Why would I be mad? Michael, if you want

to take her for a drive, feel free. I have no idea why I would be mad."

"Hmm, I'm just checking. Seems you're paying a lot of attention to her."

"What? I am not. I was just looking around. You know, a little research into the cigar industry so I can work this damn case Lewis gave me." She took a sip of her drink and finished. "Besides, she isn't a lesbian and I don't do straight women, regardless of how great they look."

"Right? She does look amazing in that dress."

"I guess."

"Okay, well I'm off. Wish me luck."

"Good luck," she said, then added, "Don't be disappointed if she turns you down flat." He didn't hear that last part. He'd already weaved his way through the crowd and was closing in on his prey.

Sofia did remind Laura of Yessenia. It had to be in their DNA, something that the tobacco bred into them. A casual fondness for polite conversation, easy compliments, and an outgoing personality that helped to convince men, mostly, that the cigar was a national treasure, and didn't everyone want to own a national treasure?

Michael suddenly appeared on her arm and he was dangling a set of keys at her. Sofia's face lit up and Laura immediately knew he was enticing her with a look or a ride in the Porsche.

Sly dog, Laura thought. *I knew he wasn't done trying to worm his way into her bed.*

❧ ❧ ❧ ❧

Sofia's gaze swept the room. While the dalliance

with Michael and his sports car had been fun, she was ready for some female company. His overt hitting on her was something she was used to, too. She did what she always did and put him down like the dog he was. Not a big ol' horn dog, but more like one of those little lap dogs that could easily be admonished and then put on the floor for their bad behavior. He'd taken it quite well, actually, and told her that he suspected she had a thing for his sister. She'd confirmed the fact that she'd like to get to know her, and asked for advice on how to achieve that goal.

His response had been rather surprising.

"She's a smart, intelligent woman and she's my big sister. I would hate to see her heart broken for just a quick fuck."

Sofia jerked her head back to study the man. "I'm not here to 'fuck' with your sister. While I don't have a problem finding a bed mate, I'm not the kind of woman who likes to try on women like shoes and see which pair fits best."

"I'm sorry, I didn't mean to imply you were a…"

"Slut?"

"I didn't say that." Michael jutted his chin out, trying to loosen his collar. He leaned back against the Porsche and swung the keys on his finger, catching them, and then reversing the action. Sofia had an urge to grab them to stop the slapping sound.

"No," She pulled her wrap around her and smiled back at Michael. "But I got the inference, Michael. I'd like to get to know your sister better, if that's okay with you."

"Like I said, she's my big sister and she's all I got. So, tread lightly on her feelings. If it's any consolation, she's a pretty good catch. She's house broken and doesn't eat you out of house and home." Michael offered up a quick laugh and extended his elbow. "Shall we?"

"Thank you for showing me your baby."

"No problem. I'd trust you with her any day. Now my sister, that's another matter."

"What if I promise I have nothing but good intentions when it comes to your sister?"

"I'm going to hold you to that promise, Sofia."

"I'll be honest with you, Michael, if I may?" Sofia pushed the button for the elevator. "I don't date much. Not because the opportunity doesn't present itself."

"Oh, I'm sure it does."

"It does, in lots of ways, but in my business women are arm candy and very few are owners of their own line of cigars. So, I know when someone is panning for gold, as you say."

"You mean a gold digger?"

They both ambled onto the elevator, turned, and reversed positions. Sofia slipped her arm through his and rested her hand in the crook of his arm.

"Exactly."

"Wait, you have your own line of cigars?"

"I do. I highly recommend them. Of course, they aren't anything like Huerta's cigars, but they can hold their own, if I do say so myself."

"Oh, shit, you're a Huerta?"

"Of course. What did you think when I invited you to the benefit?"

Michael chuckled. "Honestly, I just thought you were being nice."

"I was, but to both you and your sister. I had ulterior motives."

She winked up at him and the elevator dinged

signaling their arrival back at the lounge.

"Wow, Lala is going to be shocked."

Sofia turned and put her finger to his lips. "Nothing about who I am. I don't want to influence her one way or the other."

"She won't be influenced. Trust me, she's dealt with some power people before. She's cool."

Her finger still in place, she said it again. "Promise me. Don't say anything about who I am."

Michael crossed his heart and raised three fingers in the Boy Scout salute. "I promise."

"Thank you. Now, I'm off to find your sister and see if I can convince her to join me for dinner."

"Have fun."

She winked at him and waved him off as she went in search of a possible dinner date.

The object of her obsession was nowhere to be seen as she pressed the flesh again, frustrated that she had to. But she remembered that her father had always said, "It doesn't cost anything to be nice, but be a bitch and they'll remember it forever, mija."

She knew how to work a room, and a room full of men was a piece of cake. Like salivating dogs, she smiled, offered a few kisses on the cheek, and commented about how well they all cleaned up. For some reason, she noted, men always seemed overly pleased if you said something about them wearing their shoes, ties, their shirts tucked in, and generally looking civilized. She thanked them all for coming to support her father's charity, but that was a given. Don Roberto had made it part of his life to give back, and who better to tap than wealthy men who loved to think with their…

Sofia spotted Laura and smiled. God, she was

beautiful. Nothing striking in her features, but there was a confidence in the way she held herself. In the way she talked that made Sofia tingle like a Catholic schoolgirl doing something naughty, just waiting to get caught. She wasn't ready for the night to end yet. However, she hoped she could convince Laura of the same. The cigar club was fun, but if she wanted to get to know this American, she'd have to dump the lounge for somewhere quieter, more...private.

"Would you like to join me for a drink?" The tips of her fingers felt electric as she gently touched Laura's hand.

"What can I get you?" Laura motioned for a server.

"No, I didn't mean here. I thought perhaps somewhere less...a..." Sofia looked around the room before she spoke again, but Laura beat her to the punch.

"Male?"

"Exactly." Sofia's gaze roamed all over Laura as she took in the little black number she was wearing. "By the way, that dress look fantastic."

"Oh this? I've had it for years. It's a little something that works in a pinch."

Oh, I'd like to pinch you, Sofia thought as she twirled her finger around. Laura did as instructed, and she didn't disappoint. "Do you work out? You look great."

"If you were a guy, I'd think you were hitting on me." A complimentary shade of pink colored Laura's cheeks.

"If I were—"

"Sofia, I want you to meet some gentlemen. They're thinking of bringing your father's cigars to their club." Manny wedged himself between Sofia and Laura.

Isabella

"Tío, I was talking to someone, please." Sofia motioned to Laura.

"Oh, I'm so sorry…"

"Laura," Laura said, reminding him. "It's okay."

"Laura, right. My deepest apologies. I'm always thinking business. I'm sorry. May I borrow Sofia for only a few minutes?"

"Of course."

"I'll be right back, and you do look fantastic by the way," Sofia said as she was led away. "Manny, make this quick. I'm hungry and I want to get out of here."

Sofia was pulled up short as she stood in front of three men. Their scruffy facial hair might have been cute to a tweener, but they looked like they'd stepped out of a western. Desperados more than businessmen.

"Señorita Huerta. Sofia, right?"

"Oh Sofia, everyone wants a *Sofia*. Am I right?" One of the guys stepped up, pushed his lips out at her, and crossed his arms over his chest. "Check you out. Sofia."

Sofia cringed at the display in front of her. She didn't know who the men were, but she was about to go somewhere she hadn't had to go since her time at Stanford. Often times, because of her caramel skin and dark hair, college men assumed she was from the projects on a scholarship to Stanford and was trying to step up and out of the ghetto. She was used to setting them straight, but hadn't had to do it in a while.

"Why are you talking to me like I'm some hoodrat? I don't know you and you certainly don't know me. So, break out some paper, because I'm about to school you." Sofia leaned in and almost went nose-to-nose with the man who jumped forward. "Don't ever talk to me like you know me. I am not your sister, your mother, your tia, or your abuela. You got that?"

"Good thing, 'cause if my mother talked to me like that. Psshh." He made a gun with his fingers and fired.

"I don't know how you wormed your way into this VIP lounge." Each letter was said with such emphasis, she swore she spit on him. "But you better check yourself. You aren't in the hood here and no one has your back. You feel me?"

"Damn girl." The first man stepped between Sofia and the man-child just as Manny put his hands on him. Shaking Manny off, he said, "Hold up, hold up, we'd like to carry your father's cigars in several of our cigar lounges. We have a few up and down the state of California. Considering how much business we do, it could be a sizeable order."

One of the men gave her the creeps, the way he eyed her as if she was a piece of meat. The other kept scrubbing his chin as if he had something living in his beard, and the one speaking, well he wasn't exactly making the best of impressions as he scratched himself, even covertly. These young bucks weren't the typical cigar shop owners. Sofia had heard about a new scam involving the drug cartels buying cigar shops as a way of laundering huge sums of money from drugs. They'd make two large big buys of cigars a year, always with cash. Since it was cash, no one ever said anything, but she didn't play that way. The idea that she was helping someone launder ill-gotten gains didn't sit right with her.

"We cool, hold on. We are just businessmen trying to bring the best cigars to our customers. My boy over here, he's sorry for disrespecting you. He gets like that, you know what I mean? Me, I'm just looking to fill the shelves with some primo cigars."

"So, can we start over?" He looked over his shoulder and gave a command. "Get Tomas out of here and go get a drink. I'll join you in a minute." He looked back at Sofia. "We cool."

"I'm a little busy. So, Manny if you handle Mr…"

"Otero, Miguel Otero." He pulled a business card from his vest pocket and handed it to her.

"Fine, Mr. Otero." She looked down at a card someone clearly printed at home. "You can speak to my uncle and he'll get all of your details." She tucked the card into her purse and turned to Manny. "Un momento, Tío."

"Of course, Sofia. If you'll excuse us."

They walked a few steps away, Sofia turning so she could see the men. "Tío, I don't know who these men are, but they don't own a cigar lounge. I doubt they own a hair brush between them, so find out what you can and keep an eye on them."

"Do you think RJ sent them?"

Sofia looked skeptically at the trio who stood at the bar. "Maybe."

"I'll chat them up and see what I can find out."

"Thanks, Tío. Keep me posted."

"Of course."

"I'm going that way," she said pointing toward Laura. "So keep an eye on our friends over there." Something about them just didn't feel right. Her gut was almost never wrong, and she didn't trust her brother for a minute.

Sofia quickly made her way to Laura and stood close. "So, would you like to get something to eat?"

"Well, what did you have in mind?"

"Something ethnic? Tapas perhaps?" Laura

looked over at Michael as she hesitated. "Unless of course if you'd rather stay. I mean your brother is here, and I wouldn't want to come between family."

"He's a big boy. Besides, he looks like he's already found someone." Laura made a motion, catching Michael's attention.

"Michael. We're going to get something to eat." Laura said, looking to Sofia to confirm.

Sophia nodded. "Perfect. I'm starving."

"Did you want to join us since you're my ride home?"

Sofia deflated. She wanted to get to know Laura better, not the whole family. *Oh well, best laid plans and all.*

"Naw. See that beautiful brunette over there?" Michael pointed to a slender woman who looked like she needed a box of cookies.

"Yes,"

"Well, she came with another flight attendant who wanted to smoke a stick. She's leaving in the morning for Montreal. Perfect, huh?"

In more ways than one, thought Sofia.

"Okay, so can you get home by yourself?"

Laura looked at Sofia. "Uber okay?"

"Perfect, unless you need a ride. I mean, I have a car here as well."

"As long as I get home we won't have any problems."

"Great, don't worry. Lala... Sorry force of habit," he said, raising his hands.

"Well then that's settled. We can have the most fantastic dinner, listen to some wonderful guitar music, and get to know each other better. Verdad?" Laura gave Sofia a confused look. "Oh, it means, 'Right?'"

"Well, you kids don't stay out too late. I'll text you later to make sure you got home. I wouldn't want anything to happen to you tonight." He looked at Sofia and they exchanged knowing glances.

Michael smiled, winked at Sofia, then strode over to the waiting brunette.

"Your brother seems like a very responsible man," Sofia threaded her arm through Laura's and walked to the coat check.

Laura laughed. "Sorry, I thought you said 'respectful.'"

"Well, he seems to be that as well." Sofia smiled at the way Laura's face lit up as she laughed.

"You have a no idea," she said as she looked over at her brother.

Sofia handed their ticket stubs to the coat check girl and motioned. "There, that is mine. Laura?"

"Oh, yes. Yes, I'm sorry!" She squinted her eyes. Sofia recognized distrust on the face of the coat check girl. Perhaps it was jealousy.

Manny suddenly stood by Sofia. "Where are you going, Sofia?"

"Tío, we're hungry, so we're going somewhere a little quieter to get something to eat." Knowing it would be disrespectful if she didn't invite him, she did so with reservation, knowing that he just might say yes depending on what was working him more, hunger or sex. "Would you like to join us? I thought I would take Laura to Seville."

Manny offered a sly smile, rubbed his belly, and then lowered his voice. "Do you see that beautiful piece of prime rib over there?" He pointed to Yessenia from the humidor. "I think I'll dine on her, I mean with her tonight." Manny straightened up. "Do you think you should be leaving right now? I mean how much do you know this woman?" Manny turned his back on Laura and thumbed her way.

"That's what I'm going to find out, Tío. Besides, you're the one always telling me to get out and make friends. Now go and sweet-talk that pretty Latina. Isn't she the young lady who works the humidor?"

She knew the answer, she was just reminding Manny. She'd often told him, "Don't shit in the same field that you eat in." Dating women that he was going to see semi-regularly was the same thing. If they weren't on the same page when it came to a one-night stand, there would be hell to pay the next time he was in town. However, he was a grown man and could handle his own drama.

Manny nodded his head and then looked over his shoulder at her. She waved again and gave a full smile.

"She is."

"Good, you both have something in common, a love for cigars." Sofia moved in closer. "She does love cigars, right?"

"Si, Sofia, now go." Manny blushed, then bent down to kiss Sofia on each cheek. "Don't stay out late. We have business in the city for the next few days and then back home."

"Stop worrying, old man. Have I ever let you down? Besides, I'm sure Ms. Laura has a curfew with this being a school night and all."

"I don't go to school," Laura deadpanned the response as she walked up on the pair.

"I was just kidding." Sofia smiled and ushered Laura into the elevator.

"Tell you what, how about we don't tell each other our last names? That way we won't be tempted to Google each other during dinner."

"Hmm, okay. I suppose that's fair. Puts us on an even footing for the evening."

"It does. You don't mind?"

"Not at all."

She could see that Laura was suddenly intrigued with the idea that they wouldn't know each other's last names and wouldn't get the opportunity to look each other up. As a lawyer, her brain was probably against this idea. Sofia was sure she lived in the fact-based world where she liked to know everything about people she interacted with.

For Sofia, it was probably why her online dating experiences had failed miserably. Before saying yes to a date, she researched everything she could about a prospective suitor. She'd been catfished a time or two. However, it ended at the point when she'd called them out about their lie. She'd sent pictures of their true selves to both the dating service and the imposter. She'd heard about a high-end dating service, but twenty thousand dollars was a little steep even for her. Besides, there were no guarantees the matches they sent would result in a long-term relationship. It felt more like a high-end call service, some place you might meet someone who was marriage material, assuming they passed the credit check, the financial check, and then ponied up the steep origination fee.

Oh well, she was destined to be married to her work until her business was at a place where she could put it on autopilot and let Julian run with it. She was looking forward to a time when she could make cigars instead of enemies, but she had to deal with RJ in the meantime. What was that little bastard up to anyway?

Chapter Twelve

The restaurant was dark but ornately decorated in bright oranges, yellows, and reds. Mixed with the dark, masculine woods of mahogany, it had a warmth and charm to it. Above Laura's head, she could hear a guitar playing and what sounded like tap shoes clicking out a quick rhythm with castanets. At least she thought that's what the sound was. She hadn't played with a pair since fourth grade music class when it was international month.

"Señoras." A slender Latino swept his arm wide in welcome.

"Señoritas," Sofia corrected him, her look of admonishment practically melting the young man.

"Lo siento. I meant no disrespect."

Sofia ignored the apology and seated herself behind Laura as she scooted into the booth and quickly ordered a few things. She was too hungry to wait and hoped Laura wouldn't be upset at her presumption.

"Si, Señorita." The young man disappeared swiftly.

"I hope you don't mind but I ordered some wine and a few starters. I'm starving." Sofia smiled at Laura, scooting a bit closer. "I apologize. The music, it's a little loud and I want to be able to have a conversation. I didn't expect it to be this busy so early in the evening."

"How did you find this place? It's tucked away in south San Francisco, not exactly the Spanish part of town." She loved trying new things, so was surprised the restaurant hadn't popped up on her foodie radar. The music, the lively conversation, and the delicious smells were some things she could lose herself in dining alone, as she often did.

Before Sofia could say anything, a well-dressed, distinguished-looking man approached their table.

"Sofia." He spread his arms wide and she practically leapt into his arms.

"How are you?" Sofia kissed each cheek and pulled him into a hearty hug.

"And who do we have here?"

"Ah, Laura. This is my godfather, Señor Lopez."

"How do you do, Laura? Sofia, I'm so sorry to hear about your father."

"Thank you, Pedro. He was a good man."

"Yes, yes he was. So, how long are you in town?"

Laura could only watch the warmth between the two as they spoke Spanish. Pedro thumped his heart and drew Sofia into a tight embrace and held her. He rocked her as one would rock a child to comfort them. Then he held her out for a look and then peered over Sofia's shoulder at Laura. "That Spanish conductor is here playing the guitar. I know how you like her." He winked at Sofia. "You'll stay for dancing, yes?" Pedro hesitated, then glanced over at Laura for confirmation.

Laura looked at Sofia and then back at Pedro. "Well…" Laura couldn't help but see how giddy Sofia was at the news of the guitar player. "Why not, it's not a school night."

"Perfect. I'm sorry about my nephew earlier. He's new and well he's one of those millennials who has no manners."

"Ay, the younger generation." Sofia slapped Pedro's sleeve. "I won't be so hard on him next time, now that I know he's family."

"No, no. He needs to be schooled as they say nowadays." Pedro hugged Sofia again just as someone stepped up with a small box. Sofia took the box and smiled.

"These are for you, Papa."

"If I were only younger, Sofia." He kissed her cheek.

"You wouldn't be my godfather."

"True. Well—"

A voluptuous woman holding drinks arrived, stopping him short.

"Dos sangrias."

"Aqui, Magdalena. Well, I'll leave you two to your dinner. I'll send over the cheese-stuffed dates wrapped in bacon." He lifted his fingers to his lips. "They are to die for. Laura it's a pleasure to meet you."

"This is such an interesting restaurant. It almost looks like an old fire station." Laura smiled at Sofia, her heart racing as she was trying to come up with something to say.

"Oh it is. Look over there in the corner. That's the old brass pole the firemen used to slide down. I think Pedro has a rope around it. Last time I was here, some woman thought it would be cute to slide down the pole. Unfortunately, she'd had too much to drink and did more of a sloppy pole dance all the way down."

"No kidding?"

"No kidding. See the stairs, they're pretty wide and all of this was where the fire engines were."

"Wow, it doesn't look like it could hold very many firetrucks."

"I think there are some pictures along the walls showing the fire trucks that were pulled by horses.

See those rings on the wall?" Sofia pointed to iron rings hanging about waist-high. "They tied the horses off to those. The second floor was where the men slept. Someone who had it before Pedro completely remodeled upstairs, so not much is left, except the pictures."

"Wow, fascinating. I love historical stuff like that."

Sophia sat across from Laura smiling. Her body bobbed a little to the music from above. The wine was having an effect on her inhibitions. As usual, it was lowering the wall they were hiding behind.

"Me, too." Laura watched as Sofia smothered a giggle. "You should see the upstairs. It's beautiful. The woodwork, the stucco, they didn't hold back when they designed the building."

"I can't wait to see it." Laura's smile was infectious. "Is that clock part of the firehouse?"

Sofia looked over at the huge wrought-iron clock that had to be at least six feet across. The hands sat at 9:00 pm.

"I don't think so. I think that's something Pedro brought in."

"Oh, it's beautiful and really fits right there."

Before Sofia could reply, she was interrupted.

"Uno mas?" The waitress pointed to her glass.

"Uhm…" She looked at Laura; her glass was still partly full. "Probably not."

"Oh, go for it. We're Ubering, right?" It was the driving she was worried about, not the alcohol.

"Sure, uno mas."

"Señorita?"

Before Laura could say anything Sofia piped up. "Of course. If I can, so can you. Besides, dancing will burn off all those extra calories we're going to have tonight."

Sofia reached over and snatched a bacon-wrapped date and hummed.

"Those are so evil. I think I could eat a dozen," Laura said, reaching for the last one in the dish.

"They are good, aren't they?"

"Better than sex." Laura slapped her hand over her mouth. "I can't believe I just said that." A rose tint color started to crawl up her neck.

"You did, I heard it." Sofia giggled. *Oh, she's definitely had enough wine*, Laura thought. The waitress showed up with two shot glasses filled with a clear liquid.

"We didn't order these." Sofia stopped her before she set them down.

"From the two men at the bar." She pointed at the two men who were waving at them.

Sofia didn't return the wave and instructed the waitress to send them back. Before she could return her attention to Laura, the men were standing at their table with their drinks in their hand and the shots in the other.

"Ladies…" The taller of the two started. "These are for you." He set his on the table and motioned his friend to do the same.

"We come bearing gifts," the other said, flashing an overly white, toothy grin that clashed with his tanning booth complexion.

"Don't you know it's rude not to let a man buy beautiful women drinks?"

"Really," Sofia stiffened at the disrespectful way he was talking to them. "In my country, it's rude to assume we're interested."

"Wow, I love your accent. Where are you from?'"

"I'm from Nicaragua, but I'm half American, too. Not that it's any of your business."

"Wow, do you think you could just say my name in Spanish? I want know what it's going to sound like when we make love tonight."

"Are you kidding me, you gringos think you can buy a woman a drink and assume we'll fall at your feet and beg you to take us to bed because you're wearing a flashy suit and a Rolex?"

The tall man offered a cocky grin as he looked down at his watch, Seemingly proud that Sofia had noticed his high-dollar style.

"I think we got off on the wrong foot. Let me start—"

"Let me stop you before you start." Sofia put up her hand. "Of course, I can't speak for my friend, but let me save you the embarrassment of putting your suede loafers in your mouth again. I'm not interested. My friend and I are having a ladies' night out. Comprende?"

"Oh, I comprende, Señorita. I like the chase." He nodded to his buddy. "My friend and I own one of the biggest tech startups and we just went public today, so we thought we'd celebrate. You know, mucho dinero," he said so condescendingly that Laura gasped. He rubbed his fingers together for emphasis.

"It's okay, I speak sleaze, too." Sofia patted Laura's hand reassuringly. Sofia looked over the man's shoulder and nodded.

Each man was grabbed on the shoulder so roughly that they each spilled their drinks down the front of their pants.

"Ah pobresito. You look like you've wet your

pants, Mr. Tech Startup."

"Are these men bothering you, Sofia?" Her godfather stood between two huge sides of beef in black suits with earplugs in one ear and a bulge under their armpits.

"Si." Sofia smiled at the two men who were barely touching the floor with the tips of the suede loafers. "Next time you should treat women with more respect. Clearly, money doesn't buy manners."

The men struggled to get out of the grasp of the bouncers, then mouthed off. "Oh, I get it, a couple of lesbos, huh?" The man tried to shrug out of the bouncer's grasp. "Why didn't you just say so in the first place? Christ."

"You can bring a dog into the house, but if you don't train it to behave around company it must go outside where it belongs. I'm sorry these men are ruining your evening, Sofia. I'm sure they would like to make it up to you and buy your dinner and drinks. Right, gentlemen?"

"What? Hell no. We aren't paying for something we aren't getting—"

One of the bouncers pinched the man's shoulder tighter. "I'm sure SFPD would be happy to take this trash off our hands. Just say the word, boss, and I'll dump them on PD."

"Gentlemen, would you like to reconsider?" Pedro asked again.

"Fine."

"Good, I see we still have your AmEx card. I'll make sure their bill is taken care of and you can pick it up tomorrow."

"That's extortion."

"Technically, he's right," Laura piped up and

grimaced.

"You're right. I would hate to lose my business license because I made some apologies for harassing my patrons. Call SFPD and let's have these men arrested for harassment, drunk in public, and trespassing. Oh, and failure to pay their bill."

"Wait, wait, wait. I'm sure we can come to an agreement," the jerk offered.

"Are you sure? I wouldn't want you to do something you didn't want to."

"It's fine. I'd be happy to buy their dinner and drinks."

"And offer an apology for the disrespectful way you talked to my friend and me," Sophia added.

"Whatever."

"Then be a man and apologize. I'm losing my patience," Pedro said, dangling the platinum AmEx in front of his face with the receipt.

"My apologies for ruining your evening. My friend and I were just excited and wanted to celebrate. We made a mistake and apologize for being disrespectful."

"Are you satisfied?" Sofia asked Laura.

"Are you?"

"Hmm, I'm not sure."

"Aw come on. I'm buying your dinner and I apologized." He was practically whining now. "Come on."

"Fine, I'm satisfied, godfather." Sofia waved her hand at the men and gave a dismissive glare.

Pedro leaned over the man as he made him sign the receipt and issued a warning. "If I ever see you here again, I will have you arrested, but not before my bouncers bounce you right out of my restaurant. Do you understand?"

"Yep," he said, his contrite attitude all but disappeared as he snatched his card back.

"Aw, but let me explain one more thing. If you get any ideas about coming back here or pulling any funny business." His voice was low and menacing. "I'm calling the police and filing a report right now. So, don't even think about screwing with me, because you had better hope they get to you before I do. Understand?"

"Jesus, we said we're good. Can I go now?"

"Boys, walk them to their car, and while you're there get their license plate."

"Sure, boss."

Sofia giggled as she watched the men being ushered out of the restaurant.

"I'm so sorry, Sofia. I hope this hasn't ruined your evening. Let me get you something wonderful from the kitchen."

"Thank you, Pedro, you don't have to do that."

"Please, it would make me feel better. Yes?"

"Fine."

"Perfecto." He practically danced back to the kitchen and disappeared.

Laura was stunned.

"I'm sorry." Sofia said, patting Laura's hand.

"Don't be, it wasn't your fault. I'm just so sorry those men were so…"

"Please, they are no different from men in my country. Men are the same all over." Sofia waved the incident off. "I just didn't want to speak for you if you were interested in those guys."

"Not in the slightest. Trust me they are not my type in the slightest." Laura sipped at her sangria and looked Sofia dead in the eye.

"So…" Sofia smiled. "What is your type?"

"Hmm. Oh, god, it's been so long. I'd have to think about it."

"Why?" Sofia said, then sipped her drink

"Why?"

"Why has it been so long? You're a very attractive woman. I'm sure you have men lined up to ask you out."

The electricity between them snapped like a whip, flinging between the two, charging the air. Laura fidgeted with the napkin in her lap, pulling at a thread that had started to unravel. Like the napkin, her life was sown up tight and neat, but pull too hard on a string and it could unweave the very cloth she'd used to make up her well-ordered life. The heat of the restaurant had amped up as music replaced the hum of diners.

"I guess I'm married to my job. Or maybe I just haven't found the right—"

"Señoritas."

Thank god, a reprieve. Laura smiled at the waitress, Who had the check in her hand as her body shifted between herself and Sofia.

"I'll take that," Laura said, scooping it from the waitress as she put up a hand stopping Sofia from saying anything.

"Laura, dear."

Laura stopped fishing in her purse for her wallet the moment she heard the endearment.

"Yes?"

"This is already taken care of. Remember the little incident earlier with those men?"

"Oh right, but they really aren't going to pay for our dinner, are they?" Laura handed the check back to the waitress with her card.

"It's already been taken care of." Sofia offered a

smoldering smile that made Laura's heart quicken.

Sofia said something in Spanish to the waitress, who nodded but stayed glued to her spot. Laura looked around the room and noticed the practically empty restaurant.

"Oh gosh, I bet you want to go home, huh?"

"No hurry, Señorita. Your booth upstairs is waiting," she said to Sofia.

"I thought the place was closing," Laura said, looking around. There wasn't any music coming from upstairs now.

"Ah, no. They are taking a break. It is a special night. Tonight, they have Flamenco." Sofia snapped her fingers and struck a pose.

"Flamenco? As is Flamenco dancing?"

"Sí."

"It's that dancing from—"

"España. Yes, from Spain. This is a Spanish restaurant." Sofia winked.

"Oh. Wow, I feel stupid." Laura palmed her face. "I thought you were from Latin America. Gosh, do I feel stupid."

"No, no. I am. Nicaragua, to be exact. But I love tapas."

"But you said…Okay, I'm confused." Heat raced up her neck and she was sure she was a brilliant shade of pink now.

"Not to worry, I'll explain everything upstairs." Sofia grabbed her purse and reached for her hand. "Come, let's get up there before one of these gringos steals our booth,"

Laura felt her body infuse with warmth the minute she took Sofia's hand.

"Unless of course you need to go home. Then I'll

escort you to a cab."

Was she getting the brush-off? Sofia's tone sounded rushed, not pissed, but had she said something wrong to get the brisk quip? Oh, god this was why she didn't date—that dance that people do when they're getting to know each other, that rush to establish a connection that tells the head the heart was right, this person *is* into you.

Christ.

Had she read Sofia's body language all wrong?

Looking up at the clock, she noted the time: 10:00 pm. It wasn't exactly late, but maybe she was keeping Sofia from going home. She looked at Sofia and then back to the huge reminder. "Well…"

"You don't want to miss this guitarist. She's a world-renowned conductor who only plays here twice a year as a favor to my godfather." Sofia's enthusiasm was contagious. She reached for Laura's hand again. A sudden warmth threaded its way through her body. She hadn't felt this giddy since her first date with a girl in college. Sofia pulled her gently to the stairs and then whispered.

"Please?" Sofia's expression softened and her eyes twinkled in the low light of the restaurant.

Shit, I need whatever they're putting in that sangria, Laura thought as she nodded.

Chapter Thirteen

The cigar barons had given RJ a day to consider their offer, calling for another meeting at Rique's restaurant. *Why not?* RJ thought. The food was good and he wasn't paying, so he could play the game as long as it got him what he wanted.

RJ sat across from Don Pablo, the smoke creating a screen of sorts between the two. Glancing around the room, everyone was again enjoying his father's reserve cigars but Lewis. Lewis seemed to be hugging that stick he had up his ass.

"Lewis, relax," RJ whispered behind the back of the waitress delivering their drinks.

"I'm tired, RJ"

"Well, I need you in the game, so get your head straight." He slapped the ass of the waitress and then smiled up to the frown he received for his sexist attitude.

"So, Don Pablo." RJ set his cigar in the ashtray and slid closer to the table. Reaching for his dish, he cradled it between his leg and hip and inhaled the delectable scent. It had been a while since he'd had a home-cooked meal and this was as close as he was going to get. Estrella wasn't known for her cooking skills, but then again that wasn't why she was in his life. Lina…well, she was on her way out with her little bastards. Scooping up some rice and beans on the flat fried plantain, he shoved it into his mouth, savoring the simple fare.

"So, RJ, we're expanding our reach. We've laid out a plan and we need at least one more cigar manufacturer to join our operation."

RJ was amazed that Pablo could eat, smoke, and talk all at the same time. It was a skill RJ didn't want to acquire, but for Pablo, it worked. His girth alone proved that.

"Okay, I'm listening."

Don Pablo snapped his fingers and a woman magically appeared to start his cigar again. Why didn't RJ have someone like that? He was going to have to talk to Estrella.

"We've been approached by a group of individuals who'd like access to our distribution outlets. They are setting up cigar shops in the United States and have some heavy cash to invest. We don't want to miss out on another revenue stream, so we're opening our markets to them."

"What about your distributors?"

Distribution happened with salesmen, vendors, and a host of people who got out and humped their cigars to new opportunities, which was especially important now that cigars were facing a backlash from state and federal governments and countries. Taxes, import fees, and the like were having an influence on the industry. Don Roberto had often complained about the massive burden some countries were putting on their livelihood.

Cigars were associated with a particular lifestyle in most countries, and that lifestyle was diminishing. The rich and powerful were always going to be a group the cigar industry could count on, but they were going for the younger millennials. Don Roberto had done a lot to bring in a younger, more urban sales crew. They all had their place, right alongside the older salesmen who gave off an air of refinement. It was also the reason, RJ was sure, Don Roberto had let Sofia build her own little boutique line. The biggest growing line of cigar smokers were women, and he had to give credit to Sofia that she'd tapped into that market early and with a strong brand and image. Good-looking women sold cigars and Sofia was the perfect spokesperson for her brand.

Once RJ removed Sofia from the Huerta line, she wouldn't be able to divorce herself from the Huerta name and RJ would use that to his advantage. A Huerta in the cigar business was good for business.

Don Pablo wiped his mouth and then sucked on the 60 ring gauge like he was milking a bottle. "We aren't going to cut them out of the market, but this is a special favor to some very well-connected people." He blew a long stream of smoke up and then adjusted a critical gaze back on RJ. "You in?"

"Depends—"

"I get it, you gotta go back and get your sister's permission."

RJ bristled at the comment. He wasn't beholden to anyone and if this was the way Pablo was going to make his case for joining, he was about ready to tell the fat bastard to shove it.

"Look Don Pablo. I don't need my sister's permission. So, you better show me some fucking respect or I walk and this deal, this Cigar Baron idea you have goes down the fucking toilet. You aren't the only game in town. I'm a fucking Huerta. I've got a business that reaches into the US and Europe. I'm not some tobacco leaf humper. So, if you'd rather deal with my manflor sister, feel free. But I suspect she won't be able to supply you with the amount of cigars, or the reach you're going to need to play with the big boys." He had options and he sure as hell didn't need the cigar cartel to dictate to him. He didn't feel bad outing his sister to these men. If he was playing his cards right, he suspected he'd just killed any possibility she had doing business with men who didn't take kindly to someone living an alternate lifestyle.

"Look my friend, I was just kidding. Calm down." Pablo got up and rounded the table, slapping RJ on the back. "We have your back my friend. So, you're sister's a lesbian, huh?"

The group chuckled at the implications Pablo was throwing around as he slipped his tongue between a "V" he made with his fingers.

RJ wanted to deck the bastard, but the company he was in was thick. They always had each other's backs and wouldn't stand for one of their own getting their asses handed to them in public. He wasn't in the gang yet, so he smiled and stood. He wasn't about to burn any bridges he might want to walk back across, so he'd bide his time and play along.

"No problems, my friend. We're good. Besides, I want to hear more about this deal you're working on." RJ was getting ready to stand when Lewis's hand stopped him.

"Be careful my friend. Let's hear what he has to say." Lewis restated RJ's comment.

"I know, I'm just standing to get a smoke. Want one?"

Lewis waved his hand. "I'm good. Thank you."

"So Pablo…" RJ dropped the respectful Don title to bring the fat bastard down to his level. His father that was one thing, but Pablo—that last statement about his sister earned him nothing. "What's this little deal you guys are working on?"

Like dominos, each man around the table looked at the man next to them and then to Don Pablo. He had become the center of their attention, waiting for him to offer an explanation. Clearly, he—and his company— was the point man on the deal.

"RJ can I speak to you outside? Not all ears were meant to hear."

"What?" He pointed toward Lewis. "You can say anything in front of him. He's my lawyer and is the epitome of discretion. Right Lewis?"

His lawyer rolled his eyes before answering. "Of course. Geez."

"What the fuck is his problem?" Rique asked.

RJ put his hand on Rique's and held him down. "He's just tired, my friends. He's been travelling nonstop for several days, so that should earn him some slack, yes?"

A few grumbled around the table but kept their seats, turning their attention back to their meals and cigars. RJ noticed how Lewis's eyes roamed, lighting on each man before he turned his own attention back to his own cigar and liquor.

"Since everyone else knows what's going on, it isn't a secret, except to me. So what's this deal?"

Pablo nodded toward the doors and two men jumped to close them.

"We've got a pretty sweet deal. Friends want us to help them with a little extra money they have on their hands."

"Okay, so why don't they just invest in some real estate, or business?" RJ was connecting the dots, yet with the lack of information he was being spoon-fed, the picture was slow coming into focus.

"It's in the US and they can't move it without drawing some suspicion." Pablo took a long pull on his cigar. "So we've come up with a plan to help them out, and this is where you come into the picture. You have your own cigar houses in the US, and as such you are in a better position than the rest of us."

Pablo was right. Don Roberto had opened Huerta-only cigar lounges in cities like Vegas, Los Angeles, Tampa, New York, and Chicago. They carried only their cigars and moved a lot of product. They gave other lounges in Texas, Arizona, and along the eastern seaboard a great price and therefore guaranteed a spot in those states with a lower tax footprint. Having their single drop points in those states also meant they didn't have to worry about separate import taxes to each shop, which made them even more attractive to their vendors. His father had been smart like a fox and definitely ahead of the game. In the beginning he'd shipped cigars to his in-laws' house and used that as a drop point to avoid taxes when he was small potatoes, which helped get his foot in the door in California. Money talked, no it yelled, when the price of a stick could rise by dollars, not pennies.

"So, who are these *friends*, and how does this work?" Pablo looked at Lewis and then back to RJ. "You can talk in front of him. Besides, I value his opinion and I would ask his advice before I make a decision, so spill."

"These men have large sums of cash that they need to move through the system and get home, to Nicaragua, Colombia, and the Dominican Republic. They've opened a few cigars stores in the US and they'll be buying large quantities of cigars twice a year. That way they don't draw attention to the purchases. It's not uncommon for some cigar shops to do this, so we floated the idea to them and they are interested."

"Drug money," Lewis said, more of a statement than a question.

"It's just a reallocation of cash," Pablo corrected.

"You can call it what you want, but it's money laundering." Lewis sipped his drink, dismissing Pablo with the action. RJ knew he'd better get Lewis under control before Pablo did.

"I think what my friend is saying is, how does this affect us?"

"We get to double dip, my friend. They buy our cigars and we get a cut of the money coming back to be repatriated. Sounds like a win-win to us. Right mis amigos?" Pablo lifted his drink in salute as the cheers rose.

Drug money.

Drug dealers looking to launder their money from their drug sales in the United States could be a good influx of cash that RJ could potentially hide or explain away, but Sofia wasn't stupid. She'd figure things out, quick. That's why he needed to get the company away from her. He didn't care how the cash came rolling in so long as it wasn't tracked back to him. Doing it through a third party like a cigar shop meant it would be harder to connect the dots to Huerta. Or so he thought.

"So, RJ are you going to join us?"

"You said you were already starting to put some pieces in place. What are those?"

"We've sent a few young bucks up to the States to get the balls in the air, but they are going to need us to fund them as soon as possible."

It was definitely a tempting offer that RJ didn't think he was going to pass up, but he wanted to run a few things past Lewis before he signed on. Joining the ranks of a drug cartel had its downside, and then there was the whole he-didn't-own-Huerta-cigars-yet thing, but that was a minor detail at best.

RJ smiled and raised his glass as a cackle broke between the doors that had opened when the waitress walked through with more drinks.

Lina.

Shit.

She'd see the meeting and blow everything for him. Once she received the divorce papers, she would blow this deal and he needed time to think about it.

"Men, if you'll excuse me, I hear my wife cackling in the bar. I'm going to need to think about this fantastic offer. But I assure you that I'm leaning toward yes."

"That's excellent news. I'll have the papers drawn up and sent to your lawyer," Pablo said, nodding toward Lewis. "Tomorrow too soon?"

It would be if RJ didn't get Lina under control and out of the restaurant. "Nope, sounds good. Shall we meet again tomorrow, say two?" RJ said over his shoulder. He nodded toward Lewis who followed him out into the hallway.

"Sounds good, RJ. We'll see you tomorrow."

Everyone raised their glass and in unison said, "Tomorrow."

RJ could hear the buzz behind him and hesitated for a moment. *Fucking Lina.* It figured she'd blow this opportunity just by being in the same building. He needed to get her ass out of here before she saw the rest of the families meeting. She was stupid, but she wasn't that stupid. Rounding the corner, he spotted her leaning on a slim, tall man, her hand running up and down his back.

"Bitch," he whispered.

Lewis pulled on RJ's arm. "You don't need a spectacle here, RJ. If she gets wind of that meeting, I'm sure she's smart enough to put two and two together."

RJ jerked his arm out of Lewis's grasp. He was fuming at the public display. At least he had the decency to keep Estrella out of eyesight. Lina, on the other hand, was practically putting her hands down the guy's pants.

Lewis jerked RJ into the hallway before Lina could see them. "Don't be stupid, RJ. Those men in there are getting you mixed up with drug dealers and now that woman can put you with them. So pull your head out of your ass and think about what you want."

Lewis was right. She could put him at the meeting and she'd sing like a bird if she knew it would put him in jail and she could get access to his money. The divorce wouldn't go his way and all of his plans would be for nothing.

Bitch.

Even now she controlled his every move.

"Let's get the hell out of here." RJ moved down the hallway to the marked exit door.

Was he ever going to catch a break?

Chapter Fourteen

The lights dimmed, then suddenly a spotlight popped on and focused on a woman sitting in a chair, a guitar resting on her leg. Leaning over, her hair created a curtain between her and the crowd. A quick strum and the crowded room began clapping and cheering. Oblivious to the commotion, she started to tap out a quick tempo against the body. Laura could hear a rapid metal tapping as a woman appeared out of the darkness to the guitarist right. The quick syncopated rhythm of the guitarist and the dancer was hypnotic as they worked in unison, the beat echoing through the lofty space.

Laura was mesmerized by the way the dancer's dress flowed as she moved around the floor, wrapping around her own body and then fanning out as she turned in the opposite direction. She ran her hands over the guitarist's shoulders in such an intimate way. The guitarist plucked at the strings looking as if she was touching a lover, the way her hand glided down the neck. It was sexy as hell as the two shared an intimate exchange in front of everyone, as if no one was watching.

"She's beautiful isn't she?" Sofia said, scooting closer to Laura.

"I can't see her face."

"Trust me, she's beautiful. I'll introduce you to her later."

"Okay." Laura sensed Sofia's presence the closer she slid to her.

"I can't see her from over there. I hope you don't mind."

"No, not at all."

The dancer swung the embroidered shawl that seemed more like an extension of her body, around her as she snapped to the tempo. Gazing around the room she could see the crowd leaning in, watching her with rapt attention. She swung seductively across the dance floor, weaving around the few who sat in chairs surrounding the dance floor. Men reached for her as she swayed out of their grasp, their partners slapping playfully at their shoulders in mock jealousy as the dancer pursed her lips and shook her finger at them.

"She's just beautiful, the way she works the crowd," Laura whispered to Sofia.

"She's fantastic."

"Sexy, isn't she?"

"You like it?"

Laura turned toward Sofia, their eyes catching. "Yes, very sexy."

Sofia smiled at the comment and then slid closer. "Yes, very." Sofia's hand clasped Laura's, sending a jolt through her. The energy in the room ramped off the charts as she caressed Laura's face. "I'm sorry, I don't mean to be so forward, but…" she said, dropping her hand back to the table.

Suddenly speechless, Laura did the only thing she could think of and reached for Sofia's hand. "Don't be."

The room faded as they leaned in closer, their foreheads touching. Laura could smell Sofia's perfume. Intoxicating was the only thing that came to mind as she smiled. It seemed like hours passed as Laura studied Sofia's face. "I don't usually…"

Sofia laid a finger against Laura's lips. "Don't worry, I understand."

Laura bit the tip, running her tongue against it as she clasped her lips around it, her teeth nipping at it. Her body tingled as Sofia closed her eyes and gasped.

They had been playing at this all night, hadn't they? She wasn't one to fall so quickly to seduction games, but Sofia wasn't like any woman she'd met. Smart, confident, successful, and sexy as hell didn't hurt. She was everything Laura wanted in a woman and yet, she couldn't help but wonder why a woman like Sofia would be interested in someone like Laura. They were polar opposites in many ways. Her caramel skin, her curvy figure, and dark hair and brown eyes were a beacon to Laura's starved body. The way she toyed with men, knowing they would never have a bite of that apple was alluring, and counter to Laura's cautious demeanor.

"Can I tell you something?" Sofia whispered, her warm breath caressing Laura's soul.

"Please." Laura leaned into Sofia. Perhaps she'd had too much to drink at dinner.

"Please don't think me to forward, but I think you're—"

Laura felt like she was about to explode, hanging on the next words working their way out of Sofia's ruby lips.

"Drinks ladies?"

Shit.

Laura jumped and shifted back from the contact of Sofia's body. "Uhm…" She looked at Sofia expectantly. The crowd around them erupted into applause as the music ended and the dancer stood, one hand over her head and the other at her waste, her castanets silent.

They, too, broke apart and clapped.

"I think I'm good for now." Laura looked at Sofia.

"Maybe later." Sofia stood from the booth, her attention on the pair on the stage. The whole room was standing, calling for more as the guitarist stood and bowed, and then reached out for the dancer and swung her around her as she took her bow to the left and right of the stage. Sitting back down, she began to play again. This time the dancer went to men in the crowd and brought them on the dance floor, dancing with each of them. In an instant, the floor was flooded with people.

"Let's dance." It was more of a statement than a request as Sofia offered her hand.

"Here?"

Laura's gaze lit around the room as others were pulled or jetted onto the dance floor. Several groups of women danced together in small circles around the suddenly crowded dance floor, so they wouldn't exactly look out of place.

"Would you prefer some place more..." Sofia offered an enchantingly wicked grin. "Private."

Laura could feel herself melting at the sly way Sofia was flirting. Again she could only wonder, either the alcohol had silenced her inner critic or it had bolstered her courage, but either way she didn't feel like ducking the challenge Sofia had offered. Dumping her purse and wrap, she slid toward the offered hand.

That's what is was, right? A challenge. She thought. "Here's fine."

The half-cocky smile Sofia flashed her was confirmation of what Laura had wondered for a couple of days. The way Sofia had been checking Laura out. The opened innuendos. The sly way she'd been flirting with Laura since they'd met at the cigar lounge. *Subtle like a brick through a window,* Laura thought. Now she was almost sure they batted for the same team and she was suddenly all about being a team player.

Gliding past her and then pulling her close, Sofia ran her hand through her coiffed locks down her hips, and then it was hip, hip, glide. She stopped and turned around and swayed her hips to the beat of the Latin strains being pulled from the guitar. She motioned Laura over, her hands hypnotically beckoning Laura closer.

Without overthinking things, Laura swayed closer until she could see a fine sheen of sweat glistening on Sofia's top lip. Sofia's hands searched out her hips again and pulled her closer. Together they swayed seductively to the music.

Suddenly everyone around them disappeared, and Laura watched Sofia as she bit her lower lip, closed her eyes, and rolled with the music. The way Sofia bit her lip then closed her eyes as she pressed Laura tighter against her almost threw Laura off the cliff she'd been precariously dangling from. The Latin beat coursed through them as the tempo slowed and then quickened. Like a fine fabric she was draped over Sofia's body, moving when she moved. She couldn't tell where she ended and Sofia began. As the music slowed only a few couples were left on the dance floor. Laura leaned back and motioned toward the booth, but Sofia shook her head and held Laura tighter. She draped Laura's arms on her shoulders and pressed her mouth to Laura's ear.

"Can I tell you something?"

The warm breath almost sent her to her knees.

God her accent was as intoxicating as the wine. Before she could say anything, Sofia continued. "You are the most beautiful thing I've ever seen in my life, Laura."

She felt Sofia trail her tongue along her ear. She had to wrap her arms tighter around Sofia, fearing her knees might buckle from the declaration and the electricity that pulsed between them. She lost herself as she pushed against Sofia. Their breasts pressed tightly as she buried her face in the dark tresses that suddenly seemed to be falling around her face.

God, she wished she was anywhere but here. Her body was on fire and she didn't know if the bass of the music was thundering through her or if her pulse was exploding in her ears. She moved her mouth closer. She wanted to say something, but the way her body moved against Sofia's she was sure Sofia knew the language they were speaking in unison.

Laura leaned back and watch Sofia's eyes drop to Laura's mouth and then back up. Laura bit her lip. If she didn't know better, she would have expected a kiss, but Sofia must have read her mind as her mouth drew close to her ear and whispered, "Not yet."

❦❦❦❦

God, it had taken everything Sofia had to tell her "not yet," but she wanted to make sure she wasn't overstepping. The way Laura melted into her, touched her, peeled every nerve back and exposed her raw intensions. Was she being too forward? They'd only met a few days ago, but Sofia wanted Laura. No, want was too primal, she told herself. She needed to get to know this American. If someone were saying that to Sofia, she'd call bullshit. However, the reality was Sofia was taken with her, smitten her uncle would say.

The intensity with which Laura had studied her back in the booth had almost been her undoing, but the dancing...well, that was just blatant foreplay. She could feel herself vibrating with each sway of Laura's body against hers. The lights had dimmed and Sofia felt as if they were the only couple on the dance floor. She pulled Laura's hips into her, slipping together like a yin-yang diagram, Laura's pale hand in direct contrast her own tan hand clutched tight against her chest. Laura leaned back and offered a soft, knowing smile. She was suddenly putty, molding herself against Laura's lean frame.

She rested her cheek against Laura's face, the soft skin caressed against her own. She closed her eyes and imagined them someplace else, some place quiet, without the crowd pressing against them as the dance floor filled.

"God you're beautiful," she whispered without thinking. Laura's hand slipped around her waist, her fingertips gently spread and pressed against Sofia's back pressing her tighter against her.

"I don't want tonight to end."

"If I told you it doesn't have to, would that be too forward of me?"

"If I told you no, would that be bad?"

Sofia pulled Laura's hand up to her lips and twisted it, placing a kiss on her wrist. Opening it, she rested her face in the palm and then kissed it.

"You're killing me here."

"You've been killing me since last night in the cigar lounge." Sofia leaned back and smiled at Laura. A seductive, smoky gaze passed between the two.

"Me?" Laura pointed at herself. "You were the

one with the stiletto hanging off the tip of your toes, swinging it like a calling card to all the boys in the club."

"Me? No, I don't..."

"Don't what?"

Sofia lowered her eyes and then leaned her mouth against Laura's ear so only she could hear. "I don't like boys."

Laura turned her head just as she was about to place a kiss on her cheek. Landing on her lips instead, Sophia prolonged the contact. The warmth was more than inviting as Laura opened her mouth slightly, her tongue caressing Sofia's top lip. Electricity surged through her at the contact, her body wanting—no, demanding—more than just a kiss. Her hand threaded through Laura's hair and pressed her tighter.

She didn't know who broke the contact first, but suddenly the music was ending and people were leaving the dance floor. A slap on the back brought her back from the brink of no return.

"Sofia, how are you my friend?"

If she hadn't recognized the voice, she would have decked the person who'd just ruined her moment with Laura.

"Aurelia, how are you my friend?" Sofia kissed each cheek and gave her friend a hug.

Aurelia looked from Sofia to Laura and back to Sofia. A knowing glance passed between them.

"I'm good."

Aurelia looked at Laura, her eyebrows lifting. "Hello, I'm Aurelia, and please forgive my friend for her bad manners."

"Give me a minute," Sofia said, stepping around Laura.

"Just a minute?" Aurelia chided Sofia.

Sofia shot her a dismissive look. "Laura, this is one of the premier Latina conductors. In fact, she's the only female Latina conductor to head a major symphony."

Laura extended her hand. "Wow, impressive. I loved your playing tonight. Very…"

Sofia watched as Laura blushed.

"Very sexy, I think she's trying to say."

"Sofia," Laura turned away, her blush darkening.

"It's okay. I've known Sofia forever, she always gives me a bad time."

"Well, if you didn't have them fawning all over you after a performance—"

"Hi, excuse me. Could I get your autograph?" a young woman brazenly interrupted.

"Of course." Aurelia smiled and took the pen. "Do you have a piece of paper or something for me to sign?"

The woman pulled the corner of her dress to the side, exposing the top of her breast. "Here's fine."

"See," Sofia said softly to Laura. "What did I tell you? Just wait, it gets better."

"Thank you so much." The woman stepped closer and kissed Aurelia on the cheek, then whispered, "Here's my number." She slipped a piece of paper into Aurelia's jeans before she ran back to a booth of women who were squealing at the demonstration.

"See." Pulling the paper from her jeans, Aurelia opened it and waved innocently at the woman. Holding up she said, "She did have a piece of paper after all."

"Oh my god, does that happen all the time?" Laura seemed shocked at the display.

"Well, when you're one of the most eligible

lesbians in music, I'd say yes. Right my friend?" Sofia slapped Aurelia on the back.

"More than I'd like to admit to my wife." Aurelia pursed her lips together and turned away from the booth of women.

"Her wife is beautiful and very understanding. Where is she, by the way? I'm surprised she let you come out to play by yourself tonight."

Aurelia playfully backhanded Sofia's shoulder. "What, if you didn't scoop her up, I know plenty of women who were waiting in line to hook her."

"Uh-huh," Aurelia said and pointed at Sophia.

"No, not me. I knew she was into you. There is no coming between a woman when she's got someone in their sights, if you know what I mean." Sofia held her hands up. "So where is she?"

"She's visiting her parents. I have a concert this weekend, so we came a little early. Pedro found out I was in town and asked if I'd come and play."

"Well that was nice of you to do that for my godfather."

Aurelia lifted her hands and wiggled her fingers. "I like to keep them nimble. Besides, I don't get to play too often anymore. The travel takes up a lot of my time, besides I'm happy to help him. He gave me some of my first playing gigs while I went to college, so I'm happy to help fill seats." Aurelia looked at Laura and then back to Sofia. "So what have you been up to?"

"Lots of traveling for work. You know how it is." Sofia had barely remembered their pact about not talking about their lives outside of this moment. She almost spilled the beans, but caught herself quickly enough.

"No kidding?"

Sofia wondered if she should say anything about her father, but didn't want to bring it up if Aurelia didn't know. More importantly she didn't want to bring the evening down, when it had been looking so promising with Laura.

"So that's why are you in San Fran?" Aurelia looked over at Laura and smiled.

"That, and we had our yearly charity event. I'm also seeing my grandparents while I'm here."

"And?" Looking toward the blonde again, she quirked her head at Laura.

"Oh, we're just friends," Laura said quickly.

"Ah, friends. Right? Well, I have one more set to do. It was nice to meet you, Laura."

"It was nice to meet you, too." Laura shook Aurelia's hand just as another woman walked up.

"Hey, I'll leave you a set of tickets to tomorrow's concert. If you're interested." Aurelia smiled at the woman and took her pen, looking for paper as she walked away. "See you tomorrow."

"Thanks," Sofia said, shaking her head. "Poor woman, she never gets a break."

"Wow, I'm shocked women are so…"

"Forward?"

"Well, I was going to say pushy."

The lights lowered and Aurelia strummed the guitar again, giving it a quick tune.

"So, where were we?" Sofia scooped Laura closer and smiled.

Chapter Fifteen

Rum sloshed out of the glass on to the floor of the SUV as RJ tried to refill Lewis's glass. Both were sufficiently lubricated that the spat at the restaurant was long forgotten. RJ knew he had Lewis at a disadvantage when it came to drinking. His liver had sufficiently pickled long ago so that what little he'd had wouldn't make a dent in his mental acuity. In fact, he practically broke his arm patting himself on the back for the acting job he was doing with Lewis. Dumb bastard, wouldn't know what hit him later. The trip to Esteli was long enough that by the time they reached it, Lewis would be clay in his hands.

"Amigo, another cigar? These are more of my father's special reserve." He opened a box and showed the rare commodity to Lewis. "We shared them at the funeral." RJ shoved one in his hand, the end clipped and ready to be smoked. "Here let me light it."

Holding the flame to the tip, Lewis mouthed the end more than he sucked on it. "Damn thing won't light, man." Lewis weaved across the seat as they took a tight corner. "Hey can you tell the driver to slow down or you're gonna see this rum again. And, it ain't gonna be pretty."

RJ tapped his driver on the shoulder. "Slow down, eh?"

"Sure thing, jefe."

"RJ, I don't think you should get involved with

the men at the restaurant. They're working with the drug cartel. Those are the only kinds of people with large sums of money that need to be repatriated back into the system." Lewis slurred his words.

RJ scrubbed his day-old beard. Lewis wasn't as off as he thought.

"Well, I'll tell you what Lewis, if they have a big enough wad of cash, it can buy a lot of silence and protection. It's definitely something to think about. Besides, I haven't committed to anything yet."

"Well…" Lewis took a sip of his drink. "It's not like you have controlling interest in Huerta Cigars."

"Yet," RJ said, pointing his cigar at Lewis. "Yet, and you're going to help me get the company."

"Look, that will is pretty airtight. I mean your father thought of everything. Why don't you take the rum distillery, or the ice cream factory?"

"I don't want those. Let Sofia take them. I want Huerta Cigars. This is a man's business and some manflor is not going to get my birthright. Bitch."

RJ was seething. He had to get the cigar factory. It was ready cash if he went in with the other cigar businesses. He'd have more cash than he'd know what to do with, and wasn't that all that mattered? Well, that and watching Sofia lose everything. God how he hated that bitch. She'd ruined everything for him ever since they were kids. She was good at everything and he had to work his ass off for every little scrap his father had thrown his way, and now the bastard left him nothing. Abso-fucking-lutely nothing. She wasn't going to get it that easily; he wouldn't let her.

Lewis guzzled his drink and then extended his empty glass. "You gotta plan don't you?" Lewis slurred as he tried to light his cigar again.

"Hey, no sense in waiting until the will is contested, right?" RJ smiled and leaned back against the seat and stretched his legs out, crossing them at the ankles. "I do, my friend. I do." He pulled on the end of his lit cigar and slowly let the smoke ease out. "She's not going to know what the fuck hit her."

"Smart man," Lewis said, pointing to his head. "You're going to need to play this smart. RJ, I have no idea why Don Roberto didn't leave you something. For Christ's sake, you're his fucking son. Not like my fucking prick son who doesn't want anything to do with me. He thinks he's better than everyone else on his high-and-mighty doctor's horse. If it weren't for my money, he'd be a fucking nurse, emptying bedpans. Asshole."

RJ knew he had a hard-on for his son. He'd ranted and raved about it many times when they'd gone out drinking. Now he just waited for the—

"I wish I had a son like you, RJ. You fucking stood by your father, helped him build that empire, and all you get is dick? What the fuck is that about?"

"He doesn't deserve you, Lewis. He has no idea what a great man you are." RJ stoked the flames.

"Damn right he doesn't. He's a momma's boy, is what he is. Can't stop sucking from her fucking tit." Lewis scrubbed his face. "He was always soft. He couldn't get through a fucking day without some kind of 'attaboy' from his mother."

RJ prickled at the reference to the man's mother, especially since all he ever wanted was a relationship with his own mother, but he let it ride. He didn't want to spoil the mood. Besides, he'd get even with Lewis Worthington.

"You're a good man, Lewis."

"Damn right I am. I made that business. I bring in the high-dollar clients that put food on everyone's plate. Do you think they give a shit? Fuck no. I know they all look down at their noses at me. I don't give five shits. You see these shoes. They fucking cost more than…"

He mumbled something RJ couldn't hear. "Here Lewis, let's toast to good men." RJ slapped his chest. "We are good men."

Lewis raised his glass and beat his chest. "We are good men."

☙☙☙☙

"What do you think RJ has up his sleeve with that American?" Enrique asked.

Pablo steepled his fingers and rested them against his lips. He was wondering the same thing. What game was RJ playing with Lewis Worthington?

"I don't know, but I think we are going to find out."

"The American looks a little uptight if you ask me, Don Pablo," Julio said, wiping his mouth. "I don't like this, an Americano sitting in on our meeting."

A woman cackled over Don Pablo's shoulder.

Lina Huerta.

No wonder RJ made a dash for the door. Pablo knew she slept around, in fact she'd pulled some sheet duty with him on occasion, but he just figured it was to piss RJ off.

"Lina? Lina Huerta, what are you doing here?" Pablo tried to act surprised, but the way the men were looking at him made him want to laugh.

"Don Pablo? What are you doing down here?"

She looked at each of the men and smiled. "Is this a meeting of some secret club of cigar families?' She kissed each cheek and waved at the men.

"Oh, it's just our weekly rotary club meeting. You know, we meet to do charity work in Esteli."

"Seriously? I'm surprised RJ didn't ask to join."

"Oh, you—"

Pablo scraped Enrique's shin with his boot.

"Arg." He bent over in pain.

"Are you okay, Enrique?" Lina rubbed the bent over man's shoulders. "Hey, Pipa, I think Rique is sick. Maybe it's your cooking." Lina laughed and turned her attention back to Pablo.

"Anyway, as I was saying, you should invite RJ to your rotary meeting. He could use a little charitable giving."

"How is RJ? We're really sorry to hear about Don Roberto, what a shame. He was so young." Pablo snipped the end of another cigar and held two matches to the end.

"Yeah, a real loss." Acid laced Lina's words.

Pablo tried to stay away from scorned women. They were toxic, nasty, and bent on revenge. However, in Lina's case maybe he could use it in his favor. If RJ wouldn't tell him what was going on with Huerta, maybe he could flirt it out of Lina. He looked at Rique and nodded his head toward the door, then eyed the other men. If he was lucky, Rique would get the hint.

Rique wiggled his eyebrows and nodded toward the door, too. He then started talking to Julio and Armando. Nope, he wasn't that lucky.

Pissed, Pablo stood and stretched. "I need some fresh air. Would you like to join me Lina?" He offered a sickly sweet smile and his arm. Without hesitating,

Lina linked hers through Pablo's and smiled.

"Sure. Who am I to pass up good company?"

"Well, I'm the lucky one. RJ just doesn't appreciate what he has, now does he?"

"He never has." She smiled and waved at the bartender. "Tell Pipa I'll be right back. Save my drink."

The bartender waved her off, placed a napkin over her drink, and went back to wiping glassware.

The night air was cool and refreshing. Pablo pulled at the vest he had on and tried to tent his shirt, pulling it off his sweating body.

"So, Pablo, what is it you really want?" Lina lit a cigarette, the flame accenting the smooth lines of her face. Why RJ went out on Lina was beyond Pablo. She'd always been a looker, and if she hadn't been so quick to land RJ, Pablo wondered if he himself would have taken her on.

"Ah, cut to the chase. Why didn't you marry me, Lina?"

She threw her head back and offered that same cackle Pablo recognized from earlier. She rested her hand on his stomach and sobered.

"I didn't think you were the marrying type, Pablo. Besides, Esteban wouldn't have approved of a marriage between our families."

"Not true. You're Catholic, I'm Catholic. Is there anything else?"

She rubbed her fingers together.

"Ah." He nodded understanding. "So your father wanted you to marry up, not down? I get it."

"No, your father wanted you to marry up, not down."

He didn't respond. Esteban could be a bastard when it came to his legacy and Lina wasn't wrong.

"Just bad timing, nothing more, Lina." He patted the hand still resting on his stomach. Covering with his, he raised it to his lips and kissed the back.

"Ask me in a month and maybe my answer will be different," Lina said. She lifted her hand to his face and cupped his cheek.

"Things are going that bad at the estate, huh?"

"Well, let's just say I'm not sticking around till RJ gets his shit together."

"Things that bad since Daddy died?" Pablo broke out the crowbar and started to pry Lina open.

"Not bad, he's just..." She looked up at the stars and sighed. "I don't know why we ever married to be honest." She leaned against the wall and took a long drag on her cigarette.

"He's lucky to have you, Lina. You gave him heirs for the Huerta line. He should be down on his knees kissing your ass." Pablo leaned against the wall, his bulk blocking them from view. "I would be thrilled to have a few boys running around, calling me Daddy."

Lina's eyes picked up the reflection of the overhead light and sparkled when she looked at him. "Well, yesterday has happened and I can't go back and change anything."

"Is that why RJ looks like he could kill right now. You're leaving him?"

Lina narrowed her eyes and took all of Pablo in, assessing him. He knew she was doing the friend or foe math, deciding if she should talk or not. Why were some women so easy?

"Tell me, who is the American I saw RJ with today?"

Lina's knitted her brow and searched his face. "How do you know about the American? He's here to help RJ with something, that's all I know."

"What kind of help?"

She shrugged.

"You can tell me. Maybe I can help him before that American leads him down the wrong path. We wouldn't want RJ to compromise his inheritance with a stupid American, would we?"

"Oh, I don't think RJ needs any help finding the wrong path. He's already done that."

"What do you mean?"

"You didn't know about Estrella? I thought everyone knew about that little bitch."

"You mean that woman he's been seeing? Doesn't she work for Roberto?"

"Well, she did. Now that the old bastard is dead, I doubt Sofia will keep her on. I suspect she's going to run things her way and since Sofia can't stand Estrella." Lina ran her finger across her throat.

"Surely, you're not implying that Sofia would kill someone." Pablo quirked his smile.

"What? No, I just mean that now that Don Roberto is gone, things are going to change around the estate."

"Are you one of those changes?"

"Well, let's just say I've had my own place for a while now. The children will get an inheritance and that will take care of us for a while."

Pablo was even more confused the longer Lina kept flapping her lips. If he pumped her any more he might want to be on top of her, so she didn't get suspicious.

"Can I buy you another drink, inside?" He waved his arm wide, ushering her toward the door.

"I already have one, but when I finish that one

maybe you can buy me a bottle and we can talk about your rotary club more."

"Lead the way, lead the way." He held the door open and watched her sway her ass, sure she was trying to entice him. He searched the street to see if anyone had seen them outside.

He couldn't see anyone.

Now, if he could get Lina to spill her guts maybe he could connect the dots on why he felt something wasn't quite right at the Huerta estate.

Chapter Sixteen

They picked up where the music had left them, their bodies melded to each other. Swaying to the strum of the guitar only added fuel to the raging fire she was feeling. Laura couldn't help herself as she laid her head against Sofia's shoulder. Everything about the night felt right. It felt as if this was where she was meant to be, held by Sofia. Sofia ran her fingers through her hair, the tips gently massaging her scalp. Locking them in the tresses, Sofia gently pulled her head back and softly placed a kiss on her lips. Her eyes were smoldering as she looked at Laura. They traveled down her body and then back to what she wanted.

Another kiss.

Laura felt as if electricity was traveling between them. Ungrounded, they continued to combust as Sofia touched her face, ran her hand down the curve of her hip, and kissed her again, setting her body on fire. They were dancing all right, the dance of lovers.

Laura squeezed her legs together, the sensation, the tingle there almost unbearable. It had been months or perhaps a year since she'd been with a woman, let alone one with the passion that Sofia exuded. She'd kept her love life on a short leash, not wanting to invest the time and energy it took to sustain a relationship. She wasn't built for a one-night stand, either. Her heart often led when her mind should have taken over. She could segment her life easy enough: work, gym, chores,

ne cheek was her reward. "See, here it is." The valet
pened the passenger door for Laura, who was never
ɔ glad for heated seats as she relaxed into the soft
ather.

"Thank you."

"My pleasure, miss. Have a great evening."

"Thank you, I hope so." Laura heard Sofia say as
ne shut the door. "Do you mind if we make a quick
op on the way to the restaurant?"

"No, not at all."

"Great."

Laura noticed the line at the front of the tapas
staurant. "Wow, people are waiting to get inside."

"Aurelia is popular, but after her they'll play
atin music, so it's a win-win for Pedro."

"Well, I'm sorry we have to miss it then," Laura
ɔsently said.

As the Uber driver coasted the car to a stop at the
ght, Sofia offered, "We can go back if you want."

Laura smiled and touched Sofia's hand
·assuringly. "No, it's fine. Pancakes suddenly sound
·ally good."

"Pancakes with big fat blueberries."

"Oh my god, I love blueberry pancakes."

"Karma."

"Do you believe in that?"

"Sometimes."

"Don't you think people believe in karma when it
ιits them?" Laura said, shifting in her seat so she was
cing Sofia.

"What do you mean?"

"Well, I've represented a client or two who said
at when things didn't go in their favor. They'd say
mething like, 'Oh, I hope I'm there when karma hits

her place in Napa, and a few outings with fi
enough to fill the voids a relationship or
Looking at Sofia now, she felt the starting of
cleaving itself.

"Do you like brunch?" Sofia whispere

Surprised at the statement, she leane
looked at Sofia. "I do."

"What else do you like?"

"Hmm, long walks on the beach, suns
breath, sleeping in on the weekends." Laur;
smile. "Sounds like one of the online datin
huh?"

"No, I think it's cute. Hey, I know this
that doesn't open until eleven p.m. and serve;
until ten a.m. All this dancing is making me

"Really?"

"What, you don't think I'm hungry? I
this figure by starving myself to death." Sofi
back and bowed. "We have a saying, meat
man, or in this case woman, and bone is for t

"You're not fat."

"Well…"

Sofia pulled her closer and ran her ha
Laura's back. "Careful, I bite when I'm hungr

"Well, then we better find you some pai

Laura felt herself twirled around on tl
floor and then Sofia started for the stairs. Aurel
at them as they passed the stage, winking at
Sofia blew her a kiss. Laura hugged herself as t
from dancing was trapped against her body,
chilling her instantly. On cue, Sofia stepped be
and wrapped her arms around her shoulders.

"It'll only be a minute before the car ge
Laura turned her head trying to see Sofia. A

them' or 'Karma's a bitch and I hope karma makes them hers.' Stuff like that."

"Hmm, guess I've never thought about it that way, I guess."

Laura absently ran her finger over the vein in Sofia's hand resting on the seat between them. Mesmerized by her long, lean fingers, she slid down to the painted nail and was suddenly grabbed by Sofia's hand. Laura jumped.

"Oops, we're here."

Laura recognized The Banker Building.

"Did you forget something at the cigar lounge?" she asked, confused as the valet opened the car door.

"Sorta. Come on, let's change into something comfortable."

"Here?"

Sofia led Laura to the elevator, taking out her titanium card. "I have a condo here." Sliding the titanium card into the slot, she hit penthouse floor and caught Laura's reflection in the polished brass.

"You mean penthouse, don't you?"

"It's just a place to lay my head when I'm in town. It's no big deal, really." Sofia turned and pulled Laura close as the elevator started to fill, even at the late hour. Snuggling her nose in Laura's hair, she pulled at a pin and marveled as it tumbled down. "You look beautiful."

Laura swiped her clutch as Sofia's hand rested at her waist. "Stop, people will see," she whispered, then giggled.

"Who cares? We'll never see these people again."

As groups of people got of the elevator, Sofia moved back against the wall and watched Laura as she looked sideways at the older couple next to them. A blush crawled up her neck.

"I'm sorry, that was rude of me. I was just—"

"Don't make it worse by apologizing." Laura turned toward Sofia, her gaze more lustful that embarrassed. "I'm just not used to PDA," she said as the last couple got off, tsking as they left.

"I didn't mean…I meant…I just was lost in the moment from the restaurant, that's all."

Before either woman could say anything else the doors opened to the penthouse floor.

≈≈≈≈≈

Laura stood in the entryway, taking in the vast, ten-foot lacquered door. She felt small in comparison as Sofia waved the card in front the key mechanism.

"Lights." Sofia pulled off her wrap and tossed it onto the table with her keys and clutch.

"Dim, one, two," she said as the lights dimmed slightly.

Laura still stood just inside the door admiring the modest décor. The white plush pile of the carpet looked manicured, the way it bounced back as Sofia walked across it. She leaned against the cream couch as she pulled at one shoe and then the other.

"Please, make yourself at home."

Just like in the cigar lounge, black travertine tile filled the entryway, then broke for the white carpet. Accent lights lit colorful paintings along the wall, and over the broken glass fireplace a large tropical landscape filled the vast expanse. But that's where the similarities ended. White and glass were the theme and nothing looked out of place. It was something someone would see featured in a home magazine.

"Oh, come on. Take your shoes off and relax. I'll give you the nickel tour in a minute." Sofia smiled, pulling Laura into the living room. "Can I get you something to drink?"

"Water," was all Laura could say.

"Sit. I'll bring you some. Sure you don't want anything else?" Sofia laughed as Laura stood still looking around. "Sure I can't bring you something stronger? Wine maybe?"

Laura watched Sofia disappear and heard the clinking of ice in glasses.

"No, water's good for me."

"Okay."

Laura walked to the bank of windows that looked out over San Francisco. She couldn't see much with the fog obscuring most of the view, but looking down she could see taxis, a few pedestrians, and a bus meandering as if it didn't have anywhere to be fast. Off in the distance she could see one of the highways with its clogged arteries, cars still lined up to get out of town. On a clear day, she was sure the view alone was worth the price of admission.

"It's beautiful, isn't it?" Sofia set a tray with a pitcher of water and glasses on the coffee table. Tucked under her arms were clothing and a pair of sneakers. "I brought something for you to change into. I don't know about you, but my shoes were killing me."

Without thinking, Laura wiggled her toes that were screaming to be let out of their tight confines. Laura sat and slipped off her shoes, digging her toes into the thick pile.

"God, that feels good." She leaned back against the couch and finally sighed.

"I know, right? I hate dressing up sometimes. I

mean, I like to play dress-up for a special occasion, like dinner with someone special or the holidays, but I hate standing on my feet all night. I wonder if men complain when they have to get dressed up?" Sofia flung herself on the couch and curled her legs under her.

"My brother loves to dress up. I think he gets it from our parents. We always had to dress for dinner or my father wouldn't let us come to the table."

"Really? I could see that. He looked all James Bond tonight with his tux and cuff links."

"You noticed?"

"Oh, yes. And when he took me down to see his car. Well, you can't get more macho than that little sports car with the big engine."

Sofia's eyes twinkled as she talked, sucking Laura in even more. The only thing missing was the sound of a fishing reel and a net scooping her up as it wound Laura in. Wanting to change the subject, she motioned to the clothes Sofia had set on the couch between them.

"Are those for me?"

Patting the pile, Sofia smiled. "I hope you don't mind." She held up the sweatpants with a logo of the San Francisco Golden Gate Bridge on it, and peeked around them. "I swear I must have five of these and the fleece jacket, too. Every time I go and take friends sightseeing I'm in shorts and a T-shirt, and then the weather changes so I have to get something warm. I think the vendors have a deal with the fog makers here in San Fran. They have these all over the place. Have you noticed?"

"I know what you mean. I have a couple in my car, just in case. I think that's why I like my place in Napa so much. It's so much warmer there and the sun is always on."

They sat on the couch staring at each other, neither saying anything. Laura could feel herself melting into the soft sofa. If she wasn't careful she could fall asleep in its warm cocoon-like grip.

Setting her glass on the tray, she said, "Still feel like pancakes?"

"Of course." Sofia jumped up and reached for Laura's hand. "Here let me show you around and I'll show you where you can change." Laura was pulled along toward the dining room, next to the bank of windows. "This is the dining room. The table seats eight and this is the kitchen. I love to cook, but never seem to have time when I'm in the city. But I do use it when I have friends over and..." Popping out into the hallway Sofia continued. "This is my office, again, I don't use it a whole lot. And this is the spare bedroom and this..." Sofia stopped at a set of double doors, pushing them open.

The room was almost as big as the living room and dining room combined. "This is my sanctuary." Pointing to another set of double doors, she said, "That's my closet, small I'm sure compared to yours, and across over there is my bathroom. Come let me show it to you."

The bedroom was bathed in soft warm cream tones with a huge bed in the center. Behind it were windows that stretched from floor to the ten-foot ceilings. Laura couldn't keep her eyes off the bed. Suddenly a pang of jealousy poked at her as she wondered how many women might have shared the space with Sofia. Now why was she thinking that? God, she needed to get out of there, quick.

"Here, let me show you the bathroom."

Laura felt herself being pulled along as she still

eyed the king-size bed.

"I have a huge bathtub. I love baths. Are you a shower or bath girl?"

"Ah, bath. I love a hot bath." For some reason she was embarrassed to admit it as she looked at the tub built for two.

"I have a sauna over here. It has a setting for essential oils that get mixed with the steam. I love the way my skins feels after a sauna." Sofia closed her eyes and ran her hands over her bare arms and sighed. "It's all voice activated, and/or I can set it to go on at a certain time and when I get home it's ready. Look inside. It's huge."

Laura peeked through the glass door. The lights went on and then dimmed.

"Go inside, you can smell eucalyptus, and if you don't like that smell you can have orange or tea tree or a mixture of scents and when I want more steam, I just take that ladle in the bucket and pour water on the rocks. It's amazing."

"Wow, it's beautiful. Was this already built like this or did you design it?"

"Oh, I just remodeled the bedroom and the bathroom. I took out an extra bedroom to make the bathroom bigger."

"Your condo is amazing."

"Do you like it?"

Laura needed some air. If she stayed this close to Sofia she wasn't sure what she was going to do. She was on sensory overload and she needed a diversion.

"Wow, I'm suddenly starving. We should get changed and get down to the restaurant before it gets too crowded. Don't you think?" Pointing to the clock on the wall, Laura added, "Pretty soon all the drunk clubbers are going to be looking for something to eat."

"Oh, right. That restaurant is so small it fills quick." Sofia pulled Laura along and stopped at the spare bedroom. "Here, you can get changed in here. If something is too big let me know and I'll see if I have something smaller."

"I'm sure it will be fine."

"Well, let me get those clothes and you can get changed." Sofia said, closing the door behind her.

Laura plopped on the bed and sighed. If Sofia touched her one more time she was going to come unglued and she couldn't explain why, she just wanted to feel her hands all over her body. The dancing had been foreplay and that was putting it mildly. The kisses, the way they melded together, had been magical. Ever since last night in the cigar lounge, all Laura could think about was Sofia. The way her lips moved when she talked. That sexy accent drove her to the brink of succumbing to seduction, and Laura was sure Sofia knew it. If she didn't, god help her. No wonder her brother was hot for her. Now she knew what men felt like when a woman's pheromones were released. She was practically overdosing on them tonight.

A light tap on the door jerked her upright. Sofia peeked her head around the corner, the clothes in her outstretched hand. "Let me know if these don't fit. I'll be out in the living room."

Grabbing for the garments, she felt the electricity between them singe her as she took the clothes. God, was she going to make it through the evening? Maybe she should make an excuse and get home before she combusted.

"Thanks." She tossed them on the bed and slipped her wrap off. She reached back to the top of the dress and yanked on the zipper.

It didn't give.

Shit.

Trying again, she tugged and it still didn't move. She'd pull the dress over her head, but it was so tight she was afraid she'd rip it. Great, now what was she going do to?

Shit, shit, shit.

A few more minutes of trying to extricate herself from the form-fitting dress didn't yield any success. A light tap at the door stopped her dead.

"Are you okay in there?"

"Uhm, yeah. This is kind of embarrassing, but I can't seem to get my zipper down."

"Oh, ah…would you like to see if I can get it?"

What could possibility be the harm in that? Laura asked herself. Laura walked to the door and opened it a bit. "Sure, would you mind?"

"Let me try. This happens to me all the time. You know sometime the fabric gets caught in the zipper and it gets…" Sofia bent down to get a closer look. "Come with me, I have some tweezers in my bedroom—"

Laura panicked. "No, that's okay. I'll just rip it."

"What, no, no, I can get it. I would hate to see you rip your beautiful dress."

"Oh, this old thing."

Sofia offered a smug look. "I saw 'this old thing' at that little boutique in the mall, so it's not an old dress. Besides, I'm sure I can get it unstuck. Come with me." She grabbed Laura's hands and dragged her to her bedroom. Setting her on the bed, she said, "Stay right there while I get my kit."

"Kit?"

"Sewing kit. If I can't get it with the tweezers, I

have a seam ripper that we can take the zipper apart with and then you can just take it to a seamstress to have them reattach it."

"But—"

"It's fine. Don't worry. It happens to me all the time. That's why I have a sewing kit. With as much as I travel, I have to make repairs on the fly. Relax. We'll be eating blueberry pancakes in no time."

Suddenly, Sofia was behind Laura on the bed straddling her from behind. "Here, can you hold this?" She handed Laura a small box with needles, thread, scissors, and other sewing items. "Can you pull your hair to the side please? I don't want to get it caught in the zipper or accidently pull it when I unzip you."

"Can you see what the problem is?" Laura's body tensed as Sofia's warm breath touched her back.

"Hmm, I see what the problem is, your slip is caught in the teeth of the zipper. Damn, let me think about this."

Sofia's warm hands spread out on each side of Laura's back, sending a chill through her. The fabric of her dress was pulled taunt and then released, the zipper was worked back and forth, and the fabric finally released its binding around her body.

"There, I think I have it. No, wait...it's..." Sofia tugged again and then it all released and fell down around her hips in one slow motion. A soft kiss was planted between her shoulder blades and Sofia's fingertips trailed down Laura's spine. A hair pin was pulled, releasing the few strands that had been swept up in her hairdo and she heard Sofia release a soft moan as she planted another kiss behind Laura's ear.

"Oh," Laura sighed at the contact.

Chapter Seventeen

RJ stood at the window, half-naked and watching one of the sorting buildings start to smoke. He'd started the small fire under a pallet of tobacco in the sorting room to give himself plenty of time to get back to the house and get undressed. No one would suspect it was him if they had to come and find him at the house. Soon enough the old building would be fully engulfed and burning like a five-alarm fire. There weren't any sprinklers in the old room, just pallets of tobacco, wooden tables, stools, and an old radio that the workers listened to as they sorted. It didn't hurt that they were Sofia's bundles, either.

He didn't want to torch perfectly good tobacco for his own cigars, but burning up Sofia's product was just good business sense. It would take her a full season to recover by the time the next grow of tobacco had been brought to the factory. The fields were heavy with tobacco this year. God had been good to them with rain, few insects, and lots of sunshine. Huerta would see a banner year, and if he was lucky he'd sell what he didn't need to those gringos who always begged for a few bales for their own little lines of cigar. Sure, he'd share the wealth, just not with his sister.

Flames started to lick the sides of the building as RJ heard men yelling. A frantic knock on his door practically beat it down.

In his best sleep-laden voice, he yelled, "What?"

"Señor Huerta, the barn is on fire. Come quickly," Julian's frantic voice yelled through the door.

"What?"

"Señor, the barn. It's on fire."

RJ swung the door wide and looked at Julian. He must have been convincing, because Julian stepped back away from him. RJ scrubbed his head and then his face as if he was trying to wake himself up. "The barn..." Julian pointed toward the factory. "It's on fire. Come quickly."

"Call the men and get the water started on the fire. I'll get changed and be down."

"Si, señor. Hurry, I'll call Señorita Huerta."

"No," RJ yelled. "You just take care the fire and make sure it doesn't spread to any of the other buildings. If it does, I'll fire your ass. Understand me?"

"Yes, yes, señor. Hurry." Julian ran past his grandmother. "Señora Huerta,"

"What is going on, Beto? I smell smoke."

"It's the sorting barn, Grandmother. It's on fire."

"Oh, my god. Hurry, you can't let your father's legacy burn up. You must save it, hurry, mijo." His grandmother pushed him toward the door.

"Grandmother, let me get dressed." He pointed down to his boxers. "You don't want everyone to see me like this do you?"

"No, of course not. Hurry and get dressed. I'll call Sofia and tell her the bad news."

He grabbed his grandmother's arm and stopped her. "Abuelita..." He rarely called her that anymore. It was his pet name for her growing up. She smiled up at him as she heard the term of endearment. "I'll call her. We don't know how bad it is and no use in worrying her if we don't have to, right? Besides, she's at father's charity tonight. We can call her after the smoke clears."

With the time difference Sofia would be at the cigar lounge. Knowing her, she would drop everything and rush home. Well, there wasn't much she could do about the fire now, so why bother her? He would tell her he didn't want to bring her bad news at something so important as the event that would now be held in his honor. Besides, he still needed more time to finish some things on his end before she got home.

"Okay, but you should get down there, honey. The men are going to need someone to take charge and tell them what to do." His grandmother patted his hand still holding her arm.

Now it was his turn to smile. It was the first time since all this mess started that she referred to him as a boss at Huerta.

"Go back to bed and I'll let you know when the fire is put out. It might not be until morning, I have to assess the damages, makes some calls to our insurance agent, and get an idea of how bad this is going to hurt us. So try not to worry, Abuelita. I'll take care of everything," he said, kissing her forehead like a child.

"Hurry, RJ,"

"I will, Abuelita. Now go. I need to get dressed." He turned and shut the door behind him. Standing at the window, he watched as the flames grew higher. He wasn't going to rush out there and save his sister's tobacco, that would defeat the whole purpose of the fire. He poured himself a drink and swirled the glass, watching the amber liquid ripple. No, he wasn't going to rush at all.

⁂

Standing in the center of the smoldering ash, RJ

wanted to cut a big grin loose, but all eyes were on him at the moment. What was left of the sorting barn was a few eight-by-eight posts, only a few up to RJ's chin left standing. The corrugated tin of the building, peeled back from the intense heat, was still attached to a few of the posts. The windows, shattered to pour water on the flames, and the rest of the tin lay in piles around the scorched building.

RJ had a handkerchief tied around his face. Black soot conveniently covered any exposed skin, but his clothing for all intents and purposes remained untouched with the exception of a black stain that ran down each thigh, Both the same width and darkness. Clearly, he'd added the ash himself so it looked as if he'd been at the fire for a while. In truth, he'd stood back and watched it all go up in flames, at least what was left when he arrived.

"Julian, what the hell happened here?" RJ barked at the man.

"Señor RJ, we tried. The men they came as quick as they could. We put water everywhere, but by the time we all got here, it was…poof," Julian said, his hands exploding up. "It was already too late. I'm sorry, Señor Huerta."

RJ kicked at the ash in mocked disgust. "How much did we lose?"

Julian shrugged. "Not much, really. It was mostly Señorita Sofia's tobacco for her new line." Julian turned in a circle and pointed to the dark patches on the cement floor. "There, there, and all of that over there was her tobacco." Remnants of the colored ribbons that bound the leaves together when they were drying looked like bits of confetti strewn across the floor, mixed in with the fragments of burnt legs of tables and chairs.

"Christ, this is a disaster," RJ said, kicking at the ash again.

"I know. I don't know what Señorita Sofia is going to say." Julian pulled off his hat and wiped his forehead. "She's gonna be so mad."

"Well, it's done. There isn't anything to say. She's coming home soon so I'll be the one to break it to her."

"RJ, what the hell happened here?" Lewis stood at the edge of the building looking like he'd been hit by a bus.

"I see you combed your hair, Lewis." RJ slapped him on the back.

"Well, I heard the commotion so I came down to see what all the lights and sirens were for. What happened?"

"One of the sorting barns burned down." RJ pointed to the men raking the smoldering ash.

"No shit. How bad is this going to set Huerta back?" Lewis rubbed at the bristle on his chin and eyed RJ.

"It won't be bad. It was mostly Sofia's tobacco for her new line of cigars she was working on."

"No shit?" Lewis leaned over toward RJ and whispered, "Gee, I wonder how that happened."

"It happens all the time, my friend. This is tobacco and fires aren't new to this business. When they do, you just hope you aren't in the factory when it catches fire." RJ slapped Lewis on the back again, hoping his friend picked up on the veiled threat.

"Christ, Sofia is going to go ballistic."

"That she will, my friend, that she will. But lucky enough for me, I was in the house when it started. I have the foreman and my grandmother who saw me there. Give me a minute, I want to talk to the fire chief and see if he knows what started it."

RJ walked away and left Lewis staring at the pile
of his sister's lost dreams.

"Chief, hold on. Do you have any idea what
started the fire?"

Chapter Eighteen

Sofia sat behind Laura, her hands trembling as she ran her fingers tips down Laura's spine. Leaning in, she kissed her neck again, this time her teeth grazing the muscle that flexed at the touch.

"I wish I could say I'm sorry, but…" Sofia pulled Laura into her and rested her chin on Laura's shoulder. "I'm about to come unglued." Wrapping her arms around Laura, she was surprised when Laura leaned her head back and rested it on her shoulder. Her eyes were closed, her chest rising and lowering as if she'd been in a race. Sofia rubbed her cheek against Laura's and gently bit at her jawline. Moving lower, she grazed Laura's neck with her lips, Laura's heart racing under her touch.

Sofia didn't dare move. Too afraid that Laura might bolt, she held her, waiting for her to say something, anything. When Laura grabbed her hand and pressed it between her legs, she thought she might explode. Laura guided her hand between her panties and her body, rubbing Sofia's fingers gently against her coarse wetness. The bristle against her hand was soft and tantalizing. Sofia tried to control herself, taking measured strokes, not wanting the moment to climax too quickly. Without asking, Sofia unsnapped Laura's bra and let it fall down her arms. Her left hand cupped Laura's breast, marveling at the lack of heft, but still just enough to squeeze. Working the nipple between her finger and thumb, Sofia gently pulled as she stroked Laura. Laura pushed one of Sofia's fingers inside her and leaned back more, spreading her legs.

Christ, Sofia was about to come as she looked down Laura's lean body, a breast in one hand and the other buried between Laura's legs. The bra hung between Laura's arms like a suspension bridge waiting to be climbed. It was a memory she'd never part with no matter what happened. Laura pumped on Sofia's hand, her hips grinding as Laura pushed Sofia's hand harder against her. Laura gasped, leaned back harder against Sofia, clenched her jaw, and hissed as she climaxed.

"Oh fuck, fuck." Laura jerked as her body spasmed with each flick across her hard clit. Reaching up, she grabbed Sofia's head and turned it toward hers, kissing her hard. Their tongues battled for dominance, but there weren't any winners or losers in this battle, only lovers.

Twisting around, Laura pushed Sofia back against the bed and straddled her. Her dress pushed down to her hips, her bra tossed to the side, she rested her hands on each side of Sofia's head. Her eyes were smoldering, like something behind them was on fire.

"I'm hungry," Laura whispered as she lowered herself to Sofia's ears, her breast brushing against Sofia's T-shirt.

Sofia's voice cracked as she answered. "We can go get those blueberry pancakes now if you want."

"Uh-huh." Laura flicked Sofia's ear with her tongue. Sofia's skin prickled at the touch, goose bumps popping up all over her body.

Laura sat back on Sofia's hips and grabbed her right hand. Lifting it to her mouth, she pulled one finger to her lips and then flicked it with her tongue, a long swipe from the web of her hand to the tip, and then she slipped it into her mouth, working it back and forth.

"Christ." Sofia squirmed under Laura.

Sofia could feel Laura's tongue work the tip of her finger as she slipped another into her mouth. It sent a jolt right to her clit.

"You're killing me here."

"Oh, now you know how it feels. The way you were working me on the dance floor tonight, I thought I might come right then and there. But no, you…" She pulled the fingers into her mouth and worked them back and forth over her tongue. "You're such a tease." Laura took the wet fingers and moved them around her nipple, wetting the areola.

Sofia was almost there, one more touch and she'd be sent careening over the edge. And Laura did just that when she started grinding her hips against Sofia's sweats.

Grabbing Laura, she pulled her hard against her pubic bone, grinding against what she'd already had. She knew Laura was wet, primed, and if she was lucky, ready to come again. Arching against Laura, Sofia jerked back and forth as she climaxed against Laura.

"That's it, come for me."

No one had talked to her during sex. She couldn't focus when they did, but suddenly she was vibrating with each word Laura whispered in her ear. Pushing against Laura, she created just the right amount of pressure to climax again.

"Ay, dios mio," Sofia said, pulling Laura tight against her as she rode out her orgasm.

Chapter Nineteen

Word spread quickly around Esteli. Don Pablo came that morning to assess the damage and talk to RJ. Fire was every cigar maker's fear, and when it hit, it usually wiped out the whole section of the business. Fermenting rooms were warehoused in a different location than the drying and sorting rooms. Then there was the whole operation of making the cigars. While men did most of the heavy lifting, women did the sorting, assuming they could pass the mandatory eye test for color, first. They also did most of the rolling, wrapping, and labeling of the cigars—at least at Huerta Cigars.

RJ stood next to Don Pablo, his arms crossed and his stance wide. He wanted to look like the new Don at Huerta as they surveyed the damage. He had already brought in a few men to do the cleanup. The insurance agent had been by and taken pictures. It was perfunctory, since the fire department wasn't going to investigate. RJ had seen to that matter.

"Damn, RJ, this is my worst nightmare. You know?" Don Pablo kicked at a burnt two-by-four and then walked around the cement slab. "Do they know how it started?"

"No, they have no idea. Could have been the wiring, you know how things are around here. Workers are constantly overloading the outlets with their damn cell phone chargers and radios." RJ followed him around like a puppy dog. "Hell, just the other day I caught one of the men plugging in one of those damn vapor cigarettes."

"Why do they smoke that shit when they have cigars?" Don Pablo waved his hand at RJ "I'll never understand these young guys. Shit, if my old man had let me I would have smoked cigars as soon as I could walk. That's all I wanted to do when I was their age. Christ. What did you tell Sofia?"

"She doesn't know yet. I'll tell her when she gets back. She's out selling cigars, making me some money," RJ said, rubbing his fingers together. "Besides, what's she going to do, huh? She can't fix this."

"Hmm, how many pallets did you lose?"

"Me?" RJ pointed to himself. "None, it was all tobacco for Sofia's line of cigars."

"Oh, shit. She's going to be pissed. You better be ready for a shit storm when she finds out."

RJ smiled and slapped Don Pablo on the back as he wiped his face. "What the fuck is she going to do, my friend? What's done is done. We have fields of top tobacco out there. If she's lucky, I'll let her have a few bales to make up for the loss. But she won't be bringing out that new cigar she was hoping to release at the IPCPR in Vegas this year. Huerta comes first."

The International Premium Cigar and Pipe Retailers Association conference, IPCPR was the biggest event for cigar manufacturers, and all the houses released their premium lines at the weekend event. It was reserved for the cigar vendors, reps, and cigars shops. Everything at the event was top-shelf, and it was one of RJ's favorite events to go to. He usually hooked up with a female rep or two during the conference and wrung hands with the heavyweights in the industry. Everyone who was anyone in the tobacco industry was there, and if you were lucky enough to score an invite to a VIP event, you didn't turn it down. It was considered bad manners to decline an invitation because they were usually reserved for the heavy hitters. Most houses had grand dinners, quality liquor, and some of the best entertainment on the Strip at their VIP events. Huerta did its own version of the VIP dinner, but his father had limited it to those cigar lounges that carried their line and managed the Huerta cigar lounges. Don Roberto didn't care much for the flashy clothes, the big jewelry, and ladies in skin-tight dresses, but he wasn't dumb, either. He just knew where to spend his money. Now that RJ would be running the show, he'd show up and show off. It was going to be first class all the way.

"Be careful, RJ, she isn't going to be taking this laying down. I know your sister; she's a hellcat who doesn't take no for an answer."

"Hmm."

"Well, I have to go and check on my own house. I have some new stuff coming out and I want to make sure this..." He swirled his fingers around. "Doesn't happen to me. I'm going to go check my wiring and make sure my foreman looks in every nook and cranny."

Yep, fire scared all the families. With few building codes, lots of the cigar factories just added on rooms when then needed more space. At least it wasn't like the old days when they would just hang the tobacco out on sticks and let it dry. Today, they had big wheels in the fermentation rooms that they tied the tobacco to so it could be rotated and dried out evenly. Big windows in the factories let light and the air into the building. Too much moisture and it screwed with the tobacco; not enough and it was brittle. It was a balancing act that took place in buildings that were often old school at best. The bigger factories were quicker to modernize. Don Roberto had been receptive to adopting new technology, but little had changed in the decades of cigar manufacturing. It was still all done by hand—at least the best cigars were still hand-rolled.

"Take care, Don Pablo, and thanks for stopping by."

"Hey, I have to make sure we are all still in business. Yes?" Don Pablo pulled RJ in close as he shook his hand. "I'm still waiting for an answer, RJ. Don't disappoint me." His voice was just as firm as his handshake.

"I'm just making sure everything is perfect, Don Pablo. Trust me, everything is going to work out just fine."

"That's what I want to hear. Let me know if you need some help rebuilding. I can send some of my men over to help."

"Thanks, I'll remember that."

RJ watched Don Pablo leverage himself into the back of his black Escalade. Waving, he waited until he was out of the parking lot before cursing. "Fucking prick, don't threaten me."

❧❧❧❧

Laura rubbed her nose, thinking it was itchy. Instead, she opened her eyes to find Sofia brushing it with the petals of a daisy. Smiling, she reached for the flower, but it quickly disappeared as Sofia jumped off the bed.

"Good morning, sleepy head."

"Oh my god, what is that smell?"

"Blueberry pancakes." Sofia walked to the bed with pancakes hanging off a fork. "Since we didn't exactly make it to the diner, I thought I'd order in and have them deliver before they closed." She waved them under Laura's nose and then popped one off the fork into her mouth. "Here," she said around the pancake she was chewing. "I have everything on the balcony. It's sunny out and we don't get to say that too often in the morning in San Francisco."

Laura swung the blankets off and immediately pulled them back over herself when she realized she was naked.

"What's wrong?" Sofia reached for Laura's hand.

"I...ah...need some clothes. I don't have anything on."

"Now you're shy?" Sofia sauntered over to the bed and straddled Laura's body. The smoldering look she gave Laura went right to her head. "You weren't so shy last night."

"Well, last night was—"

"Yes," Sofia said, leaning down and nibbling her earlobe.

"Last night." Laura grabbed Sofia and pulled her down on top of her. Turning her head away, she whispered. "Can I tell you something?" she said as sexy as she could muster.

"Sure."

"I need to brush my teeth and you're lying on my bladder." She spun Sofia on her back, wrapping her in the blankets as she jetted for the bathroom door. Closing it behind her, she heard Sofia grumbling, trying to extricate herself from the pile of linen.

"Toothbrushes are on the bottom drawer, right-hand side. I'll meet you on the balcony."

"'Kay." Laura couldn't believe she was standing in Sofia's bathroom, naked. Well, she could believe it, but she…well, she just needed to come to terms with the fact that she'd slept with a woman for the first time in years.

Years?

"Has it really been years?" she said to herself in the mirror. Her body ached in places that hadn't seen sun in, yep, years. It was a good, comfortable ache though. Closing her eyes, she replayed parts of the night and felt her face heat. Oh god, she'd been so… bad. Smiling, she ran her fingers over her bruised lips and thought about all the places she'd kissed last night. Oh, she was in trouble. Finding the toothbrush she made quick work of her morning routine, just as her stomach grumbled. She was starving.

Opening the bathroom door, she peeked out to make sure Sofia wasn't lying in wait for her. Not that it would be a bad thing if she was, but she needed time to process what had just happened. She had the sensation of her world off its axis at the moment and didn't know how she felt about it. It wasn't that she didn't like what had happened, it just made hell for her well-ordered world. What if Sofia was only into one-night stands? It wasn't like she lived in the US, right? Did they talk about that? Hell, what did they pillow talk about?

"Okay, stop with all the self-talk. It was great, it was fun, and that's all it was, fun," She said as she tied the sweats. Yawning and stretching, she wandered down the hall looking for breakfast, secure in the knowledge that she was all right with what happened. Nothing more was needed. Except maybe pancakes.

※ ※ ※ ※

Sofia smiled as Laura rounded the corner, her hair still a mess. If she had her way, it would stay that way for the rest of the day.

"Trying out a new hairdo?" Sofia stood and kissed Laura, motioning for her to sit down. "I hope you like honeydew and bananas." Sofia poured coffee for Laura.

"Everything looks fabulous."

"Fabulous, really? I'll have to do this more often then. I can see you're easy to please." Sofia smiled at Laura's face as she flinched from the hot coffee. "It's hot."

"I do that all the time. I know it's hot, but I still take a big swig and burn my tongue." Laura reached for her water glass and dipped her tongue in it.

"That could be a very serious injury for a lesbian."

Laura gave Sofia a stunned look. That was the first time either of them had acknowledged the obvious.

"Don't look so surprised. Yes, I'm a lesbian. I'm assuming you are, too. Or are you one of those straight women who has always wanted to experiment?" Sofia wagged her eyebrows at Laura and took a bite of her pancakes.

"Hmm, let me think. How many drinks did I have last night? Two? Isn't that how the saying goes."

In unison they both said, "Two drinks away then you're gay."

"Or something like that," Laura said, giggling.

"So?" Sofia asked.

"So?"

"Are you, or aren't you?"

Coyly, Laura picked up her coffee cup, smiled, and said, "I'm sorry you have to ask. Clearly I didn't do a good enough job last night of showing you."

"Oh, you showed me things I never knew existed."

"Really?" Laura said, surprised.

"Yes, would you like to see me do them to you? I mean for purely re-edification purposes of course."

"I'll take it under advisement." Laura leaned back and cradled her coffee, suddenly preferring to watch Sofia eat and blush under the scrutiny.

"Eat. You'll need your energy for later. Unless of course you have an appointment."

Laura pretended to search around the room for an answer. "No, it's a Saturday, so I'm off the clock."

"Good, I'd like to schedule an appointment for today then."

"What did you have in mind?"

Before Sofia could answer, Manny appeared in the doorway. "Sofia, I see you brought a guest home with you last night." Manny tugged his robe tighter around his girth. "Good morning, Laura. How are you today?" He sat down at the small bistro table and helped himself to a pancake, filling it with eggs and fruit and then rolling it, biting the end.

"Please excuse my Tío, he has the worst table manners and timing in the world. Right Tío?"

"Sofía, please. A man has to eat."

Laura watched as Manny had two more pancakes and then coffee. Afterward, he rubbed his belly and sat back in his seat looking from Sofia to Laura and then back to Sofia. He suddenly sobered.

"I need to talk to you for a minute."

"Now?" Sofia pointed to their breakfast. "Can't it wait? I'm having *my* breakfast."

Manny leaned close to Sofia and said, "I got a call from Julian this morning."

"What? What happened?"

"Uno momento, por favor." Manny said motioning toward the living room.

"Tío, I have a guest."

Laura could see Sofia was getting agitated, so she said, "It's fine. I can go." Suddenly feeling like an intruder and that she was in the way, Laura got up.

"No, please sit. This will only take a moment." Sofia rose, tossing her napkin on the table. "Tío."

Walking into the condo, Laura could hear them talking but it was all in Spanish, and her high school Spanish was bad in high school, so she didn't have a clue what was said. But if Sofia's gestures were any indication, it wasn't good news.

Laura ate quickly, knowing she was probably going to have to leave sooner rather than later. Spearing a melon ball and a banana, she popped it into her mouth just as Manny went one way and Sofia returned and sat down. If she was upset, Laura couldn't tell. Sofia was definitely a poker player. Laura had a sense the first time they met that Sofia didn't wear her feeling out for everyone to see. Passion maybe, but raw emotion, doubtful.

"Everything okay?"

"You ever have one of those moments in life where everything is going good and then suddenly it goes sideways?"

Laura grimaced. Yep, she was probably going to be leaving sooner that she thought.

"Yeah." She sipped her coffee, waiting for the other stiletto to slip off of Sofia's toe.

"Well, not today. Would you like to join me at the symphony? Aurelia left tickets for us, remember?"

Confused, Laura asked, "Are you sure?"

"Yes, I'm quite sure I'm not ready to end our day. If you'd rather take a rain check, then I'll understand." Sofia reached for her hand and brought it to her lips.

She wasn't ready for the day to end. Hell, she wasn't sure she was treading on the ground quite yet. So, if Sofia was asking her to stay, she couldn't think of a better way to spend her Saturday. It wasn't like they were going to be seeing each other anytime soon.

"Sure," she said casually. She didn't want to give Sofia the wrong idea. It was just fun, right?

"Unfortunately, I have to leave for home tomorrow. But I would love to spend my last day with you." Sofia stood and pulled Laura to her feet, wrapping her arms around her waist and planting a kiss on her lips.

Out of the corner of her eye, Laura caught sight of Manny with a carry-on, making his way to the door.

"I'll see you at home, Sofia."

"Travel safe, Tío. Call me when you arrive home."

The door didn't slam, so clearly he wasn't upset.

"Everything okay?"

"It's perfect now. So, where were we?"

Laura pointed to her lips. "Right here."

Chapter Twenty

The slam of the front door caught RJ off guard. Steeling himself for Lina's onslaught, he changed from the small crystal to a highball glass and poured more rum. If he was going to duel with her he wanted to be sufficiently lubricated. Instead of Lina, his uncle strode through the office door.

"RJ, what the hell have you done?"

"Tío, back so soon?" He looked around Manny, expecting to see Sofia on his heels. "Where's my sister?"

"She's finishing up business in San Francisco and seeing your grandparents. I'll repeat my question. What did you do, RJ?"

"I'm sure I have no idea what you're talking about, Tío. Would you like one?" He motioned to his glass.

"Quit dicking around and tell me how the fire started." Manny pulled him up by his shirt and was practically spitting in his face. "I know you started that fire, Nephew. Especially since it was only Sofia's tobacco that burnt. So, tell me what the hell happened or I'll beat it out of you."

RJ set his glass down and pushed Manny off him. "You put your hands on me again, Tío, and I'll put you down." He cocked his fist and slammed it against Manny's jaw. Before he could get a second shot off, Manny tackled him to the floor and pinned him down.

"That was stupid, RJ. I think you need that ass whipping your father should have given you a long time ago."

RJ bucked his hips trying to dislodge Manny, but Manny was stout and a pile of bricks would have been easier to move. Twisting his wrists, he jerked his arms up and then out, and still couldn't break free. Manny's laughter only infuriated him more. He relaxed for a moment, catching Manny off guard and clocked him on the side of his head, stunning him long enough for RJ to wiggle out from under him.

Standing, he swung his leg back to kick his uncle, but Manny grabbed his leg and tossed him backward onto the coffee table, shattering it to pieces.

"Manny, what are you doing, Son?" RJ's grandmother stood in the doorway, her house robe on and a towel around her head.

"Abuelita, Tío needs to be taught some respect. He came in here accusing me of starting the fire in the drying room."

"Manny. RJ was in the house the whole time. I saw him and told him to get out to help put the fire out." His grandmother hobbled over and helped RJ get up. "I can't believe you would accuse him of such a thing. Apologize, mijo."

RJ smiled at the quandary Manny found himself in. No one disrespected his grandmother, and she wasn't above threatening to put Manny over her knee and melding out some motherly justice.

"Thank you, Abuelita. I tried to explain to him what happened but he wouldn't listen to me. Now will you believe me, Uncle?"

Manny straightened his clothes in a huff. "I'm going to the factory and check things out for myself. You better have some answers for me when I get back, Nephew."

RJ went to the door and offered, "Uncle, I already told you I don't know how the fire started."

A slamming door was the response from his uncle.

"Where is your sister, Roberto?" His grandmother sat on the couch and patted it beside her.

Picking up his glass, he raised it and motioned to her. She blushed and raised her hand to measure out a small amount with her fingers. "I'll have a drink with you, Grandson."

"You know, Abuelita, you're the only one around here who believes me. I don't know why Father did what he did. I can't believe he cut me out of the will completely."

Patting the couch beside her again, she grabbed her glass and then his hand. "You're a Huerta, honey. Talk to your sister, she will see reason. Family is family and the same blood that runs through your veins runs through hers. This isn't the time for a fight."

RJ patted his grandmother's hand. At least he had her on his side. If he could get his grandmother to argue in his defense, maybe he could get her to fight for him as well, make Sofia see reason. He'd use anyone to get what he wanted, blood or no blood.

"I love you, Abuelita," he said, kissing her on the forehead. "I don't know what I would do if you left me."

"Oh, Roberto. You must make peace with your sister. I won't be around forever and it would do my heart good knowing you and your sister are running your father's business together."

"I'll try, Abuelita. For you, I promise I'll try." He sipped his drink knowing he wasn't just lying to his grandmother, he was all but going against her wishes.

"Thank you, honey. I think I'll take my drink to my room where it's cooler. Where did you say Sofia was?"

"I think Tío said she was finishing up some business in San Francisco. She's probably visiting Mom's parents while she's up there."

He watched as his grandmother got agitated. He knew telling her that Sofia was staying to see their mother's parents would rub her the wrong way. They'd had words at his mother's funeral, or so he was told. The rift her death created between the two families was wider than the Grand Canyon and about as passable. They never spoke again, not even when his father died. So while his grandmother professed that family mattered, sometimes she just meant the Huerta side of the family mattered.

"Hmm, well I'll see you at dinner, Beto."

"Would you rather go to town for dinner, Abuelita? My friend Lewis and I found this new restaurant the other day and the food was great. Not as good as yours, of course, but why don't you let me take you to town?"

"I'll think about it. Do they have those fried plantains I like?"

"Yes, they do."

"Oh, they are so much work, I hate getting the kitchen dirty for a few fried plantos," she said, walking down the hall toward her room. "Come get me at four and we can have an early dinner."

"Of course, Grandmother." RJ kicked himself. He really didn't want to take his grandmother to dinner, but now he was on the hook. He'd make Lewis go with him. Where was Lewis anyway? RJ went to find the man so they could strategize about the will. If Manny was back then Sofia wasn't far behind, and he needed to sound convincing when she grilled him about the fire.

"Lewis," he yelled, walking through the house. "Where the fuck are you?"

≈≈≈≈

It was tougher to say good-bye to Laura than she expected. They'd spent Sunday tossing the sheets back and forth after brunch and then took a quick stroll along Golden Gate Park, people watching and getting to know each other better. She'd already made a promise to return in two weeks, even going as far as booking her flight while lying in bed with Laura. Laura had told her not to, but they were getting on like people who knew each other for years. Common interests, the symphony, and a love for helping people gave them plenty to talk about when they weren't exploring new...territories. They'd kept their promise not to divulge last names, but she'd caught a glance at Laura's license when she'd been carded buying wine at the local liquor store.

They'd gone to the airport together to prolong the agony of saying good-bye.

"Hey, give me your phone." Sofia held out her hand.

"Why?"

"Come on, give me your phone. It'll be a good thing, I promise."

Laura handed it over and smiled, leaning her head on Sofia's shoulder. "I think I'm going to miss you."

"You think?"

"Well, since I know you're coming back in two weeks, it might not be so hard."

Sofia held Laura's phone out and said, "Smile."
Laura smacked her arm.

"Let's try that again," Laura said, straightening
up and leaning in close to Sofia.

"Smile."

The phone snapped their picture and Sofia
turned it around to look at it. Tapping the screen, she
poked at the keyboard and then her phone went off.

"There, now you have my number and I have a
memory of us."

Sofia kissed Laura and held back tears as she
tried to talk. "Look, I've had a wonderful time and—"

Laura put her fingers on Sofia's lips and stopped
her. "If you're trying to let me down easy, just come
out and say it. It's been great spending the weekend
together." Laura laced her fingers through Sofia's. "So,
you live in Nicaragua, I live here, and I don't want you
to feel obligated or think that you owe me or something.
I mean, we've had a great time together. We're both
consenting adults and…well I don't want you…"

"It sounds like you're trying to let me down easy."
Sofia raised Laura's hand to her lips. "I've booked a
return trip already, so if you're telling me to piss off
then just say it while I can still get a refund."

"No, no, not at all. I'm not saying this right. I just
don't want you to think that…"

"Think…what?" Sofia smiled.

"That I'm reading more into it, if it's just a fun
weekend for you."

Sofia turned toward Laura and pulled her chin
close. "If I didn't want to see you again, I wouldn't
have just given you my number. I would have said
good night after dancing, or I might have just screwed
you at your place and left like a thief in the night."

Sofia kissed Laura as passionately as she could to convince her what she was feeling for her was the real deal. God, they were in passenger unloading and the rent-a-cop was banging on the window, telling them to move the car. Sofia motioned to the cop for five more minutes. *Five*, she mouthed back to Sofia.

"Look, I thought we had a good time. If you don't want to see me again, I get it. I'm gone today—"

"No," Laura kissed her again. "I was just being stupid and I didn't want you to think you had to see me again if you didn't want to."

"Well, I want to, so that ends the discussion. I'll see you in two weeks. I'll handle my business at home, have Julian oversee my affairs while I'm up here, and maybe I can convince you to come and visit me."

"Deal."

The pounding on the window started again. "I'm going, I'm going," Sofia said, then kissed Laura again. "You have my number. If you change your mind, text me."

"I'll see you in two weeks. Bring some cigars and we'll go to Napa, and I'll buy the wine and we can spend the days relaxing...or something else." Laura smiled and pushed Sofia toward the door. "You better go before I start to cry again."

"I'll see you in two weeks."

And with that, Sofia said good-bye to someone she was crushing on—well probably more than crushing if she was honest with herself. However, she needed to get the company settled and RJ out of the house and away from her business, by any means necessary and as soon as possible.

෴෴෴

The small plane bounced down the runway, a good landing by Managua standards. First class on Air Mexico was more like coach on an average plane, but the airport wasn't set up for big planes so the puddle jumper was the best Sofia could do. Unbuckling, she looked out the window and spotted Julian standing out in the parking lot waiting by the company SUV. She pulled her phone and looked at the picture of her and Laura together. She vacillated between thoughts of texting Laura and letting it ride for a day or two. God, it'd been years since she'd really been interested in someone and she didn't know what the dating protocol was anymore. Going with her gut, she texted Laura.

Already miss you.

Short and sweet. Now the ball was in Laura's court. If she knew her, she'd wait an hour or two and then respond. If she didn't want to see Sofia again, she'd just blow her off. That was how it worked, right?

As she got to the luggage carousel, her phone beeped.

Me too.

Sofia smiled and tucked the phone in her back pocket. Grabbing her bag, she wheeled it to the curb and the waiting Julian.

"Señorita Sofia. How was your trip?"

"Good." She couldn't wipe off the goofy grin she felt break her reserve, but important business was at hand. "So, what happened, Julian? Do we know how the fire started?"

"Sorry, jefa. I asked around and the fire department said they didn't know anything. RJ has already cleared the burned…" His hands moved around.

"Debris?"

"Yes, debris. He's already planning the new building."

"What?"

Julian threw his hands up. "Señor Manny confronted him when he got home. They had a fight in the house and your grandmother broke it up. She told me that they broke a table."

"Jesus Christ." Slipping into the back of the SUV, she pulled her sunglasses out of her purse and tapped them on her hand as if it would help her think. RJ had started that fire, she knew it, but how was she going to prove it? Slipping her sunglasses on, she said, "Take me to the factory."

"Sí, jefa."

The trip to Esteli was an hour, so it left plenty of time to think about the future, and about Laura. Pulling the phone from her pocket, she flicked it to life and smiled down at the happy faces on the screen.

Yep, she was falling. Hard.

Chapter Twenty-one

Laura's finger hovered over the keys of her phone. She was torn: should she text Sofía and let her know that she was on her way to Nicaragua and hope that they could meet on the off chance she would be available, or not because Sofía might think she was stalking her? Christ, she suddenly felt like a high school girl with her first crush. The swirling crowds, professionals pulling rolling briefcases, women with strollers, and hipsters oblivious to the masses, headphones perched at their temples that looked more like appendages growing out of their heads, filled the terminal. The bustling airport only made her more anxious as she leaned against the bistro set in the wine bar trying to figure out whether her quick trip to Nicaragua would be welcome news.

"Screw it. If she doesn't want to see me, she'll tell me." She motioned to the waiter.

Hey, I've been called to Nicaragua for a meeting. Want to meet up? :)

She texted quickly then stuffed the phone into her jacket pocket and ordered a white wine. No use in waiting for a reply. The two-hour time difference probably had Sofia busy, not to mention it was unexpected.

The waiter dropped off her wine just as her

pocket buzzed.

An answer.

She didn't want to look desperate, so she paid her tab, took a sip, and then slid her finger over the face of the phone.

Oh gosh, that's great. I would love to pick you up at the airport and have dinner, but the emergency that called me home is worse than I thought. Rain check in two weeks? :)

It was a long shot. No worries. Two weeks sounds great. :)

It had been a long shot. She was disappointed, but no harm, no foul. She had tried. She would have felt worse if she hadn't at least given it the good ol' college try. She laid her phone on the table and swiped through the pictures they'd taken. Oh yeah, she was sweet on the beautiful Latina from Nicaragua.

༄ ༄ ༆ ༆

"Lewis, this better be good."

Lewis tried to give her a hug and a kiss, but Laura stiffened and pushed him back. His hair was in disarray, he hadn't shaved in a couple of days, and if she didn't know better he looked like he'd slept in his clothes. His disheveled appearance was more than a surprise. Laura threw her bag into the back of the SUV and held onto her briefcase. His frantic phone call begging her to come to Nicaragua and handle the case was over the top, even for him. Sitting across from him, she almost felt sorry as he fumbled with a string that hung loose on his shirt.

"What the hell is going on? You call me, frantic, demanding that I get down here and so here I am. What's up?"

She wiped at her forehead. She hadn't dressed for the tropics. San Francisco had hit a balmy high of 74 that day and she'd dressed accordingly for the nighttime dip of 55. The twenty-degree flux wasn't a surprise and the wet, heavy mist one could set their watch by arrived exactly at 3:00 p.m.

"Christ, Lewis, you look like you've slept in those clothes." Laura looked around the airport, which seemed more like a small-town hub than an international airport.

"Hello, you must be Laura Worthington." A man stepped forward and offered his hand. There was something familiar about him, but she couldn't put her finger on it. Laura took in the whole picture of the man. Well dressed, clean shaven, and showcasing a grin that seemed to go on for days. She paused, then shook the extended hand.

"And you are?"

"I'm Roberto Huerta, Junior." His cocky grin and fake charm poured on like cheap wine that needed ice to cool it off. The sudden need for a shower as she pulled her hand from his grasp was evident as she slipped her hand behind her back, trying to slyly wipe if off.

Peeling her jacket off, she slung it over her arm and pushed her sliding sunglasses back up.

"You're the son in the will."

"I am."

"I can't help you." Laura shot him a no-nonsense look and then looked at her father. "I told you that this was pretty cut-and-dried, Lewis. The will is textbook, law school 101." She looked back at Roberto Junior. "You contest it and you get a dollar."

"If I do nothing, I get nothing. So what is the difference?"

"Look, I've looked over the will and..." Wrestling with her jacket, she slung it over her arm that was holding the briefcase and pinched the bridge of her nose. Pausing, she wasn't able to remember his sister's name. "Your sister and Tío are the beneficiaries. You fight it and you get the equivalent of nothing, and your kids get a token amount when they turn twenty-one."

"So, find a loophole," Roberto persisted.

"Look, there isn't one. I'm telling you, fight it and you'll get a buck and your kids lose their inheritance."

"I don't think you understand..." He loomed over her. "I said, find a loophole." Roberto looked over at Lewis who seemed to recover some of his vigor. "Tell her, Lewis. She needs to find a loophole or else."

"Or else what? Lewis, what the hell is going on here?"

"Get in the car. We're heading to the compound. We have a meeting later today with my sister and her lawyer. I want you to see what we're up against. Vamanos." RJ opened the door and practically pushed Lewis into the car. Her father was abnormally silent. While it wasn't altogether a bad thing for him, it meant he was off his feed. Something was eating him, and she could tell.

※ ※ ※ ※

RJ sat back in the limo and watched Lewis huddled with his daughter. The ride to the compound had been like a tennis match between Lewis and Laura so far. He'd tried to insert himself and calm Laura down, but she was as big of a barracuda as Lewis had said, which meant she was a first-class bitch. Well, he knew how to put a bitch in her place, and what he had on Lewis would set her straight, and quick.

"Miss Worthington. Excuse me, Laura," RJ said rather loudly.

Laura jerked her head around and glared at him. "What? I don't know what the hell is going here, but I've already told you, I can't help you."

"Well, you're down here now, so you're going to help. Or, your father, well..."

"What's he talking about, Lewis?"

"Look, let's put all our cards on the table. What do you say, Lewis?"

"RJ, I can handle this, let me talk to her."

"Lewis, you've had plenty of time to try and convince her, so I'm going to take a stab at it," he said, reaching into the seat next to him to extract his trump cards. "You don't help me and these go to the police. I'm sure you'll understand why when you see these."

Laura caught the tossed envelope and then looked at Lewis. "What have you done, Lewis, that would warrant you owing this asshole?"

Lewis looked away from his daughter as she opened the envelope. If Laura was stunned by what she saw, she didn't let on. Her stone face was going to be perfect when she confronted Sofia.

"Jesus Christ. How old is she, Lewis? I suppose you took these?" Laura shoved them back in the envelope and threw it back to RJ. "I'm sure those aren't the only copies."

"You *are* smarter than you look, Laura. You

don't mind if I call you Laura, do you? I mean since we're going to be working together to get my share of my inheritance."

"You fucking bastard."

"I don't care what you call me as long as you get my cigar company back."

Laura scooted away from her father. "You are such a fucking pig. You make me sick. You're always thinking with your dick, aren't you? But this is low even for you, Lewis."

"Family, the gift that keeps giving." RJ rubbed it in. "Ah, we're here. Now was that a fun ride. Time flies when you're having fun. Now, let's go meet my sister. Shall we?"

Chapter Twenty-two

T hanks for coming, Señor Gomez." Sofia held
up her hands. "I have no idea why he called
a meeting to discuss the will. It's pretty cut-and-dried,
but clearly he isn't giving up."

"Sofia, if he contests it, his children get nothing.
Doesn't he know that?"

"This isn't about you, me, or his kids. He wants
Huerta Cigars and he's going to do whatever it takes to
get it. I think he's responsible for the fire in the sorting
building."

"What? Oh my god."

"That's why I need to have some papers drawn
up and get him and his family out of the house and off
the compound."

"I'm worried for your safety, Sofia. He's a
dangerous man and I hear he's been meeting with Don
Pablo."

"Really? About what?"

"There is talk of the families banding together to
form some super cartel. They call themselves the Cigar
Barons."

"How original."

Señor Gomez shrugged his shoulders. "That's
the rumor."

"Hmm, well RJ doesn't have control over Huerta.
I wonder if those men know that?"

"I don't think so. I hear he's been telling them

he's in charge."

"Really? You sure do know a lot, Señor Gomez." Sofia eyed her lawyer. If he was trying to screw her, he wouldn't tell her anything. "How do you know so much?"

"Señorita, in my business, it pays to know who the enemies are and who you can trust. Besides, your father paid me very well to pay attention."

"Well, lucky for me you're my attorney."

"Jefa, RJ asked me to ask you to come to the conference room in the factory." Julian peeked around the door.

"Did he now?"

"Sí."

Calling the meeting at the conference room at the factory was all for show, a blatant attempt at a power grab. RJ wanted everyone to see her walking in with her lawyer. Talk would be spread around town before she shut the door. Speculation would rise to the level of a Greek tragedy and everyone would think Sofia was being pushed out. Well, it wasn't going to go that way if she had anything to say about it.

"Tell RJ if he wants a meeting, I'm waiting right here," she said, thumping her father's desk.

"Si, jefa."

It would give her some time to strategize with Señor Gomez and sign the paperwork she needed to have filed to get RJ evicted from the house. Better to play offense than try to figure out what RJ had up his sleeve.

"Señor Gomez, do you have the paperwork I requested?"

"Yes, right here." He patted the worn leather briefcase.

"Good. When we're done here, I want you to go to Managua and make sure it's filed as soon as possible. Then call me. I don't want to make a big scene with my abuelita in the house."

"I understand."

Sofia walked around the desk and leaned against it. "RJ has always tugged at her heartstrings with his sob story. I don't want to give him a chance to drag her into this mess." She tapped her lips with the pen she'd been holding.

No, she was definitely going to put RJ on the defensive, and if he wasn't careful, he'd be on the business end of someone's fist.

❧❧❧❧

All Laura wanted to do was lay down and forget this whole trip. The pictures of her father in indecent positions with girls barely old enough to drive had her wanting to throw up. What a sick bastard. His excuse? He was drunk. She couldn't even look at him as he started to drink himself stupid again.

God, when she got back to the States she'd recommend that he divorce her mother and leave her everything or she'd expose him for the lecherous bastard that he was. The scandal would crush her. Worse, he could be prosecuted for sex with a minor. She'd heard about men who went to foreign counties just to have sex with young girls and boys. Little did she know her father was one of those horrendous individuals.

Someone she didn't recognize walked into the room and whispered to RJ, who exploded.

"What do you mean she wants us to come to the

house? Fucking bitch. I told you to tell her to meet us here."

"I'm sorry, but she said she would meet you in the office."

"Great. Okay everyone, let's get moving." RJ waved his hands shooing them all out of the office. "We're meeting my sister at the compound."

Laura was too drained to argue. She just wanted to get to her room, sleep, and get on the first flight out of Nicaragua in the morning. What Lewis did was his business, but she'd talk to him before she left.

Lewis pulled her up short just outside the office. "You need to do this, Laura. If I go to jail down here it will crush your mother and she'll be my first phone call when they arrest me."

"Are you threatening me?" She jerked her arm out of his slimy grasp.

"No, just bringing a little reality to the game. Your mother will be devastated and she'll be the talk at the country club, at her card night with her little hens, and then there's the firm's reputation to think about. Hell, people won't be able to look at you without my name crossing their lips first. Can you handle all of that, Laura?"

"You're a grade A asshole aren't you, Lewis? You're not worried about Mom or the firm, it's your ass that you're worried about."

"Well, someone's got take care of number one," he said, pointing to himself. "I made that desk that you park your ass behind. I built that with my own hard work. You owe me." He bent down and sneered in her face. "That little prick there..." He pointed to RJ's back. "He's going to get what's coming after I get the fuck out of here. But you, you're going to be my get out of jail free card, honey."

"Go to hell. You can rot in a Nicaraguan prison for all I care, you bastard."

"I don't think you're getting it, my dear. You do this, or your poor mother will suffer, and I don't mean by gossip. RJ is a violent man and I think he would take great pleasure in hurting you, especially if he thinks he can get to me through you and your mother. Don't you get it? I'm not the only one in danger here, Laura."

Now she really did want to vomit. He wasn't sorry for what he'd done, he was pissed he'd been called on it. And now he was putting her mother in danger to save himself. She knew he was sick and now she'd seen the photos to prove it, but she never thought he would go that far. He and RJ were a perfect match after all—they both thought too highly of themselves and thought they were above reproach, and she was caught in the middle of these two sociopaths with her mother's life on the line.

Laura wished she could appreciate the landscape as they drove the short distance to the compound, but all she could see were those damn pictures and the images she conjured up in her head of her aging mom being threatened by faceless men with guns. She tried to focus on anything else to get those thoughts out of her head. As the vehicle swung up a drive, she marveled at the stucco house that sat atop the hill. Around it were tobacco plants, at least that what she thought they were. Rounding the circular driveway, the car stopped and the doors were opened. Laura was ushered through a set of massive doors and was stopped just inside.

"Now, be a good girl and think of your father during this meeting. I understand your mother is a wonderful woman, just as pretty as her pictures." She eyed RJ and sat on the bench in the entryway. He and Lewis must have come up with the same script for today's meeting.

"You know, I don't care if he rots in jail down here—"

"Oh, but you're here, too. It might be harder to get out of Nicaragua than it was to get in. So, if I were you, I'd rethink my strategy before you go in there all high-and-mighty. All you have to do is break the will and you can go home and back to your life in the US." RJ slapped his hands together. "Easy as that. Now come on, let's get this show on the road, as they say."

"You're a prick."

RJ smiled at her. "I know, and you're going to make me a very rich prick."

≈·≈·≈·≈

Sofia heard the commotion in the entryway, but waited inside the office. She wasn't about to welcome RJ and his entourage. At least it sounded like a large group milling about. She didn't have to wait long as RJ burst through the door to the office, practically swinging them off their hinges and knocking them into the walls.

"Sofia, welcome back home. Now why couldn't you come to the conference room down at the factory? I had coffee and pastries waiting for you." RJ turned toward the people following him and motioned for them to come in. "Let me introduce you to my lawyers. They are all the way from America, so I appreciate them coming down to help us settle this little family matter."

Sofia admonished him in Spanish. "RJ, you've

already been told that the will is unbreakable. You're wasting everyone's time with this crap."

Sofia turned her attention to the newcomers and froze.

Regaining her composure, she looked at her lawyer and said, "Call Manny, please, Señor Gomez."

"Of course. One moment please."

"Sofia, please let me introduce you to my attorneys, Lewis Worthington and his lovely daughter Laura Worthington. Please don't be rude to our guests. By the way, I hope you don't mind I've put them in the guest quarters."

"Mr. Worthington, Miss Worthington. I'm so sorry that my brother has wasted your time by dragging you all the way down here. I'm sure you must know that the will is ironclad." Sofia walked over and shook Lewis's hand, and then Laura's without as much as a nod of recognition. She didn't know what game was being played right now, but she was going to find out, and quick.

"Well, that's what we're here to find out, Miss Huerta," Lewis said. He took a seat on the couch and made himself at home in her own house. Arrogant prick.

Sofia sized up the man, but she couldn't see the family resemblance between him and Laura. Michael she could see clearly that he and Lewis were cut from the same cloth, but Laura…not even close.

"And you, Miss Worthington, what is your opinion on the will? I'm assuming you've looked it over." Sofia turned her back on Laura before she could answer, sitting behind her desk before she looked at her again.

"I looked at it on the way here. I've told my father

that family law isn't my forte. I believe I was brought here under false pretenses."

"Really, were you dragged here? Blindfolded and tied up and put on a plane?"

"Don't be silly, Sofia. Her father owes me a favor and he *requested* that she help him, isn't that correct, Miss Worthington?" Sofia couldn't see RJ's face as he was looking at Laura and said something softly that she couldn't hear.

"That's correct. My father did call frantic that I come down and help. I handle international law and he felt that this was in my jurisdiction. I'll need some time to go over the will completely before I can make an accurate assessment of your brother's claims to half of the Huerta Cigar company. I understand that he's only requesting that and not any of the other assets your father had, such as the rum distillery, the ice cream business, or the other land holdings."

Sofia stiffened as Laura talked. She'd done her homework, and if she didn't feel betrayed she'd be impressed with the professional way Laura handled herself.

"Well, Miss Worthington, he can't have it. There, I'm sure my lawyer can discuss this further with you and answer any questions you may have."

Manny walked through the door and stopped dead in his tracks. He recognized Laura instantly, and then looked at Sofia, puzzled.

"Tío, this is Mr. Worthington and his daughter Miss Worthington. They are RJ's lawyers. They're here to get half of Huerta Cigars for RJ."

"Are you being serious, Sofia?" Manny walked to the desk and turned toward RJ "What are you doing, Nephew? Are you trying to tear this family apart? What would your grandmother say?"

A frail voice from the door answered. "She would say that we can work all of this out for the sake of your father's memory."

"Ah, Abuelita. My apologies. Did we wake you?" RJ went over and hugged his grandmother's shoulders. "Everyone, this is my Abuelita."

"Hello, again," Lewis said.

"It's a pleasure to meet you, Mrs. Huerta," Laura said, offering to shake her hand.

"The pleasure is mine. Are you hungry? Sofia, please bring our guests something to eat."

"Grandmother, they aren't my guests. Tell RJ, he's the one who invited them."

"I'm not hungry, thank you," Laura said to the eldest woman. "But perhaps I could get a glass of water?"

"Of course. You can get her that, can't you mija?" Sofia's grandmother looked at her. She'd been raised to never be disrespectful, and she was sure that her grandmother was going to have a few choice words for her, but damn it, they weren't her guests. Besides, she wanted to corner Laura and find out why she'd lied to her in San Francisco.

"Of course, Grandmother. It would be my pleasure." Sofia poured Laura a glass and handed it to her without looking.

"Thank you."

Sofia was so close she didn't know if she wanted to pull Laura into a hug or punch her.

"Now, Señor Gomez, if you and Miss Worthington would like to talk, I'm done here. I'm sure you'll find your accommodations to your liking. If not, RJ knows where the fresh bed linens are and you'll find food in the kitchen. Help yourself."

"Sofia." Her grandmother pinched her as she passed.

"Ouch, what was that for, Grandmother?"

"For your bad manners."

"I'm too tired to argue with you. I'll speak to you in the morning, you can spank me then. Until then, good night."

Sofia heard her grandmother talking to the Worthingtons as they walked down the hall.

"You must forgive my granddaughter, she hasn't been herself since she returned from America. I think she caught a bug or something there."

Sofia rolled her eyes at the comment. Her grandmother always blamed bad behavior on a bug, stomach or otherwise. If it wasn't that it was dysentery, or some other bowel ailment.

"Great, now they're going to think I'm sick, too."

She heard Laura say, "I'm sorry to hear that. I guess she didn't have a good time on her visit, then."

"Oh, I don't know. We haven't had a chance to talk about her trip. She's kind of moody."

Suddenly, Sofia wanted to turn around and yank her grandmother out of there before she gave a blow-by-blow of her monthly cycle.

RJ cut into the conversation. "So Miss Worthington, I'm sure you'd like to talk to Señor Gomez and go over the details of the will. Why don't we let you and Lewis get busy and my uncle, sister, and I will leave you three alone."

Sofia trotted down to her room before she was seen eavesdropping. Another habit her grandmother despised, but she practiced it liberally.

There was a soft tap on her door.

"Who is it?"

"Sofia, it's me, Manny."

Sofia swung the door wide, grabbed him by the arm, and practically yanked him to the floor.

"What the hell is Laura doing here? She's RJ's lawyer? Did you know that in San Francisco? Oh my god, what are you going to do?"

Sofia opened the double doors that led out to the courtyard.

"I don't know. Yes. No. I have no idea."

🙟🙟🙠🙠

Laura sat opposite Señor Gomez as he spread out his papers on the desk. Laura couldn't help but admire the office. A picture of Sofia and her father were on a credenza behind the desk along with other photographs, but the only one that interested Laura was one of a young girl on horseback. Small, she could make out Sofia at probably nine, smiling, her father holding the horse by the reins. A large box had been moved out of the way so the lawyer had more room to make his case. The only problem as Laura saw it was that she wasn't going to be able to make it out of Nicaragua without getting RJ something. Perhaps if she talked to Sofia, she could reason with her. The look on her face when RJ introduced her as his lawyer left little doubt how Sofia felt about Laura at that moment.

Betrayal.

Sofia tried to hide it, but Laura was paid to be a people reader and she'd read Sofia the moment they'd seen each other. The way her eyes raked Laura with contempt was evident, at least to her. God, she hated her father for putting her in this position.

Pulling out her phone, she tapped out a message

and hit Send.

I'm sorry. I didn't know.

Laura hoped it would be received with the honest belief that Laura had no idea Sophia was part of this. Hell, even *she* didn't know.

"Okay, Miss Worthington. I've laid out the will and you will clearly see that there is no room for discussion. Roberto Junior is to receive nothing for his children if he contests the will."

"I've explained that to Mr. Huerta. I see that there are several companies within the umbrella of Huerta. Is there no way Miss Huerta would see a way of at least compromising and splitting the company with her brother?"

"Miss Worthington, Don Roberto made it very clear when we wrote the will that his son was to receive nothing. I talked to him and tried to convince him that even a small inheritance was in order. He did not want to hear of it."

"Why?"

"Why?"

"Yes, why? Were they estranged at the time of Mr. Huerta's death?"

"Not at all. In fact, they had been out horseback riding the day of his death."

"Really. But he wrote him out of the will anyway. Why?"

"Ms. Worthington, I have tried to explain. I know my English may not be perfect, but I am sure you understand what I've said. Don Roberto left nothing to his son, Roberto Junior."

Laura pulled out her copy of the will, translated

into English. "I've highlighted some areas I'd like to go over with you. My Spanish is pretty crappy, so hopefully we can get through this tonight and I can give my client my recommendations."

"Miss Worthington, may I give you some advice? Abogado to abogada?"

"Sure. I'm not sure I know what that means, but of course. You're Ms. Huerta's legal counsel." Laura set her papers aside and folded her hands and laid them in her lap.

"Miss Huerta has worked hard with her father to make Huerta a cigar company they could be proud of. Roberto Junior never took an interest in the company until recently."

"Why?"

Señor Gomez shrugged. "I don't know. But I can tell you that she is not about to give half, a third, or even a sixteenth to Roberto Junior."

"I'm sorry, but I have to try. He's retained me as counsel and I'm sure you can appreciate the fact that I have to at least try."

Señor Gomez reached out his hands and grasped hers. "I do understand, but you don't know Sofia. She is not about to let her brother get his hands on even…" He held up a finger. "One cigar that has the name Huerta on that band."

If only she could tell him she knew Sofia and that was why her heart was practically seizing in her chest. The palpitations when she laid eyes on her lover almost dropped her to the floor. In a second, she would have begged for Sofia's forgiveness, but her father had discreetly touched her arm as she and Sofia were introduced, a clever reminder he was still in the room and what was on the line. As for the lawyer's comment about RJ never touching a Huerta cigar, she would do her best to get a settlement and then she and her father would be out of this mess. She wasn't a good lawyer just because she could argue a case. One needed to be quick on her feet, so to speak, so Laura threw out a compromise. "What if Sofia allowed Mr. Huerta to start his own line of cigars and..." She saw Gomez start to balk at the idea, and held her hands up. "Hold on, let me finish. He starts his own small line and she gives him three to five years to launch it. I'm not sure what it takes to make a cigar, but surely three to five years is more than enough time to establish a line of cigars."

Gomez just looked at Laura, his face a void of emotion, his mouth not moving. His eyes locked with hers and he just sat there. Had the poor fellow had a heart attack, or seizure of some sort that prevented him from moving? Surely he had to know that a compromise would save thousands, if not hundreds of thousands, in legal bills?

"You have to admit it's a sound compromise. I'm sure if you discuss this with your client she would see the reasoning in it. We could tie up Huerta cigars for years until the case is settled, possibly even shutter the business until a judgment is rendered."

She didn't want to do that, and she was torn between telling her father to stick this mess up his ass and do his time in jail, or telling Sofia everything and beg her to forgive her. Surely she would be able to understand that RJ had threatened not only her, but her mother as well. But if the look tonight was any indication, she was pretty sure they were done before they'd even really started, regardless of Sofia's empathy.

"Mr. Gomez, you must see that I'm right. While

I don't have any legal authority to practice law here, I will bring in someone local and I'll handle any US claims that might be made there."

"Well, you don't have to worry about that for Roberto Junior. He doesn't have dual citizenship because his mother and father never reported his birth to the US Consulate to get a Consular Report of Birth Abroad, for whatever reason. Sofia does because she was born in the United States and the hospital birth certificate took care of those legalities."

"I see. Well, I don't know how it works here, but I'd have to take any offer made to my client before proceeding." Of course, that was only if they were already looking at going to court, but it was worth a try. She was pretty sure he knew US law, at least enough to challenge her assentation of presenting the offer. "It can't hurt." She felt like she was practically pleading with him. She'd rather spend her time trying to salvage anything she might have with Sofia than waste it filing legal briefs and interviewing lawyers here.

"I'll present your offer to my client, but don't get your hopes up, Miss Worthington. She is just like her father—very stubborn."

"I understand. I have to go to the hospital tomorrow as well as interview legal counsel here, so it will give you time to discuss the offer with your client."

"Oh, are you ill?"

"No, I need to get my client's birth records to verify your stipulation for myself. I'm assuming they will be there, or do you have a public records office?"

"I would try the hospital first. However, don't be surprised if they can't find it right away."

"Mr. Gomez, are you trying to tell me something?"

"No, not at all. It's just that we are not as up-to-date with technology as you are in the US."

"I see. Not that you have to, but can you tell me if my client has ever applied for a passport?"

He shrugged. "I am assuming so since he's traveled abroad for trade shows."

"Well, I asked him earlier and he said he didn't have a birth certificate in his possession. Perhaps Don Roberto kept a copy somewhere?" Laura looked around the room, certain there would be a safe. In a country where political strife could break out anytime, their history of the Sandinistas fighting with the government in the eighties was a good indicator how volatile the country could be in an instant. She heard stories of political figures taking homes on a whim and there wasn't anyone to stop them. How could they if the local authorities were in on it, too?

"I'll ask Sofia and let you know."

"No matter. I'll just pick up a copy, just to be sure."

"As you wish. Are we done here?"

"Yes, I think so." She stood and stretched out her hand. "Thank you for your time. Please give my best to your client, and I hope for everyone's sake she thinks about the offer. I'd hate to see her lose any of this just because they couldn't come to an agreement."

"As I said, my client is very stubborn and her father's wishes were for her to take over the company and everything it owns. He trusted her with his life and now he trusts her to Huerta Holdings."

"Well, according to the will, he left a small portion to his brother, too."

"Yes, but only for a few years. Once she has shown she can run the day-to-day operations, Manny is out. I believe the will said for a period of two years.

Then it is all Sofia's responsibility."

"See, even her father had a grace period. Perhaps she can see fit to do the same with RJ and they can work out something amicably."

"I shall present your idea to my client." Mr. Gomez turned back toward Laura before leaving. "Miss Worthington, may I give you some advice?"

"Of course."

"Be careful of the bed that you crawl into. It could have snakes in it."

"You mean my bed here?" She shuddered at the thought; she despised snakes.

"I mean your client. He's not who he seems to be."

Well, as far as Laura was concerned, he was as slimy as they came, so the snake reference was well-intended. "I see."

"It is only a warning, Miss Worthington. I would hate to see you put too much effort into a losing case."

"I understand. Thank you for the advice and I'll take it under advisement." She tucked her briefcase under her arm and followed Mr. Gomez out. "I'm a little turned around here. Can you tell me the way to the guest house?"

"Through those doors. Follow the path and it will take you right to the guest house."

"Thank you again, Mr. Gomez. I'll see you later this week."

"You shall, Miss Worthington. However, I doubt I'll have good news."

"I suspect you're right. Good night."

He left her standing there without another word. Now what was she going to do? This was beyond a delicate mess her father had created, it was a clusterfuck of epic proportion. She considered getting her bags, heading for the airport, and catching the first flight out of Nicaragua, but she doubted she could do it unnoticed. What little she knew of RJ said she knew enough that he would be at the airport with the police to arrest her just because he could. Perhaps if she pleaded her case to Sofia, she could help her. Or, Sofia would slam the door in her face.

What was she going to do now?

Chapter Twenty-three

R J spooned a mouthful of oatmeal into his mouth and cursed at the bland concoction. His doctor had advocated for a healthier diet. Lab results showed an increase in his cholesterol, his blood pressure was through the roof, and his six pack was turning into a pony keg. Once the will was dealt with his pressure would return to normal and he'd go back to his usual routine. For now, though, he'd follow doctor's orders and lay off the red meat, but he wasn't giving up the rum or cigars. Heart attack be damned. He'd purposely faced the door just in case Sofia walked by. He wanted to bend his sister's ear and hopefully persuade her to end this nonsense. He was in luck, as Sofia walked right into the dining room.

"Sister, how are you this fine morning?"

"RJ, I'm good. I hope you aren't spending too much on those lawyers. You know you don't stand a chance in hell to get Huerta cigars. Right?"

He wolfed another spoonful of oatmeal then pushed the bowl away. Grabbing his coffee, he washed it down and then mentally cursed the crap. That was his last bowl of oatmeal, ever. Before he could answer, his Abuelita walked through the door.

"Good morning. Are we in better moods this morning?"

"Good morning, Abuelita. How did you sleep?" Sofia walked over and kissed her grandmother.

"Good, mija. The nights are finally cooling down I think. Oh, it was so hot there for a while I thought I might have to go down in that room your father built for his wine."

"Abuelita, I'll have someone come and look at your air conditioner."

"No, no, mija. It's fine. I'm just an old woman who overheats when I get dressed. I'm fine, really."

RJ scoffed at the display. She would do anything to get their grandmother on her side.

Bitch.

Before he could chime in, his grandmother continued. "I hear that your lawyer has proposed a compromise, RJ. I think it's a good one. You should consider it, Sofia." She sat, placed her coffee on the table, and smoothed out her house dress.

Where had she gotten that tidbit of news? He hadn't even talked to Lewis yet this morning.

"What? Where did you hear this, Abuelita?" Sofia said, clearly surprised at the news.

Sofia glanced at RJ, narrowed her eyes at him, and asked, "What have you got up your sleeve, RJ? The will is Father's wishes. I'm not going to go against his wishes."

"You should probably talk to your attorney to find out what was proposed. I'm not going to negotiate directly with you when we both have lawyers."

He didn't want her to know he had no clue what their grandmother was talking about, but he was about to find out. Damn it all to hell. How did she know before he did? What deal had Miss Worthington proposed last night? And who had given her permission to make such a proposal? Tossing his coffee cup on the table, he wiped his mouth, walked over, and gave his grandmother a kiss.

"Good morning, Abuelita. I have some business to attend to this morning. If you will both excuse me."

Neither woman said anything as he left the room. Waiting for a moment, he heard his grandmother explain the proposal to Sofia.

"They are proposing that you let RJ build his own line of cigars. He won't use the Huerta name, but he'll be under the Huerta roof for about three to five years. Just like your father did with you, mija."

"No."

Sofia was right. No way was he going to settle for a line of cigars. He wanted it all or nothing.

ᘺ ᘺ ᘺ ᘺ

María watched her grandchildren argue about cigars when what was at stake was far more important, the family.

"I think you should accept the offer, RJ."

"Abuelita, how can you say that? It's my birthright to lead the company."

María patted RJ's hand and offered a meager smile. "The family doesn't need a scandal, RJ, and there are things that shouldn't see daylight, and you know what I mean, mijo."

"What's going on, Abuelita?" Sofía questioned. "What scandal? RJ's cheating? Pfff, everyone knows about his women. Father even knew and that's one of the reasons he didn't leave RJ the company. The children aren't his, so what could be more scandalous than that?"

"We all have skeletons in our closet, even Huertas, and I don't think any good can come from prolonging this battle between you two." María took a sip of her coffee then rested the cup in her palm. "Your father came to me when he was making up his will. He wanted me to take controlling interest in the company, but I told him that this old woman doesn't need those headaches at my age, so I gave him my advice."

"You told him to leave the company to Tío and Sofía. Grandmother, I can't believe you betrayed me like that. I can't believe it. Of all people, I trusted you most." RJ buried his head in his hand and began sobbing. "I trusted you."

María walked to RJ and tried to wrap her arms around RJ, but he threw them off. "Don't, Abuelita."

"It's not what you think, mijo—"

"Wait, Sofia is a fucking lesbian. An abomination in god's eyes and my cheating is worse than her love of women? You and Father act as if it's no big deal, but you sit and judge me for a fling or two. You and Father are hypocrites. I can't believe it. You take my inheritance but give Sofia everything." He stood, knocking his chair down behind him. "Well, I'll tell you something, there is going to be hell to pay. That barn fire is nothing compared to what comes next."

María stiffened at the threat. "Let me tell you something, Roberto Junior." She leaned into him, her finger in his face. "I've lived through things you could never imagine, and if you think I'm going to let a little whelp like you threaten me or Sofia, you've barked up the wrong puta." RJ's eyes widened. María cringed at her loss of self-control. It rarely happened, but RJ had gone too far. "Burning the fermentation barn is bad, even for you. If you keep this up, you might be the one that gets a surprise. I can't protect you anymore, RJ, if you don't calm down and take the offer. It's the only way you can survive and come out of this with your dignity. Please, RJ, do this for me."

RJ took a step back, his face reddening. "Take the offer? Do this for you? What about me? Who is looking out for RJ?" He pushed his thumbs into his chest. "You're looking out for Sofía, but who is going to help me, Abuelita?"

She'd never seen this side of RJ and it worried her. Was this what Don Roberto had seen before his death?

"Did you kill father, RJ?" Sofia made her presence known.

María sighed. This wasn't the time to ask such a question.

"Did I kill Father? So now you want to blame me for that, too? I've told you that he had an accident on that fucking horse, you stupid bitch." RJ's voice was menacing.

"Well, you just admitted to burning down the barn."

"Murder is a long way from burning down a barn, Sofía. But I can see how you'd like to use that to keep me from getting what's mine." RJ picked up the chair and slammed it back against the table. "I don't have to sit here and take this bullshit. I'll see you in court, Sofía. You aren't going to take what's rightfully mine." RJ looked at them both. "Abuelita…"

He slammed the door without finishing his sentence. María slumped into a chair at the table and sighed.

"Nana, what aren't you telling me?" Sofia said, resting her hands on María's.

"It doesn't matter, Sofía. You need to get RJ to take the deal. I'm worried that the Huertas won't be able to weather the scandal if it gets out."

"I won't say anything about RJ setting the barn on fire, Nana. But I don't trust him with Father's legacy. So, I won't sign off on anything that involves RJ and Huerta. I'm sorry, I am thinking of what Father wanted." Sofia kissed her grandmother's head and hugged her shoulders.

María knew she'd probably made matters worse, but she worried about Don Roberto's legacy, his children, and the future of Huerta. No good deed goes without a punishment.

⚜⚜⚜⚜

RJ banged on the cottage door. When no one answered, he invited himself in. It was his house, so he could do whatever the damn hell he wanted.

"Lewis! Lewis, where the fuck are you?"

He heard someone stirring behind the door to his right. Walking over, he pounded on the door and yelled. "Lewis, get your ass out here."

Laura opened the door, clad in sweatpants and a T-shirt. He couldn't help giving her a once-over.

"Don't even think about it," Laura said, disgust lacing her words.

"Good morning to you, too. I understand you made some kind of proposal to Sofia's lawyer without my permission. Is that how things are done in the US?" He sat on the couch, spread his arms across the back, and crossed his legs at the ankle. He wanted to take up as much space in the room as possible. "I don't think so. You could be fired for that, you know."

"Then fire me. I'll be on the next plane out of here."

RJ smiled. "I know that's what you want me to do, but as soon as you got on that plane, your father would be in handcuffs and Nicaragua isn't known for its luxurious jails."

"What do you want, RJ?" Laura scrubbed her face and looked around the room.

"There is fresh coffee is in the main house. However, there is a coffee maker in that little kitchen over there, or do you have a maid that makes your breakfast in the morning?"

"What the hell do you want?"

"To tell you that we aren't accepting that little deal you cooked up with Gomez."

"Fine." She stood and walked to the doorway to her room. "I have to go to the hospital to get your birth certificate. Unless you have it, of course."

"I'm sorry, I don't know where it is. You can ask Sofia if you'd like. Perhaps my father has a copy in the safe."

"No, I'll just go into town and get it. Besides, I have an appointment with a local attorney."

"Really?"

"I'm not licensed to practice law here, so I thought it would be good to have local counsel. Assuming you have to have a license, of course."

"Very good. I know just the person if yours doesn't work out." Picking up the pad and pen on the table, he scribbled a name and number and handed it to her. "I'm sure you will find them very helpful."

"Thanks. Now if you don't mind, I have to get ready and get to town."

"Please, use my car and driver. The roads here are so bad and the drivers, well they eat crazy for breakfast before getting on the road." He stood and smoothed out his pants. "I wouldn't want anything happening to you before you got Lewis out of the country and back safely on US soil." He hoped it sounded just as he meant it: a threat.

Before Laura could say anything, he slammed the door behind him. He didn't like this American and wouldn't be surprised if she sold him out. That would be a mistake, now that he had Lewis in Nicaragua. He'd play that card before anything else. Well, maybe not before anything else. He had a few other cards he was getting ready to play and she was his last resort. Always be prepared for any conclusion, he often told himself.

Sofia wouldn't win.

❧❧❧❧

Sofia had a mind to go over and pound on Laura's door, but she didn't want to give in to her rage. Hopefully it would calm down in a few hours, but something was wrong, seriously wrong. If she didn't know better, she would think Laura didn't want to be here, and what was up with that compromise Laura had proposed to her lawyer? She'd already talked to Señor Gomez this morning and squashed the idea, but RJ looked surprised when their grandmother brought it up. No matter, she wasn't slicing or dicing off pieces of Huerta, and she damn well wasn't going to let RJ profit from the Huerta name, even if it was secondhand.

She didn't have time for this crap. Her day was already packed with a visit to the factory and to check out the remnants of the burnt-out building and hiring a crew to rebuild it. Then she wanted to get out to the fields and check on things out there. A bad crop and compounded with the lost bales of tobacco could hurt them severely. Lucky for her only her tobacco had gone up in flames. She'd need to beef up security and get some cameras installed. It wasn't going to happen again. Besides, as soon as Gomez served RJ and Lina with eviction papers, the shit would blow up.

⚞⚟⚞⚟

Her day had been filled with language barriers, long lines, and finally an envelope with RJ's birth certificate. She hadn't had time to even look at it because of her tight schedule. The driver RJ had so generously provided could not seem to locate the address of the attorney she had contacted herself, which she could not dismiss as mere poor navigation. Her visit to the lawyer RJ recommended hadn't gone well, either. She knew sleaze when she saw it, and he had it crawling all over him. A verbal duel had ensued when she tried to get out of working with him, but RJ must have handed over some of the pictures of her dad and the young girls because he splashed them all over his desk, practically drooling on them himself. She'd left the office with a bad taste in her mouth, and it wasn't just because he lacked a good hygiene regimen. She was worried about the people RJ associated with down here. Clearly they could make it difficult to get back Stateside if she didn't cooperate with RJ's plan to wrestle Huerta cigars from his sister. Where did that leave her in all of this? Nowhere, she surmised. Whatever fire she and Sofia had started to stoke in the States was over now.

She'd barely had time to dash back to the estate and meet up with RJ for her tour of the Huerta factory, the fields, and the inner workings of the cigar business.

Since he didn't want anything else that had the Huerta name, she wasn't about to waste time looking at any of the other holdings.

As for her father, Lewis could be anywhere. Mostly likely he was tucked away in the bed of a woman, consoling his wounded ego. They'd had words last night and it hadn't been pretty. In fact, she was downright ruthless in her assessment of his situation. While she still worked for the firm she had to put up with his crap, but after this trip, she was sure her working arrangements would be different when she returned to the US. She wouldn't be able to look her mother in the eye if she stayed. She told her father that if he didn't leave the firm, she would. Knowing him, he'd stay and force her out. That was fine; she was due some new pasture, so to speak.

She'd quickly changed into some jeans and a loose blouse. The heat wasn't bad today, just a little too muggy for her tastes. Snatching a wide brimmed hat from behind the door, she waited by the gate for RJ. Glancing at her watch, she noted he was twenty minutes late for their tour. She was just about to leave when a Jeep pulled alongside her.

"Waiting for someone?" Sofia didn't smile, but her tone wasn't brisk.

"I'm supposed to be going on a tour with your brother."

"Really. I suppose he's late."

"Twenty minutes."

Sofia looked around the compound and then leaned over and opened the door. "Hop in, I'll give you the grand tour. That is, if you don't mind coming with the opposition."

"I..." Laura just wanted to jump in the Jeep and

give Sofia a big kiss, but hesitated even taking her up on her benign tour offer. "I probably should wait for your brother."

"I don't think he's going to make it back for the tour. It seems he's being questioned about the fire at the factory."

"Fire? Oh my god, was anyone hurt?" RJ hadn't mentioned a fire to her when she'd arrived.

"No, just all of my tobacco for my cigar line went up in smoke." Sofia adjusted her sunglasses in the mirror and looked back at Laura. "So, I don't think he's going to make it."

"You don't think so?" Laura was getting pissed that her *client*—and she used the moniker lightly— would be so disrespectful of her time. Why hadn't he left a message and let her know he was being questioned by the police?

"Oh, I know so. Come on, jump in. Besides, I know more about the estate than he does. He's a crappy tour guide. But if you'd like to go to the police station and advise your client, I am more than happy to take you there instead."

"I'm not his lawyer. If he needs one, he'll have to call a local attorney. I'm not licensed to practice law down here."

"So, why are you here then?"

"It's complicated."

"It sounds like it."

Laura gave her a questioning look.

"I mean, anything involving my brother is always complicated."

"Yeah, but not like this, I assure you," she huffed under her breath.

"Tour or police station?"

Laura looked around one more time and then down at her watch. Nodding, she jumped into the Jeep.

"Tour." She held onto her hat as Sofia gunned it out of the driveway and down the road. Holding on to the dash, she side-eyed Sofia, watching her coffee-brown hair streaming behind her as the wind caught it and whipped it around. A tight tank top showed off her tanned arms, her hands bare of any jewelry or trappings of someone with Sofia's status. She blended in with the locals and Laura was sure she wanted it that way.

They rode in silence for a mile or two before Laura couldn't stand it anymore. Turning toward Sofia, she put her hand on Sofia's hand. "Please know that I had no idea any of this was going on. I'm so sorry."

"For what? You're just doing what you were hired to do, right?"

"That's just it. I wasn't hired. My dad called me in a panic and demanded that I get down here to help him with a case."

"I understand family commitment. I would have done anything for my own father." Sofia still didn't look at Laura.

"Yeah, well I'm not that close to my father. My mother, yes. Him…" She shook her head and looked off into the distance trying to avoid Sofia's gaze. "He's just an asshole. The fact that he and RJ are friends should say all you need to know about my father."

"Yes, but sometimes family is family, warts and all."

"Imagine having RJ as your father, then you'll see where I'm coming from."

"Good point."

Sofia turned off the paved road and onto a dirt

road lined with vegetation before Laura could explain further. The ruts bucked the Jeep back and forth, almost tossing her into Sofia's seat. On one particularly bad one, Sofia stuck her hand out and held Laura back into her seat. Her hand on Laura's chest brought a flash of memory of the night they'd spent together before all of this mess landed in her lap. Pulling herself together, she focused on the plants that lined the dirt road, organized in long lines, each one almost the same size as the next except the patch that was covered with a white fabric at head height, while most of it was left exposed to the sun.

"Tobacco."

"Huh?" Laura looked around. The fields went on for acres, at least she thought it was acres, before a rolling hill took over the view.

"It's this year's crop of tobacco. Come on, I'll show you. I usually ride the fields by horseback. I love horses, and I get to see the fields better traveling them by horseback." Sofia slid to a stop on the road and geared the Jeep into Park. Walking around to Laura's side, Sofia opened the door and swung her hand wide, waiting for Laura to exit. Any other time Laura would have thought it chivalrous, but this time she didn't know what to think.

"Why are these covered?"

"We're shading the leaves for our Connecticut wrappers. These will be a milder, lighter color than our maduro or ligero wrappers, which are darker and more robust in flavor. You get seventy percent of the taste from the wrapper. Come on." Sofia pulled up an end of the fabric so Laura could duck under.

It was cooler under the shade, so Laura took off her hat and wiped her face.

"I didn't realize tobacco plants grew so large."

"Hmm." Sofia walked ahead of Laura and pushed a few leaves away. "The way the plant grows, the leaves all have a different flavor and uses. Some of it we leave on so that it gets darker, fuller, richer in flavor. The tops come off and we use that leaf—the first pick, or legro—for the bolder cigars."

Laura looked at the leaves and ran her fingers down the veins. "They look completely different than what you make cigars out of."

"Well, these are green. We pick them and dry them, then we separate them for different tastes and roll them into cigars. That's the simplified version, but I think you get the picture."

"Wow, is there a machine that picks the tobacco?"

Sofia laughed and handed Laura the leaves she'd picked off a plant. "No. When it says handmade, we mean handmade. When it's time, the men will come out and pick the plants, bundle them, and take them to the drying rooms. Then a whole process starts of fermentation, sorting by color, bundling, and then finally rolling. Some companies use rolling machines, but we still do everything by hand. It allows us to monitor the quality and ensure nothing goes in there that we haven't touched."

"Wow, I had no idea. So after all that they're ready to smoke?" Laura absently brushed the leaves against her leg as she watched Sofia's hands gesture as she spoke.

"No, they go into our humidor and sit for anywhere from weeks to months. We have some cigars that have been aging a year in our humidors."

"Really?"

"Like wine, they get better with age. I mean you

can smoke a freshly rolled cigar, but you have to smoke it right then, otherwise you want to let it age in your humidor for a couple of weeks. If you don't, it will taste awful."

Laura giggled at the face Sofia made with the statement. "That bad, huh?"

"Oh, I see you haven't had a bad cigar, have you?"

"I guess not."

"Good, don't. It will make you sick."

"Okay, I'll remember that."

Sofia and Laura walked farther into the tobacco field and out from under the fabric. She slipped her hat back on and followed behind Sofia until they were in a clearing.

"It's beautiful here," Laura said, just before she slammed into Sofia's back. "Oh, sorry."

Sofia grabbed her just as she was about to fall backward. Pulling Laura in close, they were nose-to-nose when Laura looked into Sofia's eyes. Without thinking, she brushed her lips against Sofia's and waited. Sofia pulled her in tight and kissed her hard. Angry, harsh kisses bruised her lips before she pulled back. Tears brimmed on Sofia's lashes.

"Why are you crying?" Laura wiped at the tears.

"Why are you here?" Sofia asked again.

"I didn't have a choice."

"We always have choices," Sofia said turning away from Laura's touch.

"You loved your father, right?"

Sofia nodded.

"Well, there is no love lost between my father and me, but he's still my family and my boss. In this case even that wouldn't be enough for me to help, but both he and my mother are being threatened, and I can't have that. Know that if I had a choice, I wouldn't be here. I'd be home or at my office, looking at my phone and that picture you took of us wondering if you were going to call. Or wondering if I should call you. I'd be lamenting over whether or not it would seem too soon to text, or all those stupid things we do when we like someone but have only had one date."

"We had more than a date, Laura."

Laura threaded her hands through Sofia's and rested her head on Sofia's shoulder. "Yes, we did. It was a wonderful night, and if that's all I get then I'll live with it."

"I'm not giving my brother anything."

"I know."

"I'm not agreeing to your offer, either."

"I know." Laura offered a half-hearted smile and rested her chin on Sofia's shoulder. "I wish I could change everything, but please know that I'm not here to hurt you."

Sofia touched her chin and then kissed her nose. "We should go. I'll take you to the factory and you can see how cigars are made."

Laura's heart sank. A moment lost all because of RJ and his greed. She could see now why Sofia hated her brother. Laura put him right up there with her father. Selfish, arrogant, self-absorbed assholes. Christ, just when she thought her life was going in the right direction, it suddenly had gone off the rails in less than a day.

"Would you like to join me for a cigar later?" Sofia asked, holding the door for Laura.

Maybe there was hope for them yet.

"Sure."

Chapter Twenty-four

S ofia pulled into the compound and parked
her Jeep. RJ's car was nestled into its usual
spot.

"Looks like your client is back," Sofia said,
turning off the Jeep and sitting.

"Looks like." Laura almost sounded disappointed.

"Tell you what, let's not talk about business and
I'll meet you in the courtyard off my room. We can
have a drink and a cigar there and relax."

"Isn't that what got us in this mess in the first
place?"

Sofia shot Laura a confused look.

"Not talking about our backgrounds or work? If I
would have known in San Francisco that you were the
sibling in the will, I wouldn't have come down when
my father called in a panic."

"Oh, right."

Funny how something as innocent as establishing
a boundary could be responsible for the mess she and
Laura found themselves in now.

"Well, I won't hold it against you if you tell me
why." Sofia jumped out of the car just as RJ walked out
of the house.

"Sofia. Well, this is interesting. Trying to corrupt
my attorney with your nonsense?" RJ walked over to
Laura.

"Actually, asshole, you didn't show up to give

her the tour you promised, so I did it."

"Well, that was very nice of you," he said, grabbing Laura's elbow and ushering her toward the door.

"RJ, stop." Laura yanked her arm out of his grasp. "I am not your attorney."

Sofia felt her stomach tighten in anger at the contact. She moved around the Jeep within a close enough distance that if Laura needed her she could react.

"Well, isn't this cozy? I think there might be a conflict of interest here, Sister."

"No, I just don't like the fact that you think you can treat all women like you treat Lina."

"I treat Lina the way one would treat a cheating bitch."

"That's rich coming from you, RJ." Sofia stepped closer.

"Look, I suggest that you two leave each other alone."

Sofia looked at Laura. "I'll handle my brother, if you'll excuse us," she said, dismissing Laura. Turning toward RJ, she started on him. "If you think I'm going to just roll over for the sake of the family name, you have another think coming."

The door slammed behind them. Sofia was instantly sorry for the tone she took with Laura. They'd had a great afternoon working their way through Huerta Cigars, and now it felt like a stone wall had fallen between them.

"Do you think I'm stupid, Sofia?"

"What are you talking about?"

"I know who she is, Sofia."

"She's your lawyer, RJ."

"No," he said, pulling out some photos. "She's your lover, sister dear." He handed the stack to Sofia.

Her heart sank as she looked at the photos of her trip to San Francisco. He'd had her followed.

Bastard.

"Where did you get these?"

"You didn't think I'd sit back and give you Huerta, did you?" RJ's smug smile sickened her. "If you don't rethink your position, I'll have to send these to the Bar Association and get her disbarred for her conduct."

"You fucking asshole."

Sofia launched herself at her brother and caught him with a right hook to his chin, staggering him backward. She watched him fall to the ground, pictures scattering to the ground.

"Go head, hit me again," he goaded her.

Straightening, she looked down at him, knowing she was playing into his hands.

"You aren't worth it. Besides, call the police and tell them that you got your ass handed to you by a girl. See how that works with your compañeros, forming that little Cigar Baron group you're talking about. Just don't forget to tell them that Huerta won't be a part of it."

RJ rubbed his chin and smiled. "I'm not worried, Sofia. Things will work out for me. You should be careful who you piss off, though. They have a long reach down here."

"Is that a threat?"

"Nope, just some brotherly advice." He picked up the photos and handed them to her. "You can keep these. I have copies. Besides, I'm thinking—"

"What? That you're going to come between us?

Use her as a weapon to get me to fork over Huerta? Go ahead, use them. I don't give a shit."

Sofia pushed him back to the ground as she walked around him and into the house.

"Bitch," she heard him say as the door closed behind her.

She'd finally let him get to her. Now what? The coolness of the house did little to calm her down. Her body was amped with the knowledge that RJ would try to blackmail her with her relationship with Laura. Hopefully, Laura was out; if not she'd need to warn her about RJs scheme. The dirty bastard, she'd ring his neck when all of this was over. If he thought family meant anything to her, he had another think coming. He was dead to her, officially.

Chapter Twenty-five

Laura sat on the couch and booted up her computer. The hour nap had done her a world of good to center her and get her thoughts straight. Tapping the keyboard, she coaxed the computer to life. She'd wanted to transcribe her notes for RJ's lawyer. She couldn't help herself. She hated working for the slimy man, but she felt like her reputation was on the line and anything she could do to speed up getting out of Nicaragua, she'd do. The envelope she'd picked up from the hospital slipped out of her notebook holder and fell to the floor. Sliding her finger inside, she fished out the birth certificate and looked at it.

"Shit." She reeled at the information unfolding in front of her. Jumping up, her computer clattered to the floor. "Jesus Christ." She piled all of the contents onto the chair and headed for the door. She needed to find Sofia.

Standing in the courtyard, she looked at the door to the house and the exit to the driveway, the direction she'd come trying to put as much distance between her and Sofia and RJ. She walked out to the driveway and noticed that Sofia's Jeep was gone but RJ's car remained.

Tapping the birth certificate against her palm, she turned and went into the house. The living room was buzzing with conversations and agitation. Spotting Manny hunched over talking to Sofia's grandmother, she tapped him on the shoulder.

"What's wrong?"

Sofia's grandmother looked up at Laura. Clearly she'd been crying.

"It's going to be okay, Mama." Manny patted her shoulder and turned toward Laura. "Sofia's been in an accident."

"What?" Laura's knees went weak, so she grabbed onto Manny's arm to steady herself.

"It's okay. She's at the hospital."

"I should—"

Manny shook his head. "I wouldn't. Not yet. I talked to her on the phone. She's going to be okay. She's got a nasty bump on the head and a separated shoulder, but otherwise she's going to be okay. Can't say that for her Jeep, but lucky for her she was driving the Jeep and not her Jag."

"How?"

"She said her brakes gave out."

"What? I was in the Jeep with her this afternoon. They seemed to be fine then."

"Well, good thing it didn't happen when you two were together. She'd never forgive herself it something happened when you were driving with her."

"I should go and be with her." Laura's body shook, and her head started to swim.

"She's going to be out before you even get there, so just wait."

She knew Manny was trying to console her, but she didn't want to be reassured. She needed to see Sofia for herself. Then a thought struck her.

"Do you think RJ did this?"

Manny pulled Laura away from his mother. "Don't say anything in front of María."

Laura lowered her voice. "She was fighting with RJ earlier."

"About what?"

"I don't know. I didn't want to eavesdrop, so I left."

Manny shook his head. "Fucking RJ."

"Where is he?"

"Probably in the office. He was making some phone calls when I walked by."

"Thanks." Laura walked toward the office on a mission. She was going to get this mess cleaned up right now.

RJ had his feet up on the desk, talking on the phone. When he caught sight of Laura, he motioned for her to take a seat in front of the desk. Instead, she paced back and forth waiting for him to end his conversation. When it looked like he wouldn't, she motioned for him to hang up.

"Now," she said, waving the paper in front of his face.

"What?" he said, tossing the phone onto the desk. "This better be good, Laura."

"Oh, it is, just not for you." She handed him the birth certificate and waited.

RJ blanched as his eyes moved across the paper. The color drained from his face and he stood, crumbled it up, and tossed it into the waste basket.

"That's fake, I don't believe it," he said stomping out of the office. "Fucking bastard."

Laura fished the wad of paper out and smoothed it on the desk. She had her own ace in the hole and was going home.

"Truth sucks, asshole."

Chapter Twenty-six

Sofia had walked into the office trussed up in an arm sling and straight into a ranting and raving until she saw RJ swinging a gun around. She'd just come back from the hospital and the drugs were working their magic. Maybe she was hallucinating. She had to be, as she couldn't believe what she was seeing. He'd lost his mind, and she had a front row seat to the show played out. RJ was holding court. Laura, Manny, and everyone else all stood listening as he recounted what had happened the night Don Roberto died.

"He sat on that horse like a king, sitting on a throne. His regal attitude as he told me I wouldn't inherit a penny of Huerta Cigars." RJ lit a cigar, took a long draw, and let the smoke work its way out of his mouth, savoring the audience more than the delicate hints of leather, coffee, and pepper. "Seems I'm a Huerta all right, just not the 'right' Huerta. Right, Tío? Or should I call you 'Father'?"

Sofia blanched at the revelation.

"What the hell is he talking about, Tío?"

Manny stared silently at RJ.

Sofia stepped toward RJ, but he raised the gun and pointed it at her.

"Don't give me a reason, Sofia." A demented smile cracked his face. His eyes had a crazy glint to them, showing that he meant business even if the business was insane. Sofia almost felt sorry for the bastard, but she was looking down the barrel of a gun so she wasn't in a forgiving mood. How ironic, though. RJ truly was a bastard, but he carried Don Roberto's name and she wasn't about to sully that name or her father's memory. Pointing to her left arm strapped to her body, the pain was only diminished by the hatred she had for a brother she clearly never knew.

"It's obvious you don't need a reason, RJ."

He laughed, stepping closer to her. "Oh, that. Yeah. It was supposed to be worse. In fact, you were supposed to die, but it's not too late." He looked down at the chrome gun. "I still got this." He took another puff of the cigar and blew the smoke in Sofia's face. "Hey, you know, these are pretty good. Negrilla Diabla. Somehow, I think you named this after you didn't you, Sister?"

Manny stepped between the two. "RJ, Son—"

"Oh, now you're ready to call me son. Why now? Huh, DAD? When did you know, huh?" RJ's face gleamed, slick with sweat. "Answer me, you bastard."

Sofia's mind raced while RJ's mouth ran full speed, spewing expletives as the gun arced between her, Manny, and Laura. She gave Laura a sideways glance. She stood transfixed by the waving and ranting, color drained from her already pale face. Slowly, Sofia reached for Laura's hand, threading her fingers, sliding past the slick palm. Pulling on her hand, Sofia positioned Laura slightly behind her.

"Oh god, Sofia. I'm so sorry. I had no idea this would set him off." Laura rested her head against Sofia's shoulder. Her gentle sobs rocked them both. Lucky for them, RJ was so mentally off-balance his complete focus was on Manny.

"What happened?" Sofia whispered over her

shoulder, trying not to draw attention to the train wreck playing in front of them.

"I found his birth certificate."

"And?"

Laura didn't say anything.

"What are you two bitches whispering about, huh?"

"Nothing, RJ." Laura's voice cracked.

"You're my lawyer. What the fuck happened to client/lawyer privilege. Oh wait..." RJ walked over to Laura and pushed the gun against her chest. "That's right, you're fucking my sister." He pushed it harder into her chest, sending her backward. Sofia grabbed her hand tighter, trying to hold her upright. Pain shot through her body as the torque from her arm being yanked jerked her body.

Manny put his hand on her back to stabilize her, and then stepped between RJ and Laura.

"RJ, please."

"Tell her, Tío. Tell Sofia why my father wouldn't leave me anything. Or are you too embarrassed?"

"RJ you know in your heart that's not the case. I've taken you under my wing, Son. Tried to be..." Manny choked up as he fumbled with his words. "I wanted to tell you. I begged your father to let me raise you, but when your mother died days after giving birth, he'd given your mother his word he would raise you as his own."

Sofia searched Laura's face for the truth. A nod in agreement was her only answer. She almost felt sorry for Manny as his resolve finally broke and his shoulders sagged under the weight of the truth tumbling out.

"Why?"

"Why?" Manny shot RJ a puzzled look.

"Why would she make him promise?"

"Because it was her dying wish. To spite me I suppose." Manny looked down at his shaking hands.

"Did…did you rape her?"

Sofia's heart was in her throat at the accusation that spilled from his lips. Rape? Her kindhearted uncle wasn't capable of taking a woman without her consent. She'd never even heard him speak ill of anyone. He was more of an optimist and constantly saw the good, even in a bad situation. The idea that he would force himself on a woman was beyond crazy, but then again RJ was sitting just this side of the loony barrier.

"Rape? No, I loved your mother. She was a beautiful woman. Her heart was so pure so…" He fumbled with his words again.

"Then why would Don Roberto agree to raise me as his own son, when it's clear I have a different father—his brother."

Manny looked down at his shaking hands. "He was thinking of your mother, RJ. She was frail and weak after your birth. We were all worried and we didn't want her…" Tears started to fall. "I loved your mother beyond words. She was a beautiful soul, but she knew I wasn't in a position to raise you. You needed someone more grounded, and a son would…Huerta was at a pivotal moment in the cigar industry. We all knew the scandal could hurt Huerta cigars. Your mother asked for my permission, and I thought it would be best. You'd have a family, a sister, and all of this." He raised his hands and looked around the room. "I'm so sorry, RJ. it was never my intent to hurt you. I wanted you to have things I couldn't give you—stability, love, and a future. I wasn't sure I could offer that, not at that time."

"RJ..." Sofia need to try and calm him down.

RJ pointed the gun at her head. "Shut. The. Fuck. Up. Sofia. The perfect daughter. You look just like Mom. Now I know why we never clicked as brother and sister."

"Half-sister. It seems we still share a mother," she flippantly reminded him, taking her life in her own hands. She stepped forward, letting her grip on Laura's hand and to her future go. She'd had enough of his bullshit. Stepping around Manny, she got right up in his face.

"You did all of this, RJ. My car accident, the fire at the warehouse, burning my bales of tobacco. Father's death. All of it. It was you, wasn't it?"

RJ pushed the muzzle of the gun against her chest and leaned in so close she could smell the rum oozing out of his pores. He shook like a junkie who needed a fix. His eyes were wild with hate, his mouth pulled back in a tight grimace. Spit spewed everywhere when he talked.

Christ. He was strung out. How come she didn't notice it before? The erratic behavior, the ups and downs, the depression. He not only was womanizing, he was putting all his money up his veins, or more likely in his nose, vanity being what it was to RJ.

"How did you do it, RJ? How did you kill Dad?"

"Ha ha ha, the great Sofia knows everything but she can't figure out how her father died."

"You said he fell off his horse and hit his head on a rock."

"Oh, he hit his head on a rock all right. It just had a little...help!" He spit in her face as he grunted out the last word. "I might have helped the rock a little." He sucked on his cigar again, puffing it back to lit. He blew on the end, producing a bright red cherry. Any other time Sofia would have marveled at the beauty of the glowing tip, but so close to her face she was more worried about RJ's intentions.

"Nice, tight roll. The edges burning faster than the center is a sign of a good cigar. I can smell the Ligero leaves in the middle, Sister."

He stuck the end in his mouth and raised his hand mimicking how he held the rock. He started pacing, holding a pretend rock.

"We get to the reservoir. He breaks out a couple of cigars and hands me one. He breaks out his thermos filled with rum. There we are, smoking and drinking, and then he drops the bomb on me. He says, 'Maybe you should be the one to lead the future of Huerta Cigars. Oh, not right now, but maybe not for a decade...' But he made it clear you were the anointed one." RJ jerked to a stop. He swung around to face Sofia. He raised his hand, holding the phantom rock above his head, and slammed it down in a quick and vicious stroke meant to kill. "So, I thought I would kill him before he did something permanent." A confused look replaced one of agitation. He pulled the cigar from his mouth and blew out a stream of smoke. "Do you know why he picked you?"

Sofia shook her head. She thought she knew, she just didn't want to aggravate his demented actions any further. She'd pushed her luck up to this point, and she wasn't sure he would hold up to the knowledge that her father had already told her the why and the when. At least she thought she knew the why, but now she wasn't so sure.

"Because you took the initiative to create your own line of cheap-ass cigars. Can you believe that?"

"RJ—"

"Shut up, Tío."

"Wait." Manny held up his hands. "You can join me, Son. What am I, scraps off the Huerta table? I might be small right now, but we can grow the business together. I've always hoped your father would tell you one day and we could be father and son. Huerta and Son Cigars."

"Why didn't you tell me? Huh, Dad? Clearly, the nut didn't fall too far from the family tree."

Wildly swinging the gun around RJ stopped, stepped forward, and pressed the gun against Manny's temple, going nose-to-nose with the man. "So, why?"

Everyone in the room froze. Sofia searched out Laura and nodded her head toward the door and mouthed, *Go.* She didn't want her lover hurt in any way and she already suspected Laura felt responsible for how the events were playing out. Laura had no way of knowing RJ lost his mind the day he killed their father. There was no fault to be found—RJ was just plain crazy.

The two men squared off, neither blinking as RJ cocked the hammer. The click echoed like a bomb blast.

"RJ," Sofia whispered. "If it's Huerta Cigars you want, then you can have it. Just let Tío go. Please." She shooed Laura out of the room, but not before she whispered, "Call the police."

"I love you," Laura said. Tears, black from her mascara, streamed down her face. A soft pleading followed. "Please, please be careful."

Sofia winked in agreement and offered a half-smile before turning her attention to RJ.

"Oh, now you want to share your toys? Really,

Sister? How ironic." RJ did not move. "It's a little late for that considering everything I've done. Now isn't it?"

"RJ, we can work this out."

The heat of the day was at its most oppressive, and with all the windows closed and the blinds drawn, it felt like they were already on their way to hell. Sofia wiped the sweat from her face and tried to moisten her dry lips, but her mouth felt like it was the Sahara desert. She wished she hadn't foregone breakfast. Her head started to swim, the room spun, and she stumbled toward the desk. A frail voice pierced her consciousness.

"Abuelita, you shouldn't be in here." Sofia supported herself on the corner of the desk and looked over at her grandmother. There was no mistaking her displeasing look. She was pissed, or maybe Sofia was so out of it she was hallucinating her grandmother's presence in the room.

"Beto, put that gun down. Now."

Sofia's vision tunneled and her face started to tingle. Shit, she was going to black out. Before she could do anything, her knees buckled and she fell face first to the ground. Trying to twist so she didn't land on her shoulder, she hit her head on the desk and blacked out just as a loud something ricocheted through her fog.

Bang!

Chapter Twenty-seven

Sofia! Sofia, honey. Are you all right?"

She wasn't. Her head was splitting and her left side was screaming in agony. Hell, she wasn't exactly sure she was still alive except for the pain. No one dead would feel such anguish. Forcing her eyes open, she tried to focus on the image in front of her, but the hammering going on in her head and the oppressive light flicking back and forth made her want to throw up.

"I'm going to be sick," she whispered.

"Turn her on her side. We don't want her aspirating on her own vomit."

Well, there's a nice thought. If that meant she could choke on her own puke, *then turn me on my side, damn it.* She thought about trying to move.

"Hold on, ma'am." A male voice pushed her down on her back.

"Sofia, stay down." She recognized Laura's voice. Her hand stroked Sofia's face.

Her urge to be sick was diminished as soon as Laura cradled her head in her lap.

"My grandmother…"

"She's fine."

Sofia turned her head and caught sight of RJ pinned to the ground under her uncle. Pieces of plaster rained down on them from the hole in the ceiling.

"What happened?"

Laura wiped at her face, trying to clear the sweat away. "RJ isn't Don Roberto's son. He's Manny's son."

"What?"

"Every family has its secrets, and RJ just found out why he isn't getting any of the company."

"He's lost his fucking mind."

"The police are on their way," Laura said, stroking Sofia's face.

"He killed my father. I can't believe he killed my father."

"I guess he couldn't take it when Don Roberto told him."

Tears streamed down Sofia's face. How could he? Don Roberto had raised him as if he were his own son. He'd given him everything, and that was how he paid Don Roberto back, by killing him.

"Your brother was blackmailing my father with indecent pictures of my father in compromising pictures with young girls."

"What?"

"That's why I had to help him. I'm so sorry, Sofia can you forgive me?" Laura whispered in her ear.

"It's not your fault. He had pictures of us together in San Francisco and was trying to blackmail me with you."

Sofia looked over at RJ, who was crying like a baby under Manny's arms, who had him in a bear hug sitting on the floor. Her poor grandmother was wiping his face, like she did when they were children. He'd played her, too. How could she baby him knowing that he killed her son? A mother's love was all encompassing, wasn't it?

She struggled to sit up and leaned against the desk. Laura sat next to her, her head on Laura's shoulder. How could things have gotten this bad? Sirens and red and blue lights lit up the office from the outside.

≈≈≈≈≈

"I hope you go to jail forever, you selfish bastard," Sofia spit out as they loaded RJ into the back seat.

His head hung in despair. He didn't make eye contact with her as he said, "I'm sorry, Abuelita. Please forgive me."

Their grandmother patted his back and kissed him on the cheek. "Just know that I love you, Roberto."

Sofia wanted to scream, but she just watched as RJ tossed her a slight smile. He was already working on a plan, if she knew him at all.

"Come on. Let's get you to bed," Laura said, pulling Sofia away from the commotion.

Sofia nodded, walked over to Manny, and patted him on the shoulder. "I'm so sorry, Manny."

Manny grabbed her hand and kissed the back of it. "I'm sorry, Sofia, I should have been a better father."

"It's not your fault, Tío. RJ knew what he was doing. So did Papa."

Manny hung his head, sobbing.

"Come on. Let's get you to bed," Laura said for a second time.

"I think we have lots to talk about." Sofia wrapped her good arm around Laura and leaned on her for stability. "Like maybe a trip to Napa, yes?"

"Let's get you well first, and then we can talk about the future." Laura kissed Sofia's cheek. "I'm kinda craving those little bacon-wrapped dates at our favorite restaurant."

"We have a favorite restaurant?"

"I think so."

Sofia pulled Laura in for a kiss. Screw everyone standing around watching. She wasn't about to lose the one thing that suddenly meant everything to her. Huerta Cigars would always be there, but meeting Laura had been the real treasure.

They both watched as the police car left the compound.

"Come on, you can tell me about your place in Napa."

"You bet." Laura rested her forehead on Sofia's and sighed. "Sounds like a plan."

How can you help the Author if you liked their books?

Reviews help an author get discovered and if you have enjoyed this book, please do the author the honor of posting a review on Goodreads, Amazon, Barnes & Noble or anywhere you purchased the book. Or perhaps share a posting on your social media sites to help spread the word to your friends.

About the Author

Isabella lives on the central coast with her wife, and three sons. She teaches college and in her spare time, which there seems to be little of lately, she is working on her writers retreat in the Sierra foothills. She is a GLCS award winner for Always Faithful and a finalist for Scarlet Masquerade. She also finaled in the International National Book awards and has two honorable mentions in the Rainbow Awards.

She also writes under the nom de plume - Jett Abbott. A darker, rogue who's a motorcycle enthusiast and loves people watching.

Like her fan page for the latest in news on readings, appearances and books.

https://www.facebook.com/isabella.sapphirebooks

or

www.sapphirebooks.com/isabella.html

Check out Isabella's other books

Award winning novel - *Always Faithful* - ISBN - 978-0-982860-80-9

Major Nichol "Nic" Caldwell is the only survivor of her helicopter crash in Iraq. She is left alone to wonder why she and she alone survived. Survivor's guilt has nothing on the young Major as she is forced to deal with the scars, both physical and mental, left from her ordeal overseas. Before the accident, she couldn't think of doing anything else in her life.

Claire Monroe is your average military wife, with a loving husband and a little girl. She is used to the time apart from her husband. In fact, it was one of the reasons she married him. Then, one day, her life is turned upside down when she gets a visit from the Marine Corps.

Can these two women come to terms with the past and finally find happiness, or will their shared sense of honor keep them apart?

Forever Faithful - ISBN – 978-1-939062-75-8

Life is what happens when you make other plans, and Nic and Claire have just found out that life and the Marine Corps have other plans for their lives. Nic Caldwell has served her country, met the woman of her dreams, and has reached the rank of Lieutenant Colonel. She's studying at one of the nation's most prestigious military universities, setting her sights on a research position after graduation. Things couldn't be better and then it happens; a sudden assignment to Afghanistan derails any thoughts of marriage and wedded bliss. Another combat zone, another tragedy, and Nic suddenly finds herself fighting for her life. Claire Monroe loves her new life in Monterey. She's finally where she wants to be, getting ready to start her master's program at the local university, watching her daughter, Grace, growing up, and getting ready to marry the love of her life. What could possibly derail a perfect life? The Marine Corps. Will Nic survive Afghanistan? Can Claire step up and be the strength in their relationship? Or will this overseas assignment and a catastrophic accident divide their once happy home?

American Yakuza - ISBN - 978-0-9828608-3-0

Luce Potter straddles three cultures as she strives to live with the ideals of family, honor, and duty. When her grandfather passes the family business to her, Luce finds out that power, responsibility and justice come with a price. Is it a price she's willing to die for?

Brooke Erickson lives the fast-paced life of an investigative journalist living on the edge until it all comes crashing down around her one night in Europe. Stateside, Brooke learns to deal with a new reality when she goes to work at a financial magazine and finds out things aren't always as they seem.

Can two women find enough common ground for love or will their two different worlds and cultures keep them apart?

American Yakuza II - The Lies that Bind - ISBN - 978-10939062-20-8

Luce Potter runs her life and her business with an iron fist and complete control until lies and deception unravel her world. The shadow of betrayal consumes Luce, threatening to destroy the most precious thing in her life, Brooke Erickson.

Brooke Erickson finds herself on the outside of Luce's life looking in. As events spiral out of control Brooke can only watch as the woman she loves pushes her further away. Suddenly, devastated and alone, Brooke refuses to let go without an explanation.

Colby Water, a federal agent investigating the ever-elusive Luce Potter, discovers someone from her past is front and center in her investigation of the Yakuza crime leader. Before she can put the crime boss in prison, she must confront the ultimate deception in her professional life.

When worlds collide, betrayal, dishonor and death are inevitable. Can Luce and Brooke survive the explosion?

America Yakuza III- Razor's Edge - ISBN - 978-1-943353-81-1

Luce Potter lives by a code of honor. Push her and she shoves back, harder. There's only one problem: Luce has just found out that revenge is a knife that cuts both ways. Now that her lover Brooke has survived the attack on her life, Luce has only one thing on her mind, and his name is Frank. Unfortunately, someone walks into her life that she didn't see coming. Brooke Erickson has survived an attack so brutal it's left a permanent scar on her soul. All she wants to do now is go home and finish recuperating with her lover, Luce Potter, by her side. An unexpected event puts Brooke at the head of the Yakuza family. Can she command the respect necessary to lead it through the crisis? Luce and Brooke's worlds are upending. Can each do what's necessary to survive and return to a new normal

Executive Disclosure- ISBN - 978-0-9828608-3-0

When a life is threatened, it takes a special breed of person to step in front of a bullet. Chad Morgan's job has put her life on the line more times that she can count. Getting close to the client is expected; getting too close could be deadly for Chad. Reagan Reynolds wants the top job at Reynolds Holdings and knows how to play the game like "the boys." She's not above using her beauty and body as currency to get what she wants. Shocked to find out someone wants her dead, Reagan isn't thrilled at the prospect of needing protection as she tries to convince the board she's the right woman for a man's job. How far will a killer go to get what they want? Secrets and deception twist the rules of the game as a killer closes in. How far will Chad go to protect her beautiful, but challenging client?

Surviving Reagan - ISBN - 978-1-939062-38-3

Chad Caldwell has finally worked through the betrayal of her former client and lover, Reagan Reynolds. Putting the pieces of her life back in order, she finds herself on a collision course with that past when she takes on a new client, the future first lady. Unfortunately, Chad's newest job puts her in the cross-hairs of a domestic terrorist determined to release a virus that could kill thousands of women. Reagan Reynolds has paid for her sins and is ready to start a new life. Attending a business conference in Abu Dhabi gives her the opportunity to prove to her father and herself that she's worthy of a fresh start. Her past will intersect with her future at the conference when she accidentally comes face-to-face with Chad Caldwell. Time is running out. Will Reagan confront Chad? Can she convince Chad she's changed, or will death part them forever?

Broken Shield - ISBN - 978-0-982860-82-3

Tyler Jackson, former paramedic now firefighter, has seen her share of death up close. The death of her wife caused Tyler to rethink her career choices, but the death of her mother two weeks later cemented her return to the ranks of firefighter. Her path of self-destruction and womanizing is just a front to hide the heartbreak and devastation she lives with every day. Tyler's given up on finding love and having the family she's always wanted. When tragedy strikes her life for a second time she finds something she thought she lost.

Ashley Henderson loves her job. Ignoring her mother's advice, she opts for a career in law enforcement. But, Ashley hides a secret that soon turns her life upside down. Shame, guilt and fear keep Ashley from venturing forward and finding the love she so desperately craves. Her life comes crashing down around her in one swift moment forcing her to come clean about her secrets and her life.

Can two women thrust together by one traumatic event survive and find love together, or will their past force them apart?

Scarlet Assassin - ISBN - 978-1-939062-36-9

Selene Hightower is a killer for hire. A vampire who walks in both the light and the darkness, but lately darkness has a stronger pull. Her unfinished business could cost her the ability to live in the light, throwing her permanently back into the black ink of evil.

Doctor Francesca Swartz led a boring life filled with test tubes, blood trials, and work. One exploratory night, in a world of leather and torture, she is intrigued by a dark and solitary soul. She surrenders to temptation and the desire to experience something new, only to discover that it might alter her life forever.

Will Selene allow the light to win over the darkness threatening the edges of her life? Two women wonder if they can co-exist despite vast differences, as worlds collide and threaten to destroy any hope of happiness. Who will win?

The Gate - ISBN – 978-1-943353-93-4

Valhalla is for warriors that die in battle. What of those who don't have a hero's death? Where do they go? The inter-world is in chaos and has become the heart of the battleground in the war between Paladins and Gatekeepers. Harley doesn't know it yet, but she's at ground zero. A night of drinking, to forget a cheating girlfriend, is about to change her life forever. A birthmark—or a birthright—sets her on a direct path to a woman who claims to have known her for centuries. Not ready to accept her Paladin mantel, she needs proof—and that proof is out to destroy her. A protector by birth, Dawn was bred to preserve the delicate cycle of life and death. Protecting a Paladin is to be mated for eternity, usually without the sex, but Harley's allure is universally compelling. Harley's rise in status to The Chosen complicates things further as Dawn finds herself fighting for her own heart, as well as battling her biggest nemesis and brother, Lucius. Lucius, lord of the Gatekeepers, is out to kill souls moving to their next life. He wants Harley in his corner and he isn't about to let a little sibling rivalry stand in the way, no matter what it takes. Harley find herself caught up in Lucius's tempting promise of power, but cannot shake the soul-tugging love she feels with Dawn. Will Dawn convince Harley in time to embrace her Paladin destiny and save the souls looking for their gate, or will Lucius be able to sway Harley to throw in with the Gatekeepers?

Twisted Deception - ISBN - 978-1-939062-47-5

There are two types of people who can't look you in the eyes: someone trying to hide a lie and someone trying to hide their love.

Addie Blake's life isn't black and white--more like a series of short bursts of color that sustain her until the next eruption. She isn't a ladder-climber in the corporate world. Instead, she works long hours at the office and even at home, something her mechanic girlfriend, Drake Hogan, can't stand. If Addie can't focus on Drake, then Drake finds arm candy that will. After a long week of late nights and a series of text-messaged demands, each one a bigger bomb than the last, Addie has had enough of her Motor Girl.

Greyson Hollister inhabits a world where everything is either black and white, or money green. She's a polished, certified workaholic. As head of Integrated Financial, she has built the ladder others want to climb. Now she intends to attend a business mixer to confront a rumormonger and kill merger rumors involving her company.

Detective Nancy Hill, the lead detective on the Elevator Rapist task force, has just been called in to investigate an attack at Integrated Financial. She can't quite put her finger on it, but something doesn't add up with this latest assault, and Greyson Hollister isn't exactly lending a helping hand.

A storm's brewing on the horizon. Can Addie and Greyson weather it, or will it blow them over?

Writing as Jett Abbott

Scarlet Masquerade - ISBN - 978-0-982860-81-6

What do you say to the woman you thought died over a century ago? Will time heal all wounds or does it just allow them to fester and grow? A.J. Locke has lived over two centuries and works like a demon, both figuratively and literally. As the owner of a successful pharmaceutical company that specializes in blood research, she has changed the way she can live her life. Wanting for nothing, she has smartly compartmentalized her life so that when she needs to, she can pick up and start all over again, which happens every twenty years or so. Love is not an emotion A.J. spends much time on. Since losing the love of her life to the plague one hundred fifty years ago, she vowed to never travel down that road again. That isn't to say she doesn't have women when she wants them, she just wants them on her terms and that doesn't involve a long term commitment.

A.J.'s cool veneer is peeled back when she sees the love of her life in a lesbian bar, in the same town, in the same day and time in which she lives. Is her mind playing tricks on her? If not, how did Clarissa survive the plague when she had made A.J. promise never to change her?

Clarissa Graham is a university professor who has lived an obscure life teaching English literature. She has made it a point to stay off the radar and never become involved with anything that resembles her past life. Every once in a while Clarissa has an itch that needs to be scratched, so she finds an out of the way location to scratch it. She keeps her personal life separate from her professional one, and in doing so she is able to keep her secrets to herself. Suddenly, her life is turned upside down when someone tries to kill her. She finds herself in the middle of an assassination plot with no idea who wants her dead.

Made in the USA
Columbia, SC
01 March 2020

88552391R00217